Contributions to Finance and Accounting

The book series 'Contributions to Finance and Accounting' features the latest research from research areas like financial management, investment, capital markets, financial institutions, FinTech and financial innovation, accounting methods and standards, reporting, and corporate governance, among others. Books published in this series are primarily monographs and edited volumes that present new research results, both theoretical and empirical, on a clearly defined topic. All books are published in print and digital formats and disseminated globally.

More information about this series at http://www.springer.com/series/16616

Duncan Smith

Promoting Integrity in the Work of International Organisations

Minimising Fraud and Corruption in Projects

Springer

Duncan Smith
European Investment Bank
Luxembourg, Luxembourg

ISSN 2730-6038 ISSN 2730-6046 (electronic)
Contributions to Finance and Accounting
ISBN 978-3-030-73915-7 ISBN 978-3-030-73916-4 (eBook)
https://doi.org/10.1007/978-3-030-73916-4

This Springer imprint is published by the registered company Springer Nature Switzerland AG.
The registered company address is: Gewerbestrasse 11, 6330 Cham, Switzerland

Corruption, embezzlement, fraud, these are all characteristics which exist everywhere. It is regrettably the way human nature functions, whether we like it or not. What successful economies do is keep it to a minimum. No one has ever eliminated any of that stuff—Alan Greenspan
Alan Greenspan is an American economist who served as Chair of the Federal Reserve of the United States from 1987 to 2006.

Less corruption means lower revenue leakage and less waste in expenditures, and higher quality of public education and infrastructure
In April 2019, the International Monetary Fund published the results of research they had undertaken noting that about US$1 trillion in tax revenues annually could be generated by reducing corruption. The IMF said that fighting corruption could also reduce waste, help to improve overall public trust in government and even help to lift test scores of school students.

Foreword

The American bank robber, Willie Sutton, who made well over $2 million over a 40-year career in the early part of the twentieth century, reputedly replied to a reporter's enquiry as to why he robbed banks by saying, 'Because that's where the money is'.

Institutions that give grants or make loans are irresistible to crooks and fraudsters the world over. The vulnerability of organisations which hold themselves out as grant-givers or loan-providers is a cause of enormous anxiety in the private banking and public sector; one has only to look at the billions of pounds sterling targeted by fraudsters seeking to take advantage of the UK Government's 'bounce back' loan scheme (BBLS) to help small businesses recover from the economic impact of the coronavirus pandemic to gauge the scale of fraud in this very limited area. Up to a third of the £45 billion lent through BBLS for small businesses, which can borrow up to £50,000, is already thought to have been subject to fraud. Ultimately, the public is the loser as the loans are guaranteed by the taxpayer.

Procurement fraud is an area where the public sector is particularly vulnerable. Fraudsters seeking to obtain contracts to supply goods or services make use of a range of illicit activities, from bid-rigging during the pre-contract phase to false invoicing in the post-contract phase. In extreme cases, fraudsters set up phoney companies to tender for contracts, bidding against themselves to create the impression of genuine competition and driving the price up. Cartels are set up in secret to distort competition and direct their sights at public sector institutions offering competitive tenders. The UK has seen repeated attempts to manipulate and skew the tendering process in government contracts, particularly in the health sector and defence. The amounts at stake are very high and the likelihood of detection and subsequent conviction is worth the risk for a determined organised criminal network. Detection of fraudulent attacks on the system is not as effective as it could be in many sectors and those charged with ensuring that the organisation is protected from harm often lack essential training, skills and resources to counter the sophisticated weapons and strategies adopted by today's international cyber-criminals.

There is also a prevailing suspicion, not without justification, that it would be difficult to commit procurement fraud without insider help. This is where the issue of corruption is inextricably linked to fraud.

Some years ago, legal history was made in the UK with the longest (and possibly the most expensive) fraud trial in history, arising out of a procurement fraud allegedly committed by a number of companies bidding to secure the lucrative contract to extend the then, new, Jubilee line on the London Underground rail network. The two main defendants ran a quantity surveying firm and were said by the Crown to have corrupted certain London Underground Limited personnel in order to obtain confidential financial information. This, they had then fraudulently used on behalf of client contractors in relation to the original tendering process, and later on behalf of several client contractors in relation to claims against LUL arising out of contractual variations. With the exception of one defendant, an employee of LUL, who pleaded guilty on a limited basis to the charge of corruption, all the defendants, who were charged with conspiracy to defraud LUL, denied any wrong-doing and were ultimately acquitted following a 21-month trial reputedly costing some £60 million.

Fraud against big institutions and organisations cannot be successfully carried out without the existence of a number of key factors: these include lax controls and supervision within the target organisation, complacency ('We're not at risk'), lack of fraud awareness and anticipation and poor direction and a lack of moral leadership from senior management. It is a truism that an ounce of prevention is worth a ton of enforcement—what is often described as better the railings at the top of the cliff to stop someone falling than the ambulance at the bottom when it is too late. For many years, the Fraud Advisory Panel has urged companies and professionals to gear up their fraud prevention tools to guard themselves against becoming the victims of fraud. Awareness of fraud risk is now better than it has ever been, but fraud is becoming ever more prevalent and the losses are reaching previously unthinkable levels worldwide.

Many organisations should be complimented on the recognition of their exposure to fraud and their willingness to devote resources to combatting it. Organisations I have worked with and am still closely connected to within the UK and Europe more widely have taken up the fraud challenge and have put in impressive and expensive controls and strengthened their internal investigatory departments. There are now dedicated university departments teaching counter-fraud techniques to both law enforcement and to investigators employed in public and private organisations such as the NHS and banks. Fraud networks have been set up around the UK raising awareness of fraud prevention techniques and trends in fraud and at grass-roots level, television programmes and newspaper columns highlight the common 'scams' from rogue traders to cyberattacks on bank accounts which affect us all. International co-operation in fraud law enforcement is now a highly developed tool in combating fraud.

Fraud affects everyone. We are all the losers. Procurement fraud and fraud against public institutions should never be dismissed as 'someone else's problem' for governments or the bodies themselves to sort out. Identification of fraudulent techniques and of individuals and groups who have offended before should be a top priority. Debarment processes to stop known fraudsters and those who manipulate markets and distort the integrity of competition being allowed to participate in tendering for contracts and applications for loans should be supported. Vigilance and effective action are needed from both inside the organisation and from law enforcement to make this form of crime uneconomic and those who commit it likely to be put out of business for many years and drained of their ill-gotten gains. Where the appropriate legislative tools do not exist, governments should be pressed to introduce them. Organisations can do more to protect themselves by being alert to their own exposure to fraud; the techniques they need to instal their own railings at the top of the cliff are available. They must acknowledge the need and use them.

Rosalind Wright CB QC is a barrister and a former Director of the Serious Fraud Office and the Chairman of the Fraud Advisory Panel. She was the Director of Policy and General Counsel at the Securities and Futures Authority, chairman and member of the Supervisory Committee of the European Anti-Fraud Office (OLAF), and before that, an Assistant Director of Public Prosecutions in England and Wales. She is a bencher of Middle Temple and is also chair of the disciplinary committees of a number of professional regulatory bodies. She is a member of the Exclusion Committee of the EIB and the Complaints Commissioner of the London Metal Exchange.

Rosalind Wright
March 2021

Preface

Duncan Smith is a barrister (a member of London's Gray's Inn) and was called to the Bar of England and Wales in 1989. He works in the European Investment Bank's Fraud Investigation Division as Deputy Head, based in Luxembourg and, having previously conducted investigations including into large international corporations, he is responsible for a range of policy, training, outreach, prevention and deterrence issues.

Duncan spent 10 years prosecuting corporate fraud and corruption offences at the Department of Trade and Industry and at the Serious Fraud Office, in London, UK. He then joined the World Bank's Investigation Unit in Washington DC in 2000 as Team Leader and then moved over to become policy/debarment adviser, before joining EIB in Luxembourg in early 2007.

During his time at the World Bank, he identified the need for greater coordination between international organisations in the fight against fraud and corruption. Consequently, he co-authored the IFI Task Force's Uniform Framework Agreement (2006) that harmonised the definitions of fraud and corruption across the Multilateral Development Banks and provided general principles for the conduct of MDB investigations. He is author of the EIBs Anti-Fraud Policy in 2007–2008 (and the update in 2013).

Moreover, Duncan served on the Secretariat of the Conference of International Investigators between 2004 and 2017, coordinating annual conferences for investigators from a wide range of international organisations. He was also an external expert undertaking reviews of the investigation functions at the World Food Programme (WFP, based in Rome) and the European Patent Office (EPO, based in Munich).

Duncan is the founder (in 2003) of regular coordination meetings between the Heads of Investigations of the MDBs. He is the author/co-author of a number of documents that provide a harmonised approach that each participating MDB institution can adopt, including the IFI Uniform Framework Agreement, General Principles and Guidelines for Sanctions and MDB Harmonised Principles on Treatment of Corporate Groups. In raising awareness of the work of EIB's investigation function, he has written a number of articles for the FCPA Blog.

Any opinions or conclusions expressed herein are those of the author and do not reflect the views of the European Investment Bank Group, its management, Vice-Presidents and President or the Board of Directors (or indeed of any previous employer).

Luxembourg, Luxembourg Duncan Smith

Acknowledgements

I am extremely grateful to the many people who have assisted in creating, designing and publishing this book.

It is the summation of many years of experience working as a prosecuting lawyer at the Department of Trade and Industry (as it was then called) and the Serious Fraud Office in London and then in the investigation teams at international institutions (the World Bank in Washington DC and European Investment Bank in Luxembourg).

I owe a big thank you to Jan Willem, Bernie, Johan, Dominik, Sabrina, Marco, Alex, Gijs, Monique and all my colleagues in IG/IN for their support and assistance. I am also very grateful to many colleagues for their assistance over the years in the international arena (including Steve Z, Paul LR; Franz B., Ryna F, Yannick S, Dina D and Laura V when I was at World Bank and since; Lisa R, Enery Q, Rohan S and Chiawen K from EBRD; Samir F from IDB; Peter P, Clare W and David B at ADB; David W at the Global Fund; and Brett S at UNDP). It is difficult to think about World Bank INT without considering the lives of Christina and Christian (both WB).

Thanks also to Janet & Mark for encouraging me to complete it and seek its publication.

I have a wonderful family (my wife Joanne and daughters Laura, Kirsty and Ella) all of whom have supported me at every point along my journey of recovery after my serious cycling accident in 2018—which had me in a coma for a few days and a wheelchair for a few weeks (later, during my months of recovery, I started making notes that subsequently have transformed into this book!). My family has been very kind and patient, working hard to ensure my continued health and happiness. Thank you for everything!

Any errors or mistakes are mine and mine alone.

This book is correct as of January 1, 2020.

Contents

Abbreviations

ADB	Asian Development Bank
AFD	France's Agence Francaise de Development
AfDB	African Development Bank
AIIB	Asian Infrastructure Investment Bank
CII	Conference of International Investigators
DfID	UK's Department for International Development
DANIDA	Danish International Development Agency
(US) DoJ	Department of Justice
EBRD	European Bank of Reconstruction and Development
EEA	European Environment Agency
EIB	European Investment Bank
EIF	European Investment Fund
EPO	European Patent Office
FAO	Food and Agricultural Organization
FIFA	Fédération Internationale de Football Association (international governing body of association football)
Global Fund	The Global Fund to Fight AIDS, Tuberculosis and Malaria
GTZ	Germany's Technical Cooperation Agency
IADB (or IDB)	Inter-American Development Bank
IBRD	International Bank for Reconstruction and Development (part of the World Bank)
ICSID	International Centre for Settlement of Investment Disputes (part of the World Bank)
IDA	International Development Association (part of the World Bank)
IFC	International Finance Corporation (part of the World Bank)
IFI	International Financial Institution
INTERPOL	International Criminal Police Organization
IOC	International Olympic Committee
(WB) INT	The World Bank's Integrity Vice-Presidency
MDB	Multilateral Development Bank

MIGA	Multilateral Investment Guarantee Agency (part of the World Bank)
MoU	Memorandum of Understanding
NATO	North Atlantic Treaty Organization
ODA	Canada's Official Development Assistance
OLAF	EU Commission's Office Européen de Lutte Anti-Fraude (European Anti-Fraud Office)
OSCE	Organization for Security and Cooperation in Europe
SFO	The UK's Serious Fraud Office
SIDA	Swedish International Development Cooperation Agency
UN	United Nations
UNEP	UN Environment Programme
UNDP	UN Development Programme
UNESCO	United Nations Educational, Scientific and Cultural Organization
UNICEF	The United Nations Children's Fund
UN OIOS	United Nations Office of Internal Oversight Services
UNRWA	UN Relief and Works Agency
US AID	US's Agency for International Development
VW	Volkswagen AG
WFP	World Food Programme
WMO	World Meteorological Organization
WTO	World Trade Organization

Chapter 1
Introduction

There are many international organisations trying positively to influence the way in which the world is developing. There are numerous reasons why there are so many international organisations and why they were founded—to maintain peace and stability (Organisation for Security and Cooperation in Europe—OSCE[1] and the North Atlantic Treaty Organisation—NATO[2]), to provide rules for international trade (World Trade Organisation—WTO[3]), to monitor meteorology (World Meteorological Organisation—WMO[4]), to promote cooperation between Police forces (INTERPOL),[5] to promote positive environmental practices (UN Environment Programme—UNEP[6] and the European Environment Agency—EEA[7]) to identify and name but a few. In addition, there are a number of international institutions which aim to alleviate poverty, to promote development and provide funding to poorer parts of the world.

The international financial institutions (IFIs) include major ones such as the European Investment Bank (EIB), the Asian Development Bank (ADB), African Development Bank (AfDB), the European Bank for Reconstruction and Development (EBRD), the Inter-American Development Bank (IADB) and the World Bank (hereinafter 'the six banks' or 'six MDBs', short for Multilateral Development Banks).[8] These MDBs have a wide portfolio of loans and grants to a range of beneficiaries in the public and private sectors and seek to promote development.

---

[1] www.osce.org.

[2] www.nato.int.

[3] www.wto.org.

[4] www.public.wmo.int/en.

[5] www.interpol.int.

[6] www.unenvironment.org.

[7] www.eea.europe.eu.

[8] Their websites are provided on many occasions through this book.

D. Smith, *Promoting Integrity in the Work of International Organisations*, Contributions to Finance and Accounting,
https://doi.org/10.1007/978-3-030-73916-4_1

There are also international financial organisations which have developed a more regional character (such as the Nordic Investment Bank,[9] Black Sea Trade and Development Bank,[10] Islamic Development Bank,[11] Council of Europe Development Bank,[12] Caribbean Development Bank,[13] East Africa Development Bank,[14] West Africa Development Bank,[15] Central American Bank for Economic Integration,[16] Development Bank of Latin America[17] etc.). There are also many non-bank organisations linked to or operating under the auspices, mandate or authority of the United Nations.

The list of six large MDBs (see above), as well as many of the regional banks, are international but publicly owned financial institutions ('banks') that were founded to finance and support projects that would assist in the development of poorer countries (e.g. build roads to, for example, improve access to markets, build housing, promote social sustainability, etc.). More recently, the MDBs have added environmental sustainability and reducing the impact of climate change to their list of aims and policy objectives.

Those organisations operating under the mandate of the UN tend to be more focused on specific issues such as the Food and Agriculture Organisation of the United Nations (FAO)[18] and the UN Relief and Works Agency for Palestine Refugees in the Near East (UNRWA).[19]

The opening quote from Alan Greenspan states that 'corruption, embezzlement, fraud . . . exist everywhere' including to affect the work of international organisations but that '... successful economies . . . keep it to a minimum'. This quote is accurate and graphically demonstrates the importance of integrity and how fraud and corruption can affect (even to the extent of infesting) the work of different organisations operating in different sectors and economies around the world.[20] The quote

---

[9]www.nib.int.

[10]www.bstdb.org.

[11]www.isdb.org.

[12]www.coebank.org.

[13]www.caribank.org.

[14]www.eadb.org.

[15]www.boad.org.

[16]www.bcie.org.

[17]www.caf.com.

[18]www.fao.org.

[19]www.unrwa.org.

[20]Recently fraud and corruption have tainted the US education sector, as noted by a number of news reports and articles including on 7th February 2020 one from the BBC, as follows: 'College cheating scandal: Pimco tycoon jailed for 'chutzpah': The former head of a top US investment firm has been sentenced to nine months in prison for his role in the US universities admissions scandal . . . The US college admissions scandal has seen dozens of defendants indicted for allegedly cheating and bribing to get their children into elite universities, like Yale and Stanford. The parents - many of whom are celebrities or wealthy business executives - allegedly paid a firm as much as $6.5m (£4.9m) to cheat on students' college entrance exams or bribe top coaches to offer fake

also notes that the positive aims and goals such as efforts to develop economies, provide employment and reduce starving and hunger are subject to various illegal and/or unethical practices that will reduce their effectiveness and some of the funds will be mis-applied, possibly being deliberately mis-used or stolen.

To avoid such problems completely in the global economy is not possible: in developed economies—in European countries, North America, Australia, New Zealand and Singapore, for example—it is difficult enough to promote integrity and to reduce the effect of fraud and corruption despite the presence of project staff, local regulators, accountants/auditors, active and uninhibited press, interested third parties and active local law enforcement; to avoid those problems in developing economies where such groups are not common and if they do exist, may be less effective and operate in more of a struggle, if indeed they are functioning at all, is indeed very difficult. This is the case irrespective of the treaties signed and international commitments adopted, the rules and procedures that may require the country to try to promote positive, good practices and rational assessment of the products and services on offer and assistance in monitoring developments in the project.

One of the ways in which the six MDBs have sought to deter bad conduct is by giving themselves (rather than needing to rely on others) the ability to review and, if necessary, conduct a detailed investigation of allegations of integrity violations in the projects they have funded. In particular the six MDBs have all adopted harmonised rules (and more detailed Investigation Procedures) that I helped to draft in 2006[21] with the result that the same type of misconduct, resources permitting, would be investigated in the same way by any of the six organisations.

In addition, five of the MDBs (not EIB) have signed the Cross-Debarment Agreement in 2010 so that an entity or individual that is sanctioned following a finding that the entity has been engaged in fraud, corruption, collusion, coercion (or other misconduct such as obstruction) will be excluded from winning future contracts as part of a project financed by any of them.

Such an investigation could, amongst other results, lead to an identification of the misconduct by a publicly identified company and the debarment of that entity from other, similar projects in the future. Such rules are published and each organisation endeavours to ensure they can be relied upon if the need arises.[22]

The integrity violations of fraud, corruption, collusion and coercion can present serious economic and financial challenges to a project, as well as the entity/entities concerned and can threaten not just the integrity and the successful implementation of the project but the effectiveness and compliance with laws designed to prevent death/injury of the public when the project is completed. If the newly constructed

athletic scholarships. The colleges have not been accused of any wrongdoing and are investigating the matter internally. Fifteen parents are still contesting the allegations, and their trials are expected to take place later this year. US actress Lori Loughlin … is among the 50 total individuals - including coaches and other associates - is charged in the case … ' www.bbc.com.

[21]The Uniform Framework for Preventing and Combating Fraud and Corruption, which can be found published on most of the 5 MDBs websites and at: www.crossdebarment.org.

[22]For example, the MDB cross debarment website at www.crossdebarment.org.

road, bridge or tram/railway line fails (for example, because the failure is caused by flooding after a heavy rainstorm as the technical specifications were not met), the consequences can be significant, widespread and even fatal.

To give a flavour of the sort of misconduct that is considered (not necessarily to this extent or value but nevertheless, similar) and how it might affect a project, I thought it would be useful to include the short '5 Famous White Collar Crime Cases':

> Here are some of the most famous/infamous companies and individuals that were involved in white-collar crime cases:
>
> 1) Wells Fargo Account Fraud Scandal
>
> In 2016, Wells Fargo employees secretly created millions of fraudulent deposit accounts and submitted 565,443 credit card applications without their customer's knowledge or consent to hit unrealistic sales targets and to receive incentives and bonuses on top of their salary.
>
> As a result, customers were then charged all sorts of fees for accounts they didn't know existed. Wells Fargo needed to pay $185 million in fines and refund $5 million to the customers who were affected. This is the largest penalty ever recorded since the Consumer Financial Protection Bureau was established in 2011.
>
> 2) Bernard Madoff
>
> Bernard Madoff is considered as the most well-known white-collar criminal. Madoff is a former chairman of Nasdaq and was the founder of a successful Wall Street firm. According to Investopedia, he was found guilty of 'an elaborate PONZI SCHEME, which promised large returns on investments'. He was sentenced to 150 years in prison.[23]
>
> 3) Enron
>
> This is a story of a company that was once successful but then resorted to schemes in an attempt to fabricate profits and hide losses. At its peak, Enron shares were worth $90.75, which eventually fell to just $0.67 in 2002 when the company filed for bankruptcy. They were found guilty of off-balance-sheet special purpose vehicles (SPVs) in an attempt to hide their huge debts and 'toxic assets' from both creditors and investors. Andrew Fastow the company's Chief Financial Officer (CFO) was charged since he was the mind behind these false business tactics.
>
> 4) HealthSouth
>
> According to The New York Times, auditors discovered 'HUNDREDS OF MILLIONS OF DOLLARS IN PREVIOUSLY UNREPORTED ACCOUNTING FRAUD AT HEALTHSOUTH'. This all happened in 2004. Eventually, the company founder Richard M. Scrushy was indicted on 84 counts of fraud along with at least five former CFOs who pleaded guilty to charges.
>
> 5) WorldCom
>
> Known as the 'BIGGEST ACCOUNTING SCANDALS IN US HISTORY', according to CBS News. The WorldCom investigation started when internal audits discovered 'improper accounting of more than $3.8 billion in expenses over five quarters'.
>
> These irregularities did not comply with GENERALLY ACCEPTED ACCOUNTING PRINCIPLES. As a result, senior vice president and controller David Myers resigned from his post, and 17,000 WorldCom employees lost their jobs.[24]

---

[23] The list of films in Appendix A includes one about Madoff.

[24] an entry posted on September 18, 2019 by Robert: http://www.crimecitycentral.com/5-famous-white-collar-crime-cases/. There are further examples of individual and corporate misconduct in the two series of documentaries entitled 'Dirty Money' on Netflix.

Of course, simpler, more straightforward misconduct such as making and using false guarantees or manufacturer warranties, forged bank statements, mis-statements or significant exaggerations about conduct undertaken in previous projects, deliberately using false information to make a bid more attractive and over-invoicing (e.g. to try to cover the costs of bribes paid to those who evaluated the best bidder and awarded the contract) can equally affect the projects financed by or are being undertaken by international organisations.

This book:

- Is for lawyers, non-lawyers and students alike, some of whom work (or have the ambition and desire to work) for an international organisation or with agencies/charities that work with or co-finance projects with international organisations (including in operations, law, procurement, accountancy and other relevant fields), as well as for those people studying these and other integrity-related topics—although some sections are quite technical, I have tried to write in pragmatic (and not too legalistic) language;
- Provides a better understanding of how fraud and corruption can distort markets and indeed how such conduct can and does impact the projects and activities of many international organisations and some suggestions to how to prevent/deter it;
- Looks at the risks of fraud and corruption arising and gives examples of the sorts of problems that could be faced;
- Reviews possible controls and safeguards (that can be used by the project team, commercial companies and others) to reduce the possibility of fraud or corruption affecting the project;
- Provides a list of 'red flags' (or possible alerts) of fraud and corruption;
- Reviews the mechanisms that are available to international (and also to some domestic) organisations to investigate and conduct proactive reviews;
- Summarises the capability of international organisations to sanction entities and individuals that have engaged in such wrongdoing;
- Reviews interesting and relevant cases that have been prosecuted by domestic law enforcement agencies around the world but have affected international organisations;
- Provides some ideas about places to go to get more information and advice; and
- Identifies a number of possible ways to deter/prevent such conduct.

However, this book will not discuss the actual size of the problems faced—many different countries have actual (or at least potential) integrity violation problems. Each one also has their own selection or combination of their own individual problems (partly based on national sociology and culture, also the effectiveness of law enforcement agencies and the potential deterrent effect).

In an article by Haoliang Xu (UN Assistant Secretary-General, UNDP Assistant Administrator and Director of UNDP's Bureau for Policy and Programme Support) entitled 'Ensuring Sustainable Solutions to Combating Corruption' that was posted on December 6, 2019, he said:

> After years of apathy, cynicism and denial, corruption is no longer a taboo subject. Anti-corruption is now an integral part of global, regional and national development agendas.
>
> In many countries, there is still a huge gap between the existing anti-corruption laws, policies and institutions, and their effectiveness. Addressing the issues of money laundering and illicit financial flows, and ensuring transparency in beneficial ownership and ethics and compliance in both public and private sectors, continue to pose demanding challenges.[25]

It is, of course, possible to try to measure or quantify the size of the problem with a survey or to rely on the findings of Transparency International's yearly Corruption Perception Index.[26] This is a well known measure (on a numerical ranking but, as importantly, relative to other countries) which is an assessment of the views of informed business people and country experts about the levels of public-sector

[25]www.undp.org/content/undp/en/home/blog/2019/ensuring-sustainable-solutions-to-combatting-corruption.html. He went on to suggest four next steps:

> Learning from our anti-corruption work in the past decade, we... have identified four key priority areas of interventions for the 'Next Generation of Anti-Corruption Programming': Sustainable Development Goal 16 (#SDG16) and anti-corruption; technology and innovation; business integrity; and social accountability.
>
> **SDG 16** gives us a tremendous opportunity to integrate anti-corruption policies in the national development agendas. Increased investments on SDG 16 will significantly help strengthen the overall ethics and integrity infrastructure in a country, including credible electoral processes and strong political parties, parliaments, anti-corruption institutions, judiciaries, media and civil society organisations. These investments will help countries move from transparency to accountability - ensuring transparency is not only important, but also that accountability requires making those in power answerable for their actions, sanctioning when necessary and addressing impunity.
>
> **Technology and innovation** such as big data analytics, artificial intelligence and blockchain technology hold remarkable potential to detect, predict, prevent, and deter corruption. Whilst recognising the corruption risks in the use of new technologies, our aim for the next generation of anti-corruption programming is to harness the benefits of the Fourth Industrial Revolution, built upon the digital revolution.
>
> **Business integrity**. The Panama and Paradise papers – the work of investigative journalists around the world on illegal and hidden money in offshore jurisdictions – uncovered a complex network of politicians, businesses and other interests. They revealed a close link between corruption, organised crime and money laundering, and the need to ensure transparency in beneficial ownership, national capacity to prevent illicit financial flows, and an effective international mechanism in the return of stolen assets.
>
> We therefore aim to address corruption not only as a crime and an impediment to development, but also as a direct threat to peace and stability. Strengthening business integrity is crucial in fighting corruption, but promoting a fair business environment will require the collaborative efforts of government, businesses, and civil society, as well as an independent media, to address the challenges.
>
> **Social accountability**. In the long run, social accountability through a proactive and inclusive engagement of all sections of society is key to preventing and combating corruption. Civic engagement is instrumental in institutionalising integrity, ethics, and moral standards in public and private sectors.
>
> Taken together, these four aspects will help ensure that we increasingly see the results of the progress we have made in the policy space for sustainable impact.

[26]www.transparency.org/cpi2018.

corruption. This ranking indicates the size and extent of the problems and, perhaps as importantly, whether the situation is getting relatively better or worse.

However, it is very difficult to measure accurately the size of the problem with corruption. There is not only the cost of bribes paid to consider (perhaps as a percentage of the value of the contract or other benefit provided) but also the effects and value of contracts awarded, fines not imposed or other related costs. This may even include money laundering—providing advice about how to launder large quantities of potentially dirty money could be a sign of corruption. This is potentially bad for certain countries that may be thought of as less corrupt when it is also a preferred destination for illicit proceeds (such as Switzerland and the UK).

There are also barometer surveys and different national and comparative studies with different scopes by the Global Corruption Barometer,[27] Afrobarometer,[28] and the World Justice Project Rule of Law Index[29] (to name but a few). These studies can provide important data about actual and perceived corruption in specific jurisdictions around the world, as can also be gleaned by gathering data on the number and types of investigations being conducted by local law enforcement agencies. Those cases can sometimes provide fascinating (and sometimes quite specific) details such as how much was paid in bribes, who the bribes were paid to (i.e. to which officials), what value of contracts was awarded in return and the nature and type of the bureaucratic and control process(es) that was/were avoided or had to be deliberately undercut as a result.

There is also significant research being done by Mihály Fazekas[30] to analyse Big Data. He works at the University of Cambridge, UK as the scientific coordinator of the Horizon 2020-funded project DIGIWHIST[31] which used a 'Big Data' approach to measuring corruption risks, administrative capacity and transparency in public procurement in 33 European countries. On its website, it notes that DIGIWHIST was seeking:

> . . . to increase trust in governments and improve the efficiency of public spending across Europe. It will do this through the systematic collection, structuring, analysis, and broad dissemination of information on public procurement and on mechanisms that increase accountability of public officials in all EU and some neighbouring countries.
>
> The project will compile and evaluate micro-level data using information from individual public procurement transactions and winning firms' finance and ownership structures. This data will be linked to information on aggregate asset and income declarations data in order to detect potential conflicts of interest in the system of public procurement, and more specifically, to identify systemic vulnerabilities in the respective legislations and their implementation.[32]

---

[27]www.transparency.org/research/gcb/global_corruption_barometer_2019.

[28]www.afrobarometer.org.

[29]www.worldjusticeproject.org.

[30]www.mihalyfazekas.eu.

[31]www.digiwhist.eu. DIGIWHIST is an abbreviation of 'The Digital Whistleblower' and works towards: 'Fiscal Transparency, Risk Assessment and Impact of Good Governance Policies Assessed'.

[32]http://digiwhist.eu/about-digiwhist/.

At EIB, the definition of Prohibited Conduct (which includes fraud, corruption and collusion) is included in a detailed Anti-Fraud Policy (publicly available on the EIB website[33]). The definitions of fraud, corruption, collusion etc. are aligned with the ones agreed by the MDBs in the Uniform Framework in 2006.[34]

The EIB Anti-Fraud Policy has the following (MDB-harmonised) definitions (bold added):

'... **Prohibited Conduct** includes corruption, fraud, coercion, collusion, obstruction, money laundering and financing of terrorism defined as follows:

a. A **corrupt practice**, which is the offering, giving, receiving, or soliciting, directly or indirectly, anything of value to influence improperly the actions of another party.
b. A **fraudulent practice**, which is any act or omission, including a misrepresentation that knowingly or recklessly misleads, or attempts to mislead, a party to obtain a financial or other benefit or to avoid an obligation.
c. A **coercive practice**, which is impairing or harming, or threatening to impair or harm, directly or indirectly, any party or the property of the party to influence improperly the actions of a party.
d. A **collusive practice**, which is an arrangement between two or more parties designed to achieve an improper purpose, including influencing improperly the actions of another party.
e. An **obstructive practice** is (a) deliberately destroying, falsifying, altering or concealing of evidence material to the investigation; and/or threatening, harassing or intimidating any party to prevent it from disclosing its knowledge of matters relevant to the investigation or from pursuing the investigation, or (b) acts intended to materially impede the exercise of the EIB's contractual rights of audit or access to information or the rights that any banking, regulatory or examining authority or other equivalent body of the European Union or of its Member States may have in accordance with any law, regulation or treaty or pursuant to any agreement into which the EIB has entered in order to implement such law, regulation or treaty.

   Money laundering and financing of terrorism are defined in EC Directives8 on the prevention of the use of the financial system for the purpose of money laundering and terrorist financing, as amended and supplemented from time to time (hereafter 'AML/CFT Directive'), as follows:
f. **Money laundering** is

   (i) the conversion or transfer of property, knowing that such property is derived from criminal activity or from an act of participation in such activity, for the purpose of concealing or disguising the illicit origin of the property or of assisting any person who is involved in the commission of such activity to evade the legal consequences of his action;
   (ii) the concealment or disguise of the true nature, source, location, disposition, movement, rights with respect to, or ownership of property, knowing that such property is derived from criminal activity or from an act of participation in such activity;
   (iii) the acquisition, possession or use of property, knowing, at the time of receipt, that such property was derived from criminal activity or from an act of participation in such activity;

[33] www.eib.org.

[34] www.crossdebarment.org.

(iv) participation in, association to commit, attempts to commit and aiding, abetting, facilitating and counselling the commission of any of the actions mentioned in the foregoing points.

g. **Financing of terrorism** is the provision or collection of funds, by any means, directly or indirectly, with the intention that they should be used or in the knowledge that they are to be used, in full or in part, in order to carry out any of the offences within the meaning of Articles 1 to 4 of the Council Framework Decision 2002/475/JHA of 13 June 2002 on combating terrorism.'[35]

[35]The EIB's Investigation Procedures are also available at: www.eib.org/en/publications/anti-fraud-procedures.htm.

Chapter 2
International Finance

Finance for large or complex development projects can be obtained from a wide range of different sources, including from both public and private (i.e., commercial) sources.

2.1 Public Versus Commercial Banks

There are advantages and disadvantages with both types of financiers, including factors such as:

- the rate of interest that is paid back to the lender;
- the premiums paid according to the risks that may specifically impact the borrower;
- the region in which the project is to be implemented;
- the knowledge and support from the lending entity (or entities) in case there are difficulties, unexpected problems or costly adjustments to be addressed; and
- the level and degree of involvement of staff monitoring and specialists assisting in the implementation of the project.

On the latter point, the extent and degree of involvement of staff from the lending organisation(s) is likely to be linked to the nature, type and purpose of lending organisation(s); there is likely to be much less involvement and project scrutiny in a straight commercial transaction to lend funds than in a transaction with a publicly-owned institution seeking to assist in progressing the wider development agenda as well as to ensure the particular project is successfully but also by doing so, help to build the effectiveness and efficiency of the borrower and its governmental bodies more generally.

The world is not short of commercial financiers who aim to lend money at a relatively high rate of interest in order to cover their costs, produce a profit and to

D. Smith, *Promoting Integrity in the Work of International Organisations*,
Contributions to Finance and Accounting,
https://doi.org/10.1007/978-3-030-73916-4_2

address the risks of possible non-repayment by the borrower. Nevertheless, in most cases funds provided by international organisations such as those examples mentioned below are generally chosen (sometimes there are two or more international organisations who combine and provide finance) not only because there is no, or not much, profit element included in the costs but also because such organisations can provide knowledge and assistance in terms of the development objectives and how the aims of the project could be achieved.

2.2 Public Banks

2.2.1 The World Bank

The World Bank Group states on its website that it has the following mission: 'To end extreme poverty: by reducing the share of the global population that lives in extreme poverty to 3 percent by 2030'; and 'To promote shared prosperity: by increasing the incomes of the poorest 40 percent of people in every country'.[1]

This is clearly developmental in nature and, in association with those goals, the World Bank also is a source of financial and technical assistance to developing countries around the world. It is not a bank in the ordinary sense; it is an international organisation with a focus to reduce poverty and support development by lending funds and promoting positive changes.[2]

The World Bank Group was originally established in 1944 to help rebuild Europe after World War II, but has advanced its mandate to re-focus on development around the world. It comprises five institutions managed by their member countries:

IBRD International Bank for Reconstruction and Development;
IDA International Development Association;
IFC International Finance Corporation;
MIGA Multilateral Investment Guarantee Agency; and
ICSID International Centre for Settlement of Investment Disputes.

The World Bank Group is headquartered in Washington, DC and has 10,000 plus employees, some of them located in more than 120 offices worldwide.

The World Bank provides low-interest loans, zero to low-interest credits and grants to developing countries and thereby supports a large range of investments in projects for sectors such as education, health, public administration, infrastructure, financial and private sector development, agriculture and environmental and natural resource management. Some of the projects are co-financed with governments, other

[1]www.worldbank.org/en/who-we-are.

[2]For more background on the history, role and work of the World Bank, you can read an interesting book about the former World Bank President, James Wolfensohn, entitled: The World's Banker by Sebastian Mallaby (Yale University Press, 462 pages).

multilateral institutions, commercial banks, export credit agencies and private sector investors.

The World Bank also provides or assists with financing projects through trust fund partnerships with bilateral and multilateral donors and the Bank helps to manage such initiatives that address needs across a wide range of sectors and developing regions.

2.2.2 European Investment Bank

The European Investment Bank Group (EIB and the European Investment Fund, EIF) is a bank owned by the member states of the European Union and is based in Luxembourg.[3] Although it makes a profit from its activities, there is no yearly payment of profits to shareholders (as would be the case in the commercial sector) but the profit is added to its capital.

EIB works in both the public and private sectors and makes loans, guarantees, and provides technical assistance and venture capital for projects that are expected to further EU policy objectives. In particular, EIB provides loans (funded by borrowing from the capital markets) to small and medium-sized businesses (SMEs), less-developed European countries, environmental improvement and sustainability, energy security, trans-European networks and knowledge economy projects.

As EIB will rarely finance more than 50% of the cost of a project, borrowers often use EIB financing in conjunction with third-party financing. Also, the agreement of the EIB to participate often attracts additional financing from other parties. Whilst approximately 90% of EIB lending occurs within the EU, 10% occurs outside the EU such as in Southeast Europe, Middle East, Africa and the Caribbean.

The European Investment Bank was founded in Brussels in 1958 when the Treaty of Rome was signed. In 1968, the bank relocated to Luxembourg. The EIB Group was formed in 2000 and is composed of the EIB and the European Investment Fund (EIF), the EU's venture capital organisation that provides finance and guarantees for SMEs. The EIB is the EIF's majority shareholder and holds 62% of the shares.

The EIB is both an EU entity and a bank. As a result, the EIB must adhere to both public and corporate governance principles. The institution has three decision-making bodies: the Board of Governors, the Board of Directors and the Management Committee. The Board of Governors sets the direction of the EIB, the Board of Directors oversees the strategic direction and the Management Committee supervises the daily operations of the EIB. The bank has shareholders who are the Member States of the EU.

[3]More details are available about the role and work of EIB at: www.eib.org and EIF at: www.eif.org.

2.2.3 Other MDBs

The other international public banks (**Asian Development Bank** or ADB,[4] **African Development Bank** or AfDB,[5] **European Bank for Reconstruction and Development** or EBRD,[6] and **Inter-American Development Bank** or IADB[7]) were created and/or have developed to offer similar services with more focus on their particular continent/region. They look to assist the poorer countries, and indeed some better-off countries with a need to access finance or perhaps because they were facing higher risks of a range of different types of risks. More recently, they have all put investigation units in place and have adopted sanctioning methods. Indeed five of the MDBs (not EIB, which has lower levels of international immunity and is therefore potentially subject to legal review of any decision, including sanctioning decisions, by the European Court of Justice, which is also based in Luxembourg) have joined together to sign and enforce the Cross-Debarment Agreement.[8]

EBRD is somewhat different as it is more focused on the private sector and is seeking to support private sector business after the collapse of communism in Eastern Europe and the former Soviet Union (and more lately the events of the Arab Spring). EBRD has since said that their work has expanded to 'strengthen developing economies across three continents by making them competitive, well-governed, green, inclusive, resilient and integrated'. It was created in 1990 and is based in London.

In particular the public banks have provided expertise and finance for a range of projects that have sought to improve development, transport and energy, to reduce the number of poor people and have assisted the growth, economic progress and governance of nations.

2.2.4 Bilateral Agencies

Funds are also available from (public) bilateral aid agencies such as:

- US AID[9]
- Canada ODA[10]
- France's Agency France de Development (AFD)[11]

---

[4]More details are available about the role and work of ADB at: www.adb.org.

[5]More details are available about the role and work of AfDB at: www.afdb.org.

[6]More details are available about the role and work of EBRD at: www.ebrd.com.

[7]More details are available about the role and work of IADB at: www.iadb.org.

[8]www.crossdebarment.org.

[9]www.usaid.gov.

[10]www.international.gc.ca.

[11]www.afd.fr.

- Sweden's SIDA[12]
- Denmark's DANIDA[13]
- GIZ[14] in Germany and
- the UK's DfID.[15]

The funds are sometimes provided based on the political developments or crisis situations in the recipient country; sometimes the funds are what is available to be provided (no matter of the overall cost) and sometimes funds are provided in partnership with other institutions.

Such areas could include projects in the area of;

- housing
- access to drinking water
- education
- transportation and
- power generation

which are amongst the key factors in the life and functionality of the country. Some of the public banks and development agencies have even agreed to lend money for 'budget support' to finance other normal or specified types of spending when a government has long term deficits.

2.3 Other International Organisations

Funds and/or assistance (which can be as equally vulnerable to fraud and corruption) can be provided (or lent) to a country/region by a number of other international organisations, some from the United Nations (such as the World Food Programme[16]) or with a different geographical focus or regional mandate (not included in the six major MDBs above, such as the Asian Infrastructure Investment Bank,[17] Black Sea Trade and Development Bank,[18] Islamic Development Bank,[19] Caribbean

[12]www.sida.se.

[13]www.um.dk/en/danida-en/.

[14]www.giz.de.

[15]www.gov.uk/government/organisations/department-for-international-development.

[16]www.wfp.org.

[17]www.aiib.org.

[18]www.bstdb.org.

[19]www.isdb.org.

Development Bank,[20] Council of Europe Development Bank,[21] Nordic Investment Bank,[22] Development Bank of Larin America[23] or the Red Cross[24]).

On occasions, this assistance is provided in an emergency scenario, when most attention is on avoiding a certain type of catastrophe (war, hunger, disease, pollution, other environmental problems, etc.) and time is of the essence but, in some cases, more thought and planning about anti-corruption and fraud prevention measures could be beneficial to prevent or minimise the misuse of funds.

2.4 Key Parts of a Project

One of the possible advantages of a project being financed by an international organisation is that specialists (e.g. engineers, medical and health staff, lawyers, staff with wide experience of similar projects) working for the international organisation(s) can provide technical advice and/or assistance—frequently their knowledge is based on involvement in similar projects developed in other (sometimes neighbouring) countries to the borrower. Knowing how different types of projects are likely to develop, what are the key features and a reasonably accurate estimate of timings and knowledge of complex procurement processes may lead to much more effective project planning and implementation.

Other advantages for the effective implementation of a project can come from other staff such as environmentalists, country specialists and sustainability specialists who can all provide a contribution and suggestions based on their expertise and previous experience to the planning and implementation of a project.

Equally, if there is any domestic political pressure to focus on using local contractors and suppliers irrespective of the costs or to implement the project according to local laws and practices (rather than to adopt international processes which are designed to provide reasonably competitive costs), it may be that the assistance of an international organisation's staff is not necessary and even unwelcome. Consequently, obtaining a loan from a bank (possibly a commercial one that is either less interested or less able to get involved in the particular design and implementation issues) would be the borrower's aim.

[20] www.caribank.org.

[21] www.coebank.org.

[22] www.nib.int.

[23] www.caf.com.

[24] www.icrc.org.

2.4.1 Dedicated Project Office

Normally, a government borrowing funds for a specific purpose in a project would set up a separate office to deal with the numerous and various requirements—financial, procurement-related, environmental, as well as administrative. Such a dedicated office could recruit financial, legal and administrative staff as well as experts from the particular industry associated with the project (e.g. power generation or transmission, road or railway construction) and be able to provide guidance and focus during initial discussions that will be required and, in fact can be key to ensuring that the project has the best chance of being implemented easily, on budget and successfully as designed.

Such an office, sometimes called the Project Implementation Unit ('PIU' in abbreviated form), can be located near the project for good access by contractors and suppliers or may be located far away but in a place that is close to other government departments with better access to interested parties. There are lots of benefits associated with such an office being set up including their capacity to correspond knowledgeably about the project and to conduct a series of sometimes high value procurement processes to see what equipment (and potentially what technological solutions) are available to any particular issue facing the project. A project office, especially if it is located close to the project site, can also supervise and gain knowledge about progress, both in terms of actual construction but also in terms of how progress is forecast, hearing of important rumours, etc.

One of the downsides with such an office, or individuals based there especially in a developing country where wages are low, is that they can see and hear about large sums of money being allocated for different aspects of the project and consequently become tempted to engage in fraud or corruption, for example by generating illegal profits by misusing confidential information or agreeing to rig the procurement processes to favour certain suppliers. If the funds are to be misused or misapplied, sometimes the pressures come from other or multiple parts of the government (or even senior elected figures such as Ministers or even the Prime Minister/President).

2.4.2 Contractual Terms

The funding from an MDB is normally provided under a specific legal agreement (known as a finance contract). The terms and conditions may vary depending on the type of loan, the mandate under which it is being provided, the way(s) in which the project is foreseen to be implemented, repayment obligations, etc. Such terms and conditions as are important or necessary for the organisation providing the money will be included in a finance contract (or whatever it is called); normally there are standard terms and conditions that have been developed by the funder's legal department and they can be tailored to the specific needs of the project, country, etc., by the operational people and negotiations with the borrower.

The legal agreement (or contract under which the finance is provided) may also require the borrower to use certain processes in the implementation of the project (such as standard international procurement processes, standard bidding documents, etc.).

2.4.2.1 EIB's Information and Visits Clause

The Agreement can also provide the terms and conditions upon which the lender can choose to take a closer look at the circumstances surrounding the project if the need arises, for example to monitor developments/progress, review the effect of certain aspects on indigenous communities or if there is an allegation that fraud or corruption has occurred, that the funds are being misused or that the funds not being put to the purpose(s) intended.

Under clause 8 of the agreement with EIB, the borrower of the funds is obliged to:

(i) provide information about financing, procurement and implementation of the project, including giving notification to the lender of the funds of any event that might substantially affect the project;
(ii) provide accounting information and notify the lender of certain events (such as one that would materially affect the implementation of the project); and
(iii) allow visits by staff from the lender (and others, such from the European Community, authorised to visit) to the sites and works of the project, interview the borrower's and other staff about the project and those affected by it and review documents in relation to the project implementation.

2.4.2.2 WB's Disclosure of Fees Paid to Agents

The World Bank uses text in their Standard Bidding Document to have the bidders in a procurement process disclose the amount and identity(ies) of recipients of fees paid to third parties.

This information gives the local project team and the World Bank staff (particularly their monitoring staff and, if required, their investigators) details of funds (commissions, gratuities and fees) paid to agents or intermediaries who have been used to help them prepare and/or submit their bid.[25]

Page 66 para. (l) contains the standard language for the disclosure of commissions, gratuities and fees paid to intermediaries during the bidding process and contract execution:

[25]The link to the World Bank webpage where all the standard bidding documents by type of procurement process can be accessed is: https://projects.worldbank.org/en/projects-operations/products-and-services/brief/procurement-new-framework#SPD.

Letter of Bid

....

(l) Commissions, gratuities, fees: We have paid, or will pay the following commissions, gratuities, or fees with respect to the Bidding process or execution of the Contract: [insert complete name of each Recipient, its full address, the reason for which each commission or gratuity was paid and the amount and currency of each such commission or gratuity]

Name of Recipient
Address
Reason
Amount
If none has been paid or is to be paid, indicate 'none'.)

This type of clause is particularly important because bribes and kickbacks are regularly paid via third parties to mask the money trail. If an accurate disclosure is made and there are suspicions about the award of the contract, it gives investigators a starting point for their 'follow the money' inquiries. If, as is sometimes the case, this information is false, made-up or left entirely blank, that constitutes a misrepresentation and can be sanctionable.

2.4.2.3 EIB's Covenant of Integrity

The EIB Guide to Procurement[26] contains, at Annex 3, the following declaration (which is a Covenant of Integrity) that should be completed by bidders and submitted along with the bidding documents and addresses the following integrity issues:

2.4.3 Undertaking on Prohibited Conduct

'We declare and covenant that neither we nor anyone, including any of our directors, employees, agents, joint venture partners or sub-contractors, where these exist, acting on our behalf with due authority or with our knowledge or consent, or facilitated by us, has engaged, or will engage, in any Prohibited Conduct (as defined below) in connection with the tendering process or in the execution or supply of any works, goods or services for [specify the contract or tender invitation] (the 'Contract') and covenant to so inform you if any instance of any such Prohibited Conduct shall come to the attention of any person in our organisation having responsibility for ensuring compliance with this Covenant.

We shall, for the duration of the tender process and, if we are successful in our tender, for the duration of the Contract, appoint and maintain in office an officer, who shall be a person reasonably satisfactory to you and to whom you shall have full and immediate access, having the duty, and the necessary powers, to ensure compliance with this Covenant.

[26]www.eib.org/publications/guide-to-procurement.

2.4.4 Undertaking on Exclusion/Debarment

We declare and covenant that neither we nor anyone, including any of our directors, employees, agents, joint venture partners or sub-contractors, where these exist, acting on our behalf with due authority or with our knowledge or consent, or facilitated by us, (i) is listed or otherwise subject to EU/UN Sanctions and (ii) in connection with the execution or supply of any works, goods or services for the Contract, will act in contravention of EU/UN Sanctions. We covenant to so inform you if any instance shall come to the attention of any person in our organisation having responsibility for ensuring compliance with this Covenant.

If (i) we have been, or any such director, employee, agent or joint venture partner, where this exists, acting as aforesaid has been, convicted in any court or sanctioned by any authority of any offence involving a Prohibited Conduct in connection with any tendering process or provision of works, goods or services during the 5 years immediately preceding the date of this Covenant, or (ii) any such director, employee, agent or a representative of a joint venture partner, where this exists, has been dismissed or has resigned from any employment on the grounds of being implicated in any Prohibited Conduct, or (iii) we have been, or any of our directors, employees, agents or joint venture partners, where these exist, acting as aforesaid has been excluded or otherwise sanctioned by the EU Institutions or any major Multilateral Development Bank (including World Bank Group, African Development Bank, Asian Development Bank, European Bank for Reconstruction and Development, European Investment Bank or Inter-American Development Bank) from participation in a tendering procedure on the grounds of Prohibited Conduct, we give details of that conviction, dismissal or resignation, or exclusion below, together with details of the measures that we have taken, or shall take, to ensure that neither this company nor any of our directors, employees or agents commits any Prohibited Conduct in connection with the Contract [give details if necessary].

We acknowledge that if we are subject to an exclusion decision by the European Investment Bank (EIB), we will not be eligible to be awarded a contract to be financed by the EIB.

2.4.5 Books and Records Inspection

We grant [indicate the name of the Project Promoter], the European Investment Bank and auditors appointed by either of them, as well as any authority or European Union institution or body having competence under European Union law, the right to inspect and copy our books and records and those of all our sub-contractors under the Contract. We accept to preserve these books and records generally in accordance with applicable law but in any case for at least six years from the date of tender submission and in the event we are awarded the Contract, at least six years from the date of substantial performance of the Contract.

For the purpose of this Covenant, Prohibited Conduct has the meaning provided in the EIB's Anti-Fraud Policy - EIB's Anti-Fraud Policy for definitions (http://www.eib.org/infocentre/publications/all/anti-fraud-policy.htm)

Note: This Covenant must be sent to the Bank together with the contract in the case of an international procurement procedure (as defined in article 3.3.2). In other cases, it must be kept by the promoter and available upon request from the Bank'.

2.4.6 Monitoring Project Developments

The lender should not just provide the finance for a project. In many cases, the borrower will experience some major or minor technical problems and/or a lack of knowledge/experience in implementing such a project and so it may become necessary for the staff of the lending institution to sometimes take an active role in assisting with the project's implementation, for example by providing advice, helping the borrower address environmental concerns and/or monitoring of procurement.

The inspection and visit rights contract clause quoted above can prove important (if not decisive) to the resolution of a problem, especially if there is an allegation of misconduct in connection with the implementation of a project. For example:

- the rooms don't measure up to the ones in the original plans or pictures (smaller rooms are cheaper to (a) build; (b) decorate and (c) maintain/heat than larger ones);
- the road is not built at all or is not built wide enough or even that the road is not built in the way most roads have been according to the technical specifications (maybe the sub-strata or drains are built incorrectly or are missing entirely and therefore the road is less likely to function properly or even survive when it faces the first monsoon flooding or other adverse conditions);
- the trains are poorly matched with the terrain (lots of stations and steep hills and tight curves on the route vs long, flat straights with few stops) and/or design of the route;
- the power station generator is not as effective as originally thought because the equipment is incorrectly assembled/constructed, or is otherwise ineffective;
- the newly constructed building is in danger of falling down if it has not been constructed with appropriate safeguards and in line with local regulations, for example in a locality with high risks of strong earthquakes or other natural disasters;
- the building(s) do not exist—they were to be constructed in areas that are difficult to visit and whilst the paperwork supplied by the borrower claims they were built and paid for, in some cases this is not true. The building(s) were not erected and, although visiting them is difficult (maybe they were to be built in remote locations, in former war zones or there are other practical difficulties accessing them), it is possible to obtain recent satellite imagery demonstrating conclusively that the construction has not occurred;
- A tribe or other landowners says it has been cheated or illegally deprived of land without appropriate contact or consultation.

Some of these issues can occur in a project no matter how big or small it is, merely because of inexperience or lack of knowledge, mismanagement or unfortunate gaps in monitoring or data. They may also occur because of:

- corporate fraud;
- a desire by project officials to try to gain personally;

- corruption between the key commercial players and project or government officials; and/or
- a need to address (or even avoid the effects of) laws/regulations.

2.4.7 Project Supervision

The lender would generally have a team of experts on hand to implement the project, to monitor developments, to advise on implementation of key aspects of the project and to help the borrower (whether it is national or local government or otherwise) with any technical issues that materialise.

Project staff should adapt the processes to that location, brief government officials on the progress on the various aspects that are being implemented and those planned to be implemented in the future and review and, if necessary, provide answers to questions from the borrower's (or lenders) staff. They can also provide brief updates and reports to the lending institution about progress, even to provide an assessment of the strengths and weaknesses of implementation when the project is completed.

2.4.8 Project Completion

The completion of a project is usually an occasion for celebration—farmers and industrialists being able to reach markets quicker because of the construction of a new road or newly refurbished old one, there are fewer or no power cuts because of the construction of a new power station or distribution system, passengers can travel quickly and directly by train between two previously unconnected cities, teachers having a weather-proof room (or series of rooms, even an entire school) in which to gather and teach children, etc. This will be explored in more detail below.

That is, unless the project is badly affected by fraud and corruption and therefore, in the end, what results is not fit for purpose and may even need further taxpayer funds to maintain it in its current state.

Chapter 3
Types of Support

The nature and type of support provided by an international financial institution depends on the issues to be addressed. For example, the loan may be directed towards the construction or refurbishment of a transport link (such as railway, port/dock, road or airport), construction of housing, provision of new buildings for schools (or other educational needs such as supply of new school books or updating of the curriculum), provision of clinics, hospitals or other medical facilities or equipment, support for SMEs in a particular sector, or even the provision of food, drink or shelter in an emergency situation.

3.1 Specific Issues vs General Mandate

Each institution has a number of tools it can utilise to impact the area of concern (or reduce the impact of a situation) in line with its mandate.

For example, some organisations are focused on certain specific issues—the UN's Food and Agriculture Organization (FAO)[1] or the International Fund for Agricultural Development (IFAD, working towards the eradication of poverty and hunger in rural areas of developing countries)[2] are focused on avoiding mass starvation and provision of food supplies. Other organisations have a wider remit which may in part overlap. There is also the World Food Programme (providing emergency relief and humanitarian support)[3] which, for example, is working to prevent the misuse of food relief for hungry people in Yemen. The same is true of

[1]www.fao.org.

[2]www.ifad.org.

[3]www.wfp.org.

D. Smith, *Promoting Integrity in the Work of International Organisations*,
Contributions to Finance and Accounting,
https://doi.org/10.1007/978-3-030-73916-4_3

an organisation working to promote health or to combat disease (the Global Fund[4] or the World Health Organisation[5]) which may have very focused health-related goals that may overlap with or complement projects financed by the MDBs.

Chronic malnutrition has profound, long-term effects on health and life prospects for a given population. The World Food Programme works with governments and partners to help vulnerable groups, such as women, children, and people receiving treatment for HIV and tuberculosis, to access nutritious diets. Their programmes include distributing Specialised Nutritious Foods, fortifying staple foods, designing/implementing school feeding and enabling dietary diversification.

More than 80% of the world's people who face food insecurity live in countries prone to natural hazards. Such disasters can disrupt agricultural production and weaken livelihoods, resulting in an equivalent rise in poverty and hunger. The World Food Programme works with governments and communities to try to reduce the impacts of disasters on the population's food security by trying to build resilience, strengthening emergency preparedness and improving early warning systems to give quick and better information.

3.2 Loans Versus Grants

Some organisations give (rather than lend) funds. This sort of transaction generally occurs with the poorest countries. The inability to require repayment of the funds occurs in cases where there is a genuine shortage of funds to repay a loan by the recipient country. Providing funds rather than lending them can also be facilitated by trust funds that can be established and maintained with specific purposes and/or countries in mind.

In some opinions, the receipt of funds without incurring an obligation to repay them also may make it more likely that the funds will be misused. As there is no obligation to repay, will the recipient use the funds prudently and carefully? Will they plan, use and manage how those funds will be distributed and for what aspects the funds will be used as carefully as if they had to repay them?

The International Development Association (IDA),[6] part of the World Bank, has assisted many such nations to move towards the Millennium Development Goals. Examples of funds provided for assistance (i.e. not lent) include their use in roads in Azerbaijan, access to education in Haiti and good governance in Ethiopia.

The African country Chad has also received funds to help support the national budget '.. to improve the management of fiscal resources and risks, and implement structural reforms to foster growth, while ensuring the protection of the most

[4]The full name is: 'The Global Fund to Fight AIDS, Tuberculosis and Malaria'; their website is: www.theglobalfund.org.

[5]www.who.int.

[6]www.ida.worldbank.org.

vulnerable'. The World Bank Board of Executive Directors approved a grant totalling $65 million for these purposes to Chad under the Economic Recovery and Resilience Development Policy Operation. This is the first of two development policy operations for the 2018–2019 period. This Programme in Chad follows an emergency budget stabilisation operation implemented in 2017. It is a medium-term measure supporting Chad's ongoing efforts to improve the management of fiscal resources and risks and to implement structural reforms to foster growth, whilst ensuring the protection of the most vulnerable.[7]

3.3 Trust Funds

One of the particular problems for a recipient of trust funds is that there are sometimes higher levels of interest from the financiers of a trust fund about how the funds are being used and therefore there are higher levels of supervision involved. If such funds are suspected of being misused, there are higher levels of political concern and with them, publicity. This occurred for example in projects financed in Bosnia i Herzegovina after the break-up of Yugoslavia and the resulting civil war, such as de-mining projects of areas close to or even containing urban areas after the war finished.

Whilst all projects are important, the impact of such safety-critical issues can be life-threatening (like whether a designated area of land has been searched and, in the case of finding landmines, that they are safely and sustainably removed or dealt with by experts)—has the designated area truly been searched? Are children who walk across the land to school genuinely safe? A fraud in misrepresenting that an area has indeed been properly searched (when it has not) has a significant and direct impact if a landmine blows up and a victim is hospitalised or worse, killed. Alternatively, if there are groups of searchers not interested or willing to compete effectively in a procurement process to award further de-mining contracts, land likely to have been mined is not later searched with significantly higher chance that a landmine can be triggered and someone thereby injured or killed.

3.4 Variety of Finance

The World Bank stated that there is a range of financial support that can be provided to a country in need by one of the public banks. Indeed, it was listed on the World Bank website[8] in January 2019 as being the following:

[7]www.worldbank.org/en/news/loans-credits/2018/09/12/chad-first-economic-recovery-and-resilience-development-policy-operation.

[8]www.worldbank.org.

'**Investment Project Financing** provides IBRD loan, IDA credit/grant and guarantee financing to governments for activities that create the physical/social infrastructure necessary to reduce poverty and create sustainable development'.

Investment Project Financing (IPF) is used in all sectors, with a concentration in the infrastructure, human development, agriculture, and public administration sectors. IPF is focused on the long-term (5 to 10 year horizon) and supports a wide range of activities including capital-intensive investments, agricultural development, service delivery, credit and grant delivery [including micro-credit], community-based development, and institution building.

Unlike commercial lending, Bank IPF not only supplies borrowing countries with needed financing but also serves as a vehicle for sustained, global knowledge transfer and technical assistance. This includes support to analytical and design work in the conceptual stages of project preparation, technical support and expertise (including in the areas of project management and fiduciary and safeguards activities) during implementation, and institution building throughout the project.

Development Policy Financing provides IBRD loan, IDA credit/grant and guarantee budget support to governments or a political subdivision for a programme of policy and institutional actions to help achieve sustainable, shared growth and poverty reduction.

Development Policy Financing (DPF) provides rapidly disbursing financing to help a borrower address actual or anticipated development financing requirements. DPF aims to support the borrower in achieving sustainable development through a programme of policy and institutional actions, for example, strengthening public financial management, improving the investment climate, addressing bottlenecks to improve service delivery, and diversifying the economy. DPF supports such reforms through non-earmarked general budget financing that is subject to the borrower's own implementation processes and systems. The Bank's use of DPF in a country is determined in the context of the Country Partnership Framework (CPF).

The DPF policy emphasises country ownership and alignment, stakeholder consultation, donor coordination, and results, and requires a systematic treatment of fiduciary risks and of the potential environmental and distributional consequences of supported policies. DPF can be extended as loans, credits, or grants. Funds are made available to the client based on:

- maintenance of an adequate macroeconomic policy framework, as determined by the Bank with inputs from IMF assessments
- satisfactory implementation of the overall reform programme
- completion of a set of critical policy and institutional actions agreed between the Bank and the client.

Development Policy Operations: Prior Actions are policy and institutional actions deemed critical to achieving the objectives of a programme supported by the development policy operation. These present the legal terms defined in the loan agreement that have to be met for each operation before disbursement. A database of prior actions for all development policy operations since fiscal year 2005 is updated annually at the end of each fiscal year by the Operations Policy and Country Services Vice Presidency.

Program-for-Results links disbursement of funds directly to the delivery of defined results, helping countries improve the design and implementation of their own development programmes and achieve lasting results by strengthening institutions and building capacity.

Trust funds and grants allow scaling up of activities, notably in fragile and crisis-affected situations; enable the Bank Group to provide support when our ability to lend is limited; provide immediate assistance in response to natural disasters and other emergencies; and pilot innovations that are later mainstreamed into our operations.

Private sector options for financing, direct investment and guarantees are provided by MIGA and IFC. Guarantees can also be provided through the World Bank (IBRD/IDA) for private sector projects.

Customised options and risk management

Multiphase Programmatic Approach allows countries to structure a long, large, or complex engagement as a set of smaller linked operations (or phases), under one programme. It can be applied to Investment Project Financing and Program-for-Results and is not a stand-alone instrument.

Chapter 4
Projects

4.1 Types of Projects

International organisations are on the lookout for projects that would benefit from finance and also, in some projects, their expertise. In fact, there are many applications for loans submitted to one (or more than one) of the international banks with the mandate and jurisdiction to provide funding from countries around the world.

The 'subject matter' or classification of a project is one of the reasons for the numerous applicants—it's not just about the organisations lending or allocating (and the countries borrowing or receiving) large sums of money, their involvement and the need to have international experts (consultants) is sometimes about the subject matter (for example, the cross channel tunnel financed by EIB) and the fact that the government is taking some action to try to overcome some urgent or long-standing problem. Borrowing from an international (public) bank may be cheaper too—the international organisations are not intentionally making a commercial rate of interest (although the rates are adjusted to accommodate risk factors, etc.).

The following is a list of the types of projects that may receive finance from some (or all) of the international banks—each organisation has its own assessment of applications based on its own rules and policies about its financing of particular types of projects, so an application for a particular proposed project might not be accepted by all of the international banks; there are, though, many projects that can be co-financed by two or more organisations:

- Agriculture
- Climate Change
- Education
- Energy and Power

D. Smith, *Promoting Integrity in the Work of International Organisations*,
Contributions to Finance and Accounting,
https://doi.org/10.1007/978-3-030-73916-4_4

  - Generation
  - Renewables (hydro, wind, solar, biomass)
  - Distribution

- Environment
- Fisheries
- Forestry
- Information and Communications Technology
- Gender
- Health
- Human capital
- Irrigation
- Manufacturing
- Mining and Extractive Industries
- Private Sector
- Public Administration (central, regional or local government)

  - Economic Governance
  - Financial Management
  - Governance
  - Law and Justice

- Tourism
- Transport Infrastructure

  - aviation
  - ports
  - rail
  - roads
  - other
  - urban infrastructure
  - waterways

- Urban Development
- Waste Management
- Water and wastewater

There are many commonalities in the risks of fraud or corruption in any of the projects in the above list; of course, the more specialised the work to be undertaken on a project is, the more specialised the knowledge needs to be to defraud it as well. Nevertheless, basic construction frauds, misrepresentations about what work has been undertaken and bribes paid in return for the award of a contract can be initiated in a wide range of projects.

However, the fraud and corruption which can impact a project may not be foreseen or planned in the implementation but it may be planned over a longer time, in other words new buildings may ultimately be put to uses other than the one (e.g. a simple school) that was the focus of the project or in the award not of construction contracts but in the (longer term) maintenance contracts.

4.2 Project Procurement

Procurement is a procedure for obtaining various bids (including prices) for goods, works (including construction) and services in a competitive market.[1] Each international organisation has rules (to try to ensure that the process is efficient and a genuine competition) that would be required to be followed for the acquisition of equipment and contractors/suppliers in a project being implemented, although some accept that local rules (and there are numerous variations) from certain jurisdictions can be followed.

There are few limits to the places from which the goods and services can be made and delivered, although generally the longer the distance for transportation, the more expensive is the delivery, especially if the equipment is of a large size and/or is delicate and sensitive to knocks, bangs and scrapes. Some corporations have won many bids by taking an aggressive (sometimes even as a loss-leader) stance to the various elements in a costing of a good or service to be supplied for a project. Bids can be submitted from any number of suppliers/contractors but of course the number of bids may depend on the subject matter of the bids, the ability to transport the equipment, etc.

For example, there are only a limited number of producers who have the technology, knowledge and experience to bid for the production of high-speed trains or power generating equipment whereas the construction of railway stations and four-lane roads are less sophisticated and therefore may be the subject of more bids to undertake such construction work. The circumstances of the project are also important—where is the project located (ie. is it land-locked? How will deliveries be made?), whether early payments will be forthcoming and whether the project manager (be it a public or private agency) has a good reputation and is reliable in paying its suppliers or getting into disputes (real or made-up) to delay payments to a supplier.

4.3 Possible Problems in Procurement

The risk of fraud or corruption affecting a particular procurement process in a project depends on a number of factors including the sector involved, the opportunity to hold a fair and reasonably well organised procurement process, the number of potential bidders and whether they are located locally, regionally or internationally (perhaps even on another continent). There are a number of factors (which may be directly or indirectly linked to the status of the project or may be completely

---

[1]For more info, please see wikipedia at: www.en.wikipedia.org/wiki/Procurement, www.projects.worldbank.org/en/projects-operations/products-and-services/brief/procurement-policies-and-guidance or www.eib.org/en/about/procurement/index.htm.

unrelated to the project) that can affect the pricing of a bid in a procurement process to ascertain the most appropriate and cheapest/best supplier.

In general, the website Wikipedia states the following about corruption:

> Corruption is a form of dishonesty or criminal offence undertaken by a person or organisation entrusted with a position of authority, to acquire illicit benefit or abuse power for one's private gain. Corruption may include many activities including bribery and embezzlement, though it may also involve practices that are legal in many countries.[1] Political corruption occurs when an office-holder or other governmental employee acts in an official capacity for personal gain. Corruption is most commonplace in kleptocracies, oligarchies, narco-states and mafia states.
>
> Corruption can occur on different scales. Corruption ranges from small favours between a small number of people (petty corruption),[2] to corruption that affects the government on a large scale (grand corruption), and corruption that is so prevalent that it is part of the everyday structure of society, including corruption as one of the symptoms of organised crime. Corruption and crime are endemic sociological occurrences which appear with regular frequency in virtually all countries on a global scale in varying degree and proportion. Individual nations each allocate domestic resources for the control and regulation of corruption and crime. Strategies to counter corruption are often summarised under the umbrella term anti-corruption.[2]

The following issues are more specific problems that should be avoided if possible in a procurement process:

Under-Pricing: Occasionally a firm puts in a low priced bid, designed to have a high chance of success winning the contract. The pricing in such a low (possibly under-priced) bid may be dependent on the status of the company and whether it has sufficient work to keep its employees busy; the price(s) used in the bid may also be a function of whether there are politics involved (local, national or regional) or whether subsidies are available.

Low bids are also often made in the knowledge (or assumption) that connections with corrupt officials will allow key price elements to be increased after the event, so an initial low bid actually turns into a high final price.

Overpricing: there are a number of factors why a firm may submit an expensive bid - if a firm does not have the time or resources to calculate and submit a competitive bid that has a legitimate chance to win the procurement (but nevertheless wants to maintain its image in the market), if there is no real desire to win or even if there is such a desire but the firm gets its calculations wrong (or makes incorrect estimates of certain costs), a bidder can submit a bid that is overpriced.

Alternatively, the firm knows that its (high) bid will be accepted because other bidders will be disqualified or because the technical specifications have been 'hard-wired' to give them an advantage.

Possible Collusion: if there are good relations between some or many of the bidders locally or regionally, it is possible that the bids could be tainted by collusion and that (the designated or agreed) winner submits the lowest priced bid (irrespective

[2]www.en.wikipedia.org/wiki/Corruption.

of whether the price of the bid is providing reasonable value for money) and the others submit supporting but credible bids at varying but importantly at (pre-agreed) higher prices. In some cases, the winner is chosen by rotation and all bidders will win a contract in due course 'when it's their turn', in other cases the winner is consistently pre-determined and the losing bidder (sometimes more than one) is never the winner, but gets a share of the over-pricing profits to ensure that it or they will continue its support of the collusive scheme and in future bids.

Alternatively, some or all of the bidders are in fact part of the same group or entity but with different names, addresses, etc., (or an affiliated entity).

Coercion (Physical or Economic): In some cases, one or more sets of bidders are threatened (with poor assessment of their bids or even disqualification from the process) by project officials if certain conditions are not met or certain payments are not agreed to be made. Even if their bid is close to what is required in terms of substance and price, the assessment of all of the bids can be manipulated to ensure that the result (and the most favoured bidder) will also do what is necessary to meet any informal agreements or 'local conditions'. The reverse is unfortunately also true, namely that a bidder can make threats to the project managers about the economic viability of the project (or even the physical safety of the project officials and their families) if they are not awarded a sizeable contract.

Each of the international organisations have clear rules forbidding these types of fraud, corruption, collusion and coercion and mis-use of the funds but such rules do not mean that prohibited conduct is not attempted during the bidding process and may even be successful.

There have been cases (subsequently uncovered) where:

(1) a group of bidders submitted prices (at first appearance, the prices appeared competitive) that had actually been calculated using a formula and in consultation/agreement with the bidders;
(2) the bidders had agreed to submit bids containing documents all prepared by one of the bidders (in particular, false bank guarantees); or
(3) the bidders have colluded not just about the pricing/content of the bids but also subsequently about their responses to be given to questions asked by investigators about the similarities in the bids, the lack of competitive pricing and whether there was any collusion!

4.4 Project Implementation

There are a number of possible vulnerabilities to fraud or corruption during the course of a project being implemented. Such risks may not only depend on the type of project being worked on but also the people that are involved, from the agency implementing the project and related government agencies (such as the provision of construction permits for a newly built building etc.) but also in the firms and corporations (and any local partners) that have been selected to supply goods and services, as well as the entities undertaking important related construction and other works.

As with any series of potentially high-value transactions, there is, of course, the risk that entities will try to cheat to increase profits or reduce losses, will engage in deliberate deception or make misrepresentations (through the misuse of accountancy documents like invoices, or otherwise) that can be used to attempt to gain unduly or that funds will be stolen by individuals for personal gain.

If the funds are misused, the likelihood is that the funds will be transferred elsewhere at an early stage, with appropriate camouflage about the reasons and logic/documents for the transfer being put in place if necessary. Maybe there has even been agreement during the procurement exercise for the fraudulent or corrupt conduct to occur not during the procurement process itself but at a later stage, e.g. as part of the billing process.

As was recently discovered in Mozambique, there is the possibility of overstatement of the number of people affected or involved—there were reported to be 30,000 'ghost' or fictional government employees in that African state.[3] Overstatement (and the opposite, understatement) can be common but can sometimes directly (and significantly) influence what is being developed—such as the following (and numerous other) questions. How many civil servants are to be housed in a building? What is the likely rate of attendance at a local hospital or medical clinic? How many cars would drive along a new road or take a shortcut over a new bridge? And if it was charging a fee, how many could pay? If a high speed train connects two cities, how many more people will travel on the faster link? All of these questions need solid data/answers in order to try to prioritise potential projects that will be developed ahead of those that may be a good idea or strategically important but not economically viable.

Once the construction of the basic structure (road, road bridge, railway/tram line, power station, etc.) has been completed, the project may have some additional aspects that become necessary before the project has been fully effective and implemented.

4.5 Controls

This is a short overview of the possible controls that can be put in place (with the broader framework being discussed in greater detail in Chaps. 7–9).

One of the controls that can be used to check how the project has developed and, in particular, whether there are any red flags of misconduct or misuse of the funds is

[3] On 11 December 2018, the BBC publicised that 'Mozambique's government has discovered more than 30,000 ghost workers on the civil service payroll. The civil service said some were paid for jobs they had not done, others were dead or fictitious. The fraud had cost the government around $250m (GBP198m) between 2015 and 2017...' www.bbc.com/news/amp/world-africa-46520946.

for the lenders to utilise the right, normally included in the standard terms of the contract, to review the books and records for the project. This would apply to the books and records kept by the project agency/PIU as well as those retained by the contractors, consultants and suppliers working on the project.

(i) **Good communication with the borrower**: keeping in close contact with the project managers (whether this is by mail or less formally by phone or email) and ensuring that there is active communication of issues can in some cases reduce the size of the problems that develop and the time needed to spent to unravel or sort them out.
(ii) **Covenant of Integrity:** as noted above in Chap. 2,[4] the EIB requires that bidders submit a positive declaration or Covenant of Integrity with their bids. This includes a declaration of whether the bidder has been debarred by any other MDB, thus putting the project team on notice that greater monitoring may be necessary if the bid is nevertheless successful.
(iii) **Declaration of use of Agents:** given that third parties can be heavily involved in the agreement for corruption or fraud to occur in the procurement process, the World Bank seeks to ensure that the use of such third parties is disclosed - see the text in Chap. 2. If there are suspicions of corruption, this declaration gives investigators the starting point of who to ask whether the process was tainted by bribery and, if so, who was involved.
(iv) **Site Visits**: one of the ways in which the project can be monitored and it's progress assessed is by regular visits to key places associated with the project. Indeed as noted above, the legal agreement would normally contain language to provide financiers with the right to visit the project and conduct inspection (also as specified above). Such language may also be used for visits which form the basis of conducting a proactive review (called Proactive Integrity Reviews at EIB and elsewhere or as Detailed Implementation Reviews at the World Bank). These will be discussed in greater detail in Chap. 11.[5]
(v) **'No Objection' to key contract awards**: sometimes the financier(s) will provide oversight and assistance, by providing that proposed awards of key contracts to be subject to their own review and approval and perhaps that of other lender(s).

    This in reality allows the lender(s) to oversee the procurement decisions, review the bidding documents and the assessments that have been made of the various proposals and to assess whether there are any problems, strange selections or even red flags of fraud or corruption arising from the bid evaluation process.
(vi) **Books and Records**: as noted above, one of the terms (usually included in the loan agreement) is that the lender can request access the books and records of the project, not just those maintained by borrower but also those maintained by

[4]Pages 19–20.

[5]Page 118.

private contractors, suppliers and consultants as far as they record details of or relating to the project.

Maintenance of such books and records is not only required by national legislation (or rules issued by a regulator), which prescribes not just which documents should be preserved but for how long but in some cases is also required by the contract awarded under a project.[6] Of course, there may be other reasons to preserve such books and records and these reasons may determine the length, number and type of the documents that are kept. If the company is involved in lengthy and detailed litigation arising out of the contract, the policy of retention/destruction would need to be put on hold and the relevant books and records retained for a more lengthy time period, dictated by the need to use or refer to the documents in the litigation, disclosure of documents to court, use, inspection and analysis of original documents, etc.

For example, the US Fraud and Corrupt Practices Act (FCPA) requires corporations to 'make and keep books, records, and accounts' but there are some implications about creating and preserving accurate books and records. Corporations are also now encouraged to ensure that they retain the numerous (non-email) apps employees use to communicate with colleagues and suppliers, as well as to calculate estimated costs. However, the retention, uploading, searching, and producing of legacy data can be costly in terms of time/resources and may offer little or no measurable benefit to the later reviewer, so such retention could be time-limited and the information should be preserved only for business reasons. The entity should also have a workable archive facility for storing such documents and data which would also have a clear policy on the retention period and document destruction, striking a balance between the risks of premature destruction and over-retention.

Of course, retention of documentation is important not just for the entity's business and tax records (requirements of national legislation where the entity is registered) but also, if retained, as evidence in a civil or criminal process. If it is not retained because the document was disposed of in accordance with their retention policy, the proceedings may be put in jeopardy.

4.6 Project Completion

Once the construction of the basic parts of the project has been completed, as noted above the project may still have some important aspects (such as road signage and lane markings in a road project or timetable development and management of passengers for a rail/tram project) to be undertaken before the project has been fully implemented. The project managers can, of course, take a deep celebratory breath once the construction has been properly undertaken on a project but just

[6]For example, the requirement in the Covenant of Integrity used by EIB, see the EIB Covenant of Integrity above, pages 27–29.

because there is a new concrete building that looks like a power station doesn't mean that the turbines are efficiently producing electricity.

There are key stages in the completion of a project that will cause changes and adaptations to the focus for the project team—once successful construction has occurred, they will have to start to focus more on the finer details (eg. of timetabling and customer service to get the trains running regularly, or the ability of the generators to work efficiently perhaps in combination with existing equipment).

This change of focus may also mean the risk of fraud and corruption changes or possibly diminishes (e.g. if the construction is satisfactory or the technical equipment has been delivered correctly and is in apparently good working order). However, this does not mean that the risk of fraud and corruption will completely disappear—there may be other civil works contracts to be awarded/undertaken and there are possibilities of other contracts (e.g. maintenance contracts and other ongoing tasks, such as collecting fares, etc.) linked to the work of the project but not necessarily included in the project specifications. Nevertheless the project team may need to select and award the contract(s) and the work to be done.

Chapter 5
Cyber Crime, Data Security and Data Protection

International organisations are no less likely to be the target (and therefore the potential victim) of fraudulent behaviour by criminals than anyone else. Indeed international organisations are frequently even deliberately targeted specifically because their staff may be known in a wide range of jurisdictions and because of the numerous high-value transactions that are regularly being conducted (in a range of currencies and with a range of potential beneficiaries), hence the possible chance to introduce a false or deceptive claim and have it overlooked, thereby gaining significant benefits of a fraudulent transaction.

The nature of possible cyber crimes can vary according to the location of the institution, the robustness of its IT systems and the processes that the organisation has put in place to guard against it, including possible fraudulent claims. The internal systems that have been put in place by an organisation may also have been sensitised to send alerts to the possible victim and/or not automatically processing certain types of transactions that have been submitted deliberately as an intended fraud including:

- Falsely claiming to be an employee and seek salary and benefits payments;
- Falsely claiming to be a borrower and seeking (additional) disbursements/ payments;
- Falsely claiming to be a contractor or supplier to the organisation itself and requesting payment of (false) invoices;
- Being the victim of an email scam (of various types);
- Having legitimate staff (who do actually work for the organisation) have their identity stolen and misused;
- Having the organisation's identity stolen and thereafter replicated on another website which misuses or misrepresents the true situation (eg. in connection with fees payable for processing an application).

Data security is crucial to keeping the funds of the organisation secure and making sure that no-one receives the funds wrongly or that the entities or individuals doing the work are being appropriately reimbursed. In some cases, formal letters

D. Smith, *Promoting Integrity in the Work of International Organisations*,
Contributions to Finance and Accounting,
https://doi.org/10.1007/978-3-030-73916-4_5

requesting payment by legitimate borrowers have been intercepted and replacement letters were subsequently sent with the same request for payment but with different (i.e. the fraudster's) bank account details in it. Whilst some 'Know-Your-Customer' (KYC) checks would uncover such an attempt, if there is pressure to complete the transaction (along with many other transactions), any corners that are cut leading to few or no KYC checks on the recipient's bank account could lead to the request for payment being approved and the fraudster receiving significant funds.

There have, regrettably, been cases of 'phishing' where the organisations web site (or parts of it) have been copied with the exception that any application for funds has the payment of a fee linked to it, which is not the case for any of the legitimate MDBs. Indeed, people could have been cheated out of large sums sometimes by criminals operating an email account similar to (although not exactly the same as) the name of an employee of the organisation concerned (so any quick background checks may have been satisfied) but then the victim, when they have paid the requested fees, has failed to receive the promised (or any) funds. Consequently, identity checking and KYC processes are key to fraud avoidance.

Data Security Data security is increasingly important around the World given the quantity and nature of data that can be stored. This is because, at a personal and commercial level, the data is of great potential value, especially if an identity can be stolen and the accessible data can be misused with a wide range of consequences, both cultural and economic. This also includes personal concerns over privacy. However, greater security and protection measures merely reduces risks in the misuse of data but does not automatically inspire higher levels of trust.

Given the rapid speed of IT-related developments and the nature/extent of the potential damage, there are many questions to be considered, including:

- Can policy changes and resulting new legislation improve the responses by organisations/corporations and the general public to avoid or mitigate the cyber threats?
- How can individuals and organisation/companies improve their systems to guard against potential insecurity? and
- Are there any ways to protect particularly vulnerable people from the effects of cyber crime?

Data Protection At the same time as facing the threat of cyber crime, international organisations try to be as open and accountable as possible with data and the flow/availability of information. Some European organisations such as EIB, are also subject to European data protection rules.

The latest European rules are contained in the General Data Protection Regulation (GDPR). It replaces the Data Protection Directive 95/46/EC and is designed to change the way data is managed and processed. More specifically, the GDPR aims to harmonise data privacy laws for the European Union and the European Economic Area (EEA) to ensure that all citizens have equal data privacy. It also deals with the disclosure of personal data to places outside the EU/EEA area. The regulation generally aims to give control of personal data to individuals regardless of the person's (or data subjects') citizenship. It will affect commercial entities as well as public and government agencies.

This law has important impacts on the storage and processing of data/information retained for investigations and whistleblowers data. For example in Germany, the German Data Protection Authority (DPA) issued specific whistleblower—related guidance. More specifically, the collection of personal data from a whistleblowing hotline is allowed if it relates to fraud, corruption and insider trading amongst other topics. Having legitimate interests in the processing of the data is crucial and necessary in a whistleblowing context.

The German DPA has recommended that a whistleblower submit their report anonymously (as opposed to the other option of identifying themselves in the report to their employer and giving consent for their identity to be disclosed to the alleged perpetrator). The only restriction is that disclosure does not have to take place when it must be kept secret because of overriding legitimate interests of a third party.

As less than half of EU member states have comprehensive whistleblower protection laws, it is hoped that the new provisions of the GDPR will ensure a more consistent protection of whistleblowers across the EU.[1]

[1]FCPA Blog article entitled 'GDPR: What are the grounds for processing personal data during an investigation?' by Lara White, Andrew Reeves and Sarah Greenwood, dated September 10, 2019 which notes that: 'The GDPR applies to organisations that are established in the EU (regardless of whether the personal data that they process is of EU data subjects or not). The GDPR also applies to the processing of personal data by non-EU entities, where such processing is in the context of offering goods or services to data subjects in the EU or in the context of monitoring of the behaviour of data subjects in the EU' and that personal data is 'defined very broadly in the GDPR as any information relating to an identified or identifiable natural person. In practice this means that data collections and reviews will nearly always involve the processing of personal data'. Also, the article notes that it is 'much more difficult to rely on an employee's consent as a grounds for processing' and that 'If consent cannot be relied on, another ground for processing will need to be identified (usually the employer's legitimate interest in reviewing the data)'.

Chapter 6
Money Laundering and Other Illegal Conduct

The work done in projects by many international contractors also requires, among other things, the coordination and management of international money flows. This is part of what is required for the effective management of the contract(s), to deliver the goods or perform services in another country and make payments in and receive funds from various countries (if they are outside of the EU Eurozone) in a different currency.

A further problem arises if payments are to be made for fraudulent or corrupt purposes, as it is possible that those involved can be breaking the laws of the borrowing country (where the project is being implemented) and indeed the laws of the country in which the corporation is based or head office is located (usually it would be both if fraud or corruption overseas is made illegal in the home state). In addition, the entities intending to engage (or continuing to engage) in criminal misconduct may also be in danger of breaching laws against money laundering in related, third party countries that have little or no connection with the actual project but are involved (e.g. by the location of bank accounts) in the movement of funds or other related banking transactions such as purchasing/transferring currency. One example of this would be where the project official seeking a bribe maintains a (secret) bank account in Switzerland or another jurisdiction merely to maximise privacy and convenience, maximise the secrecy and security of the account as well as to facilitate the payment/receipt of bribes.

One situation which may create legal liabilities on the persons involved is the need to gather sufficient local funds so that a corrupt entity has the ability and resources available locally to pay bribes to those influencing/managing the project and making key project decisions. That may not be the case when 'secret' accounts are used to receive the bribes overseas. Another could be that the pay-offs are made by the organiser to the other involved parties for deliberately submitting a losing but otherwise compliant bid in a collusive scheme.

It would be difficult for investigators from a law enforcement agency to obtain sufficient evidence of such payments, to determine the amount and timing of them

D. Smith, *Promoting Integrity in the Work of International Organisations*,
Contributions to Finance and Accounting,
https://doi.org/10.1007/978-3-030-73916-4_6

and to see whether the conduct amounted to bribery/wrongdoing without relying on a Mutual Legal Assistance requests from other jurisdictions to gather evidence of the payments and details of the bank accounts making and receiving the payments (including the identity of the account holder(s)).

Active investigation by an interested but otherwise unconnected law enforcement body based in a third country could also be more difficult, with political as well as legal barriers to be overcome at the various stages at which the body seeks cooperation and assistance from agencies in other countries.

If the suspect(s) are put under formal investigation, they may well be interviewed under caution about the circumstances of the projects, payments, etc. Lying, sometimes on oath (to deny the criminal misconduct or to attempt to provide an innocent explanation to law enforcement officers that what was done was not criminal), may also be an additional criminal offence if the evidence gathered clearly contradicts the testimony.

6.1 Recent Money Laundering Issues

There have been a number of recent high-profile money laundering issues:

- **Danske Bank**: approximately €200 billion in suspicious transactions flowed from sources in Russia and Azerbaijan through the bank's branch in Estonia between 2007 and 2015. It is possibly the largest money laundering scandal ever in Europe, maybe the world. The Organized Crime and Corruption Reporting Project (OCCRP), founded in 2006, as a consortium of investigative centres, media and journalists, stated 'the Azerbaijani Laundromat (was) a general-purpose money laundering scheme and slush fund used by the ruling elite in Baku'.[1]
- **Troika Laundromat**: OCCRP and its reporting partners revealed a unique new Laundromat, created by a prestigious financial institution to channel billions of dollars out of Russia. This time, the work shows not only its beneficiaries but also exposes its mastermind and operator—Troika Dialog, once Russia's largest private investment bank. The scheme involved a large set of banking transactions and was revealed after documents were obtained by OCCRP and the Lithuanian news site 15min.lt from multiple sources. The data represents one of the largest releases of banking information ever, 1.3 million leaked transactions from 238,000 companies. The Laundromat allowed Russian oligarchs and politicians to secretly acquire shares in state-owned companies, to buy real estate both in

[1]www.en.m.wikipedia.org/wiki/Danske_Bank_money_laundering_scandal; see also www.bloomberg.com, www.ft.com and www.theguardian.com.

Russia and abroad, to purchase luxury yachts, to hire music superstars for private parties, to pay medical bills and more.[2]

- **Swedbank**: Raids were undertaken by the Economic Crime Authority in Sweden and investigations are being conducted in Sweden, Estonia, and the United States following Swedish broadcaster SVT uncovering that Swedbank is under investigation for being linked to the Danske Bank situation. At least 40 billion Swedish crowns (approx. £3.3 billion) is thought to have been transferred between accounts at Swedbank and Danske in the Baltics between 2007 and 2015.[3]
- **Standard Chartered**: in April 2019, the bank Standard Chartered had to pay $1.1 billion to settle US and UK investigations into its anti-money laundering controls and violations of US sanctions.[4]

The huge money flows in these cases[5] have been transferred over a long period of time and effectively laundered.[6] Such illegal financial movements may generate significant criminal and civil liability issues for the entities concerned, in addition to serious and possibly lasting reputational damage and major changes to compliance/

---

[2]www.occrp.org/en/troikalaundromat/; see also www.theguardian.com/world/2019/mar/04/qa-what-is-the-troika-laundromat-and-how-did-it-work and www.amlc.eu/investigation-into-the-troika-laundromat.

[3]www.reuters.com/article/amp/idUSKCN1S10DK; www.ft.com/content/c10076e2-d920-11e9-8f9b-77216ebe1f17.

[4]www.nsbanking.com/news/standard-chartered-bank-fine/amp/ See also: https://home.treasury.gov/news/press-releases/sm647 and https://www.thetimes.co.uk/article/standard-chartered-in-1bn-settlement-l2vs9bhgg.

[5]There are other cases, such as Westpac, one of Australia's biggest banks, which lost two executives after the company was hit with claims that it had systematically allowed money laundering on its watch. The company announced in November 2019 that CEO Brian Hartzer will step down in the wake of allegations that the bank had violated money laundering and terrorism financing regulations many times. Lindsay Maxsted, who serves as chairman of the board, will also move up his retirement to the first half of 2020. AUSTRAC, an Australian regulator that fights financial crime, said that Westpac failed to report more than 19.5 million instructions for transfers in and out of Australia between 2013 and 2018. Commonwealth Bank (Westpac's competitor) paid a fine of A$700m for similar breaches in 2018. Further info at various media including: www.bbc.com.

[6]See also FCPA Blog article: Why does Scandinavia have so many money laundering scandals? by Jesse Van Genugten, December 13, 2019 in which it is stated: '... on November 29, the Norwegian government announced that it had begun investigating DNB ASA ... for its role in channeling illicit funds to Namibian officials as bribes in exchange for increased fishing quotas in the country's territorial waters'. It is the third major bank in Norway, Sweden, and Denmark to face serious questions regarding the institutions' handling of funds ... Danske Bank, the largest bank in Denmark, admitted earlier this year that its Estonian subsidiary helped thousands of its customers launder tens of billions of euros as it ignored warnings about the suspicious nature of the transactions. Likewise, authorities allege that Swedbank, which is headquartered in Stockholm, Sweden, helped to launder as much as $23 billion since the start of the decade. News reports indicate that most of those illicit funds came from Russian sources ... the rapid exposure of the illegal activities in the Scandinavian financial institutions, both alleged and proven, indicates that substantial steps are being taken to eradicate money laundering in the region.

customer KYC processes.[7] Indeed, it is estimated that over $2 trillion is being laundered through various jurisdictions each year around the world.[8]

However, in part because of these events, there are various efforts to tighten regulations. The EU's Fifth Anti-Money Laundering Directive (AML5) is an update to AML4 and aims to bring a greater degree of transparency to ownership of business in the EU. One of the important provisions included in the AML5 Directive is that companies should both be required to report and have access to information on the ultimate beneficial ownership of businesses in the EU. In addition, the Directive aims at extending coverage to virtual currencies and electronic transactions. The deadline for EU member states to put AML5 into effect in national law was January 10, 2020.

FATF In addition, a list of states at high-risk of being involved in money laundering has been developed by the Financial Action Task Force (FATF), an international organisation founded by the G7 in 1989 to develop policies to combat money laundering (and terrorist financing was added to its remit). There are 39 members of FATF including the US, Canada, Brazil, Australia, New Zealand, Turkey, India, Russia, Singapore and fifteen EU Member States.[9]

According to its website:

> The Financial Action Task Force (FATF) is an inter-governmental body established in 1989 by the Ministers of its Member jurisdictions. The objectives of the FATF are to set standards and promote effective implementation of legal, regulatory and operational measures for combating money laundering, terrorist financing and other related threats to the integrity of the international financial system. The FATF is therefore a 'policy-making body' which works to generate the necessary political will to bring about national legislative and regulatory reforms in these areas.
>
> The FATF has developed a series of **Recommendations** that are recognised as the international standard for combating of money laundering and the financing of terrorism and proliferation of weapons of mass destruction. They form the basis for a co-ordinated response to these threats to the integrity of the financial system and help ensure a level playing field. First issued in 1990, the FATF Recommendations were revised in 1996, 2001, 2003 and most recently in 2012 to ensure that they remain up to date and relevant, and they are intended to be of universal application.

[7]In the same article: Why does Scandinavia have so many money laundering scandals? by Jesse Van Genugten, December 13, 2019 there is also mention of KYC developments: '...as a precautionary and reactionary measure, the Nordic region's six major banks founded a customer checking center in July, a joint Know-Your-Customer (KYC) registry to combat financial crimes and centralize compliance efforts'.. Notably, the Nordic KYC platform is not unique. There were, for example, recent launches of Afreximbank's Mansa platform to monitor customer data for counterparties in Africa and CordaKYC to serve as a consolidated blockchain platform for nearly 40 institutions in 19 countries . . . These multilateral efforts of course indicate that Scandinavian banks are not the only entities that seek to face head-on the vexing issue of conducting customer due diligence.

[8]For more info, please see FCPA blog entry: When it comes to AML, doing better means seeing better By Elsa Chan, Wednesday, May 29, 2019.

[9]www.fatf-gafi.org/about/.

> The FATF monitors the progress of its members in implementing necessary measures, reviews money laundering and terrorist financing techniques and counter-measures, and promotes the adoption and implementation of appropriate measures globally. In collaboration with other international stakeholders, the FATF works to identify national-level vulnerabilities with the aim of protecting the international financial system from misuse.[10]

Originally, a Task Force was set up to look at:

> ... money laundering techniques and trends, reviewing the action which had already been taken at a national or international level, and setting out the measures that still needed to be taken to combat money laundering. In April 1990, less than one year after its creation, the FATF issued a report containing a set of *Forty Recommendations*, which were intended to provide a comprehensive plan of action needed to fight against money laundering.
>
> In 2001, the development of standards in the fight against terrorist financing was added to the mission of the FATF. In October 2001 the FATF issued the *Eight Special Rec*ommendations to deal with the issue of terrorist financing. The continued evolution of money laundering techniques led the FATF to revise the FATF standards comprehensively in June 2003. In October 2004 the FATF published a Ninth Special Recommendations, further strengthening the agreed international standards for combating money laundering and terrorist financing - the *40+9 Recommendations*.
>
> In February 2012, the FATF completed a thorough review of its standards and published the revised FATF Recommendations. This revision is intended to strengthen global safeguards and further protect the integrity of the financial system by providing governments with stronger tools to take action against financial crime. They have been expanded to deal with new threats such as the financing of proliferation of weapons of mass destruction, and to be clearer on transparency and tougher on corruption. The 9 Special Recommendations on terrorist financing have been fully integrated with the measures against money laundering. This has resulted in a stronger and clearer set of standards.

Nowadays, FATF sets standards and promotes effective implementation of legal, regulatory and operational measures to combat money laundering, terrorist financing and other related threats to the integrity of the international financial system. FATF can also identify jurisdictions with weak measures to combat money laundering and terrorist financing (AML/CFT) and publicly list them. In 'naming and shaming' them, the countries can also be subject to increased public pressure.

As demonstrated above in Chap. 5, money-laundering or conspiracy charges can also be included as part of white collar prosecutions (especially in the USA) because it is hard to commit most other white collar crimes without actually also committing an offence of money laundering or agreeing with others to commit the offence. A classic example of this occurred when the US DOJ brought a new and additional indictment against 16 parents involved in the college admissions scandal early in 2019 - they were parents who had not already pleaded guilty to bribery and so, in addition to the existing charges, the parents were additionally charged by the US DoJ with conspiring to commit fraud and money laundering.

Given the relative ease of establishing these offences, such charges can add significantly to the pre-trial pressure faced by defendants as well as adding to the possible penalty if the defendants are subsequently convicted.

[10]https://www.fatf-gafi.org/about/.

For compliance and due diligence purposes, when facing particularly difficult questions about beneficial ownership, corporate associations, and possible AML, having: (1) the right, up-to-date; and (2) the maximum quantity of information; (3) at the right time; is a key driver to ensure that fact-finding processes result in well-informed and appropriate decisions. As a result, an organisation may wish to seek a data provider that can provide new or changes to the information (including as far as possible available information on Ultimate Beneficial Ownership) being reflected in the systems within minutes rather than weeks, as well as data providers giving as accurate and as complete information as quickly as possible.

As a result, an organisation can make decisions including those about AML risk, more quickly and on a better, more reliably informed basis. Indeed, at a recent G20 Summit, there were desires expressed about improvements and to implement international standards.

If organisations are to improve their decision-making and thereby safeguard their reputation, the compliance team will be key. As opposed to a box-checking exercise, compliance teams can use updated information and technology to allow informed corporate decisions to be made and thereby minimise the risks of doing the wrong type of business.

Nevertheless, even with faster, more reliable data and better technology, after the recent high profile and large volume money laundering listed above, financial institutions are likely to face increasingly demanding AML compliance standards.[11]

6.2 Freezing Orders

One way in which some organisations and countries have tried to combat the use of stolen and laundered funds is by using judicial orders to freeze the assets of the perpetrators. Surprisingly the ECJ recently ruled in the case of *Klyuyev* v *Council*, that the Council of the European Union had acted improperly by continuing to freeze the assets of the former President of Ukraine, Viktor Yanukovych, his son and several members of Yanukovych's administration. The people who were the subject of the freezing orders had earlier been charged with serious offences such as misspending and embezzling government funds in Ukraine.

As a result of the charges, the Council of the European Union froze their assets as a way of (a) sanctioning them and (b) showing broader support for human rights and the rule of law in Ukraine. From then on, the Council extended the freeze on the assets every year as the owners were facing charges related to those funds and freezing the assets was necessary to assist in those trials in Ukraine.

This extension of the freezing orders was challenged by Andriy Klyuyev, a former top official in Yanukovych's administration but other members (Yanukovych

[11]FCPA blog article: 'When it comes to AML, doing better means seeing better' by Elsa Chan, May 29, 2019.

himself and his son, as well as other members of the administration) were also plaintiffs in the case.

The plaintiffs were successful as the ECJ held that the Council of the European Union did not perform its due diligence in reviewing whether the Ukrainian legal authorities protected the plaintiffs' rights that were guaranteed by European Union law. More specifically, the ECJ held that the Council could not demonstrate that the legal authorities in Ukraine had protected the rights in question. Consequently, this case is an important reminder that no matter how bad the appearances nor how guilty people might appear, before they are formally convicted, there are rights that should be protected.[12]

6.3 Virtual Currencies

Wikipedia notes that virtual currency, or virtual money, is defined by the European Central Bank as 'a type of unregulated, digital money, which is issued and usually controlled by its developers and used and accepted among the members of a specific virtual community'.[13] It also notes that the European Banking Authority defines virtual currency as 'a digital representation of value that is neither issued by a central bank or a public authority, nor necessarily attached to a fiat currency, but is accepted by natural or legal persons as a means of payment and can be transferred, stored or traded electronically'.[14] In 2013, the US Financial Crimes Enforcement Network (FINCEN) noted that virtual currency does not have legal tender status in any jurisdiction.[15]

One of the advantages is that it is easy to store and transfer such currency as distinct from real notes and coins, especially on-line, digital ones (there are other versions, such as coupons). However, virtual currencies pose a number of regulatory challenges for central banks, financial regulators, fiscal authorities and ministries of finance. For example, the US SEC warned investors in May 2014 about Bitcoin.[16] There are some cities, like Istanbul, Turkey that aim to become a digital global financial centre under the supervision of the Turkish Banking Regulation and Supervision Agency and to attract foreign funds for capital markets and non-bank (cryptocurrency) financial institutions.[17]

---

[12]FCPA blog article: In Europe, freezing assets can violate human rights By Todd Carney, Monday, July 22, 2019.

[13]www.en.wikipedia.org/wiki/Virtual_currency referring to the ECB.

[14]www.en.wikipedia.org/wiki/Virtual_currency referring to the EBA.

[15]www.en.wikipedia.org/wiki/Virtual_currency where F/N 3 refers to 'FIN-2013-G001: Application of FINCEN's Regulations to Persons Administering, Exchanging or Using Virtual Currencies'.

[16]www.forbes.com/sites/michaelbobelian/2014/05/09/sec-warns-investors-to-beware-of-bitcoin/#332bcb9116c3.

[17]See FCPA Blog article: 'Bitcoin threat' spurs central bank digital currencies by Selva Ozelli, July 24, 2019.

In addition, China has been developing the DCEP (Digital Currency Electronic Payment), a central bank-issued digital currency which would be rolled out first in seven institutions (The Industrial and Commercial Bank of China, China Construction Bank, The Bank of China, The Agricultural Bank of China, Alibaba, Tencent and Union Pay). Moreover, The People's Bank of China (the country's central bank) is planning to conduct the initial pilot for the DCEP for the city of Shenzhen (and possibly the city of Suzhou) and to be generally available to the general public later. The DCEP would be pegged at a rate of 1:1 to the national currency, the RenMinBi (RMB) and the ultimate aim would be for the DCEP to become a global currency like the US dollar.[18]

[18]See FCPA Blog article: 'China marches toward creation of a global digital currency' by Selva Ozelli, December 11, 2019.

Chapter 7
Possible Controls

There are a number of different ways to try to reduce or eliminate the misuse of funds, integrity violations or the chance of fraud and corruption occurring in projects that are utilising the funds provided by international organisations. They include actions undertaken for or by the project team itself, actions taken by commercial companies to avoid getting into difficult situations (or even committing criminal offences) and other ways in which fraud, corruption and illegalities can be deterred or prevented.

Some of the controls that can be taken directly in connection with the project include official statements made by a bidder in a procurement process (or the entity chosen to be awarded the contract) such as EIB's Covenant of Integrity or the World Bank's Declaration of Use of Agents.

One important element in the use of each of the controls is the ease with which the control can be introduced and enforced; there are some that are likely to be highly effective but are inefficient and/or expensive to implement. In some situations where issues such as the politics of a country can determine the appropriate control framework to be used, there are significant limitations or restrictions to the things that otherwise can be done or measures that can be taken.

However, in most situations, there are a number of possible measures that (depending on the time and resources that are available to the project team and others) can be implemented and relied on to reduce the main fraud and corruption risks. These possible controls are as follows:

7.1 Project Controls and Management

The definition of 'project management' by Wikipedia is 'the practice of initiating, planning, executing, controlling, and closing the work of a team to achieve specific goals and meet specific success criteria at the specified time'. In some countries, the

D. Smith, *Promoting Integrity in the Work of International Organisations*,
Contributions to Finance and Accounting,
https://doi.org/10.1007/978-3-030-73916-4_7

required skills and experience to do this effectively are thin on the ground, occasionally not available at all. Consequently, in such situations there needs to be as many ways to help the borrower as possible.

In the way projects ideally function, are specifically defined and are designed to produce a positive outcome (e.g. build a road or school, refurbish and re-equip a hospital, etc.) within a period of time and with a limited budget (of finance obtained by the borrower from different sources), good project management is important. In some cases, projects are time-limited and/or they need to be put in place or implemented by a certain date. Hence, there is greater pressure on the project managers and the processes they rely on to provide reasonable outcomes within the envisaged time period.

Although some countries are very familiar with the concept (and requirements/ restrictions) of a project and have conducted many similar sorts of exercises over recent years, there are some countries that either: (1) have resisted this and would prefer not to internationalise their projects; or (2) have minimal governance or weak/ ineffective controls in place. They may also have civil servants, politicians and others who are not familiar with the rules imposed on them by borrowing funds from international organisations, so there needs to be a quick learning loop.

There may also be a certain degree of political or developmental reluctance to internationalise work (through the use, for example, of international designs or using procurement processes to potentially bring in big, international firms) that the project managers or government officials believe can be undertaken by local firms or it could be a learning opportunity for local firms to do something previously only talked about, not done. This may require not only a willingness to participate but also the development of distinct, perhaps even new, technical skills and management strategies. However, it may not be possible to do this effectively within the project's constraints (time, budget, quality, etc.).

7.1.1 Terms and Conditions of the Project Loan

The project agreement signed by the MDB and the borrower will specify the terms and conditions that are applicable. At a basic level, this will include how much money is being lent, the interest rate payable for lending the money (assuming its a loan and not a grant), the conditions and timeframe under which the loan are expected to be repaid, what the purpose of the money is and the ways in which the borrower can identify the contractors and consultants.

In more detail, the financing organisation will include rights for them to monitor the progress of the project, such as by having the right to visit key project sites and inspect developments. This visits clause is normally included in financing agreements signed by EIB (and included in procurement via the Covenant of Integrity).

7.1.2 Procurement Documents

As discussed above, some organisations such as the World Bank and EIB require certain language or covenants to accompany the bid or standard bidding documents (templates containing certain language that includes statements on certain things) to be used in the major project procurement process.

Intermediary Payment As noted above,[1] the World Bank requires bidders to state if they have paid an intermediary, and if so, how much and the name and address of the intermediary. If the bidder has made a payment but realises the implications and therefore wishes it not to be made public, any failure to disclose the payment would be a misrepresentation and sanctionable as a result.

This is done to increase accountability as payments to an intermediary can account for bribe payments, and if there are other suspicions about the procurement process, the details are useful for investigators in order to trace the payment(s) and identify who benefited.

One document required to be used in procurement processes in projects financed by the EIB is the Covenant of Integrity.

Covenant of Integrity As noted above,[2] Annex 3 of the EIB Guide to Procurement currently provides the standard wording to be used when an individual or corporate entity is submitting a bid as part of a procurement process. The wording is applicable to all contracts outside the EU (there is no threshold and it applies to both public & private sectors). In particular, the wording of the Covenant of Integrity requires tenderers (extended also to their sub-contractors) to declare if: (i) they have been excluded by an EU Institutions or another MDB or (ii) to declare if the firm or group has been convicted of any criminal offence(s).

As noted above in Chap. 3, the Covenant further provides a declaration that the bidder is willing to keep records for possible review and auditing (also extended to all subcontractors) in relation to their implementation of the contract on this project. It should be noted that this obligation is not wider and only applies to the firm's books and records recording the way in which it has implemented the contract (a wider and more general obligation to keep books and records for all of their transactions may be required by one or more applicable laws).

7.2 Project Boss/Staff

The staff who work on the project may be incentivised to manage the project funds carefully and to seek that the funds are not misused. There may also be an element of wanting to 'cash in' if the funds are being misused but that none of the over spent or

[1]In Chap. 2, page 23.

[2]Also in Chap. 2, page 24.

under-utilised funds will be payable directly or indirectly to them. In a situation where civil service wages are low and/or are paid unreliably, such large projects may appear to those close by to be a gold mine when anyone (and possibly most of the project staff) involved can seek to gain benefits irrespective of whether the project may be affected negatively.

This can normally be a force for evil in such projects and has to be a negative factor which can reduce or even cancel out the positive impact of the successfully completed project. Nevertheless, it is possible that with good levels of transparency and honest senior managers (or even the possibility of negative publicity linked to the staff heavily involved with the project) the project can be successfully implemented or if there are such negative approaches, they can be minimised.

It is possible that if such approaches are not reduced, local law enforcement (perhaps prompted by a referral from or with the assistance of the international organisation(s) that are involved in financing and working towards the successful implication of the project) may take an interest in the project too, not because they can add to the construction methodology or can bring additional socio-economic observations to the projects operation, but the need for law and order to be established and to have it play out over the full timespan of the project.

7.3 Press Coverage: Active Journalism, an Independent Press

Depending on the firms selected to participate in the project (big corporations or 'names' sometimes attract attention if they bid and win contracts in a high-profile or technically ambitious project) and depending on the country and the freedom and availability of the press (to make independent reports, to conduct investigative work and to report the results), there can be widespread publication for: (1) reports of the project that are positive or supportive; and (2) in case there are problems such as mismanagement or suspicions of criminal misconduct, more critical pieces.

In a wider context, there may be international journalists involved in reporting about the project if it is novel, innovative or using new techniques. This can also be the case if there are law enforcement investigations into international entities as part of a larger or wider situation, such as have occurred to Siemens and Alstom (see Notable Cases in Chap. 14). Such media reports can be widespread and in some cases the journalists are very well connected or informed about the nature of the suspected criminal conduct under investigation and the actions such as search warrants being executed, arrests conducted and/or interviews of senior managers taking place.

This can provide a difficult environment to try to have a positive reporting line for the media experts, especially those working in the large entities seeking to put a more positive spin on the negative reports, which if there is good evidence gathered by the law enforcement officers upon which a prosecution can be based may cover a considerable time period.

Such prolonged and negative publicity can be quite an additional deterrent not just concerned with people's (negative) views but also creating negative pressure in the market on their share price; this is the reverse of wide-ranging reports and a rise in the share price when there are positive reports in local and sometimes international press about the effectiveness and efficiency of the entity.

There are some concerns that the move to a digital age will limit the number and coverage by journalists from independent newspapers of the major developments in infrastructure projects.

7.4 Third Party Monitors

Civil Society In some situations, there are local, national or international charities or other Non Governmental Organisations (NGOs) who know in detail about the subject matter of the project and therefore can take a particular interest, and even participate in the planning and implementation of a project.

Such examples are projects about the environment or climate change mitigation, and social development projects which deal with education, healthcare and disabilities such as blindness or deafness.

As they are knowledgeable on the factors surrounding the project, they may sometimes gain an official role and purpose but, in any event, they may seek to be involved in an informal way. This can sometimes be very useful as they can bring interested parties together and may even know from previous experience whether certain individuals and entities are reliable to perform substantial tasks as part of the project. They may also know of those individuals and/or entities that are known to have engaged in integrity violations in other similar projects and therefore are significantly less reliable and may even have previously been debarred by one or other organisations.

Third Party Independent Monitors There are certain projects in which a third party monitor can participate and function successfully. Depending on the type and nature of the project, there are a limited number of entities that are able to do so. As such, the position of being an entity that conducts inspection, verification, testing and certification of all matters related to the project, or more focused on the key elements of the project, can be quite tricky and time-consuming food not technically challenging.

To provide third-party technical inspection work for a particular project needs to be rational, well organised and well planned, for example to occur during a number of years whilst construction of a certain feature (such as a long road or railway bridge), attention needs to focus on how such an inspection or testing will occur and where it will take place. In addition, a team of experts will need to be deployed on site (wherever that may be and however their inspection and testing may be carried out) to conduct a wide range of technical inspections, including welding testing and non-destructive testing.

Such firms may require a network of offices and laboratories around the world from which to organise and undertake the work as well as to write it up and issue accurate reports.

Effective Ongoing Monitoring of/by Third-Parties It can be useful to hire an independent third party to observe and monitor the internal processes of an entity to ensure that corruption is not being used or planned. It is also possible to seek clarity by greater monitoring of others in the entity's supply chain.[3]

Bear in mind that for the US DoJ, one of the 'fundamental questions' to ask when evaluating a compliance programme: 'Does the corporation's compliance programme work in practice?' It may not be an easy question to answer, especially if you are directly involved; potentially easier to seek an objective, third party opinion.

Management of contracts could be assisted with standard compliance clauses and to frequently, if not continuously, look to identify red flags related to third parties that may become hot topics: political developments, regulatory changes and undesirable events. This sounds onerous but does not necessarily need to be so—a well-designed and operated system can also be a valuable commercial resource, providing data that can reveal market interdependencies, vulnerabilities and risk profiles, whilst at the same time preventing harm to the reputation and revenue of the company.

7.5 Credibility

The credibility of a large company participating in a project may be, in some ways, as important as the credibility of the project itself. Credibility as reflected in: (1) stock market price; and (2) the company's own publications (such as Annual Reports published and sent to many stakeholders including global shareholders). A rising share price and reliable dividend payments are the basic measurements used to judge publicly-quoted companies.

More subtle but equally as important may be the way in which other market participants, potential shareholders and national regulators view the firm. Is it reliable? Does it have an active and reliable compliance department? Is it working against negative forces which may end up in criminality?

Of course, the credibility of the company can go up and down. If the company is stated publicly by a law enforcement agency to be under investigation, or there are a series of press articles about peculiar or integrity-challenging conduct, the credibility of the company may decline. That may be the situation for a lengthy period of time if there are issues of great complexity or lots of international transactions to be

[3]FCPA blog article: Stopping corruption: third party monitors, Wanted: Third-party management that's truly 'preventive' by Sviatlana Pisaryk on May 31, 2019: 'The best approach... is to monitor third parties based on the risk they pose to your organization. The first step to strong third-party monitoring is proper understanding of the risk a third party poses to your organization'.

explored, let alone that it may take longer to gather the evidence in a reliable way, for example from other countries if necessary.

The period in which there are potentially international press reports will be extended by many months if charges are laid against individuals (who were company representatives, possibly they were senior managers) and/or entities, and the case is then prosecuted in the courts. The fact that court proceedings are occurring may broaden the range of parties interested, including national regulators which may review related transactions or issues, write reports on the assessment and their findings and take further actions, which in turn could generate further negative publicity.

The situation becomes much more dramatic (and the negativity so much more acute) if there is some catastrophic event or accident that results in people being injured or killed. Newly constructed items like tunnels, road bridges or railway lines, if they collapse, are dysfunctional or break and injure or kill members of the public, can create a wave of negative publicity. Furthermore, enquiries and investigations may not be able to start effectively (or may be impeded or significantly delayed) until resulting legal proceedings have been completed.

7.6 Politicians

Depending on the size, nature and impact of a project, it is possible that local and national politicians will take a view and provide high-profile opinions on whether it is succeeding, and if not how it could be improved.

This is particularly true of a large-scale transport project, such as a road or rail project, in which there are large numbers of the population affected/impacted. The higher the number of interested people:

- The more likely the project will come under political review;
- The more likely the press will follow the political discussions;
- The more people will follow the developments in the project to see if it has a realistic purpose and is well managed;
- The higher profile would be given to reports of fraud, corruption and other integrity violations by people or companies connected to the planning and implementation of the project; and/or
- The more widespread would be press inquiries and reports published about the project.

7.7 Financier's Involvement/Monitoring

In addition to providing financial assistance to a project, the institution (or institutions, if there are a combination of financiers) can and do provide advice, know-how, and an independent view and expertise about the project and the technical issues that may be involved, as well as various mechanisms for those people who are interested in gaining more information or wish to complain about how they have been negatively affected by the implementation of the project.

7.7.1 Monitoring by Institutional Representatives

In particular, the organisation will have a small team of officers available to monitor the progress of the project, to discuss related issues with the borrower and even to raise for discussion and take a view on the possibility of lending for related or follow-up projects.

Such officials will not only receive and read reports on the progress that are sometimes issued by the borrower (on detailed issues such as soil testing, advances in the project procurement, etc.) but will also regularly visit the project to inspect key sites and to see how progress is manifesting itself.

Such visits can also be useful to get a sense of how well the project team is functioning, whether budgets are being met, and whether fraud, corruption or other integrity violations are suspected to have been perpetrated or allegations of such misconduct are perhaps even being investigated by local law enforcement organisations. If they are and weaknesses in the way the project is being managed or the way the project controls are functioning, the visitors can seek appropriate changes to the planning and implementation of the project.

7.7.2 Complaints Mechanism

There are a range of functions at the 6 MDBs to try to address problems that have been identified and complained about by people affected by the project.

The World Bank has the Grievance Redress Service (GRS)[4] which is an important mechanism for promoting transparency and accountability in the World Bank-financed operations. 'By providing an avenue for project affected people and communities to raise concerns directly to Bank Management, the GRS assures responsiveness to stakeholders' concerns and facilitates a collaborative approach to finding timely, effective and lasting solutions. Since its creation in March 2015, the GRS has forged a close collaboration with task teams across the World Bank in working with complainants to understand their concerns and identify and monitor actions to resolve them. By fostering dialogue and acting as a facilitator in conflict resolution, the GRS embodies the Bank's emphasis on proactive problem-solving and the delivery of effective and sustainable solutions'.

---

[4]www.projects.worldbank.org/en/projects-operations/products-and-services/grievance-redress-service.

EBRD has a Project Complaint Mechanism.[5] The Project Complaint Mechanism (PCM) is the EBRD's accountability mechanism that has been established to assess and review complaints about Bank-financed projects. It provides individual(s) and local groups that may be directly or adversely affected by an EBRD project, as well as civil society organisations, a means of raising complaints or grievances with the Bank, independently from banking operations.

The EIB also has a Complaints Mechanism to and through which members of the public can complain.[6] There is an initial compliance review and the outcome of the inquiry will determine whether:

- the complaint points to a failure to comply with EIB relevant provisions;
- outcomes are not consistent with the desired effect of the EIB relevant provisions; or
- EIB relevant provisions are not adequate to handle the issues raised by the complaint.

The Complaints Mechanism will also consider how the EIB has ensured the promoter's compliance with national law and other criteria. However, the Complaints Mechanism is not a legal enforcement mechanism.

The objective is to allow the Complaints Mechanism to form an independent and reasoned opinion regarding the issues raised by the complaint, which shall be independent of those responsible for the activities challenged by the complainant. The outcome will be one or more of the following:

- no maladministration found;
- problem solved during the complaints handling process;
- no further action required;
- recommendation in case of maladministration;
- suggestion of corrective actions.

A Conclusions Report will be prepared and submitted by the Inspector General to the EIB Management Committee.

7.7.3 Investigations and Sanctions

As described in Chap. 12 in greater detail, the financing MDB(s) has (have) the capability to undertake investigations into allegations of fraud, corruption, collusion and coercion in the projects it (or they) have financed.

As described in Chap. 13, if the investigation demonstrates that there has indeed been misconduct and gathers appropriate evidence to prove it, the MDB can pursue a sanctions case against the responsible party or parties. If the case results in a

[5]www.ebrd.com/work-with-us/project-finance/project-complaint-mechanism.html.

[6]www.eib.org/en/about/accountability/complaints/index.html.

debarment decision and the entity and/or individuals are prevented from getting new contracts on MDB-financed projects for a period in the future, this fact is also published. Indeed, if there is a debarment decision of longer than 1 year, it is recognised as cross-debarred by other MDBs too.

7.8 Liability

If liability issues develop in a project, those who are alleged to be responsible may face consequential legal proceedings that materialise as a result. Normally there is a time lag between the presence of representatives of the contractor or consultants on the ground and the initiation of proceedings following the event(s).

Such proceedings could be used to reclaim funds that were allegedly misused or possible overpayments made to a contractor (or vice versa by a contractor claiming non-payment of legitimate bills) but a borrower would normally only sue for work not undertaken, equipment wrongly supplied or if there is clear blame to be attributed to negative events such as a newly constructed bridge collapsing (and possibly injuring or even killing innocent passers by).

Of course, such events should not happen if the bridge has been designed and built properly but even government bridge inspectors and construction monitors who are required to inspect the work and certify certain aspects of it, may seek bribes to overlook certain technical changes from the design that had not previously been approved or product substitution in the quantities of materials used.

In a very difficult and potentially political situation, it is possible that such proceedings are started (with a tactical and political aim) to try to influence the actions of the contractor.

7.9 Prevention

Preventing integrity violations can occur in a number of ways: training the organisations staff to spot and understand the risks; staff with experience in different countries sharing and discussing strategies to deter fraud and corruption in the country concerned; and by issuing reports on best practices and successful measures are three of many ways.

If there are some key aspects that need to be addressed before a project in a particular place can be successful, certain factors can be raised (and maybe even dealt with) in advance. If necessary, preventive measures can be added, potentially as conditions of the loan or in a longer-term relationship to wait and look for positive measures being taken by the borrower.

In certain cases, it may be necessary to develop a Counter Fraud Function and the development of measures and initiatives to tackle the problem of fraud. A Preventive Services Unit (PSU)—like the one founded by the World Bank's Integrity Vice

Presidency in January 2008[7] or the team that undertake Proactive Integrity Reviews at EIB[8]—can develop appropriate knowledge, expertise and respond to internal calls (from the organisation's own staff) as well as external requests for specific advice and assistance in the design of projects. In doing so, it can be important to utilise lessons learned that have been developed from previously completed detailed investigative and/or proactive review work in similar circumstances or situations.

The issuing of preventive reports can allow for broader circulation and discussion of positive and negative issues as well as best practices identified in preventing and mitigating risk of fraud and corruption in other projects. Indeed, the transfer of such detailed knowledge (into practical advice and training) gained from an earlier investigation(s), diagnostic and analytical activities can lead an organisation to change the methodology it uses to try to prevent fraud and corruption in projects and adapt or adjust them in certain countries.

Prevention of integrity violations in projects can work in two different ways: (a) by improving the range and type of activities that can be financed by international organisations; and (b) by working closely with project teams in designing, developing and implementing pragmatic and effective approaches that can mitigate fraud and corruption risks.

For most entities in the public or private sector, it is important to find the right balance between prevention and detection versus crisis response capabilities to address whatever issues occur.

[7] www.siteresources.worldbank.org/INTFIDFOR/resources.

[8] www.eib.org/attachments/general/combatting_fraud_and_corruption_en.pdf.

Chapter 8
Corporate Safeguards

In situations where multinational (and even large domestic) firms are involved in bidding for and being awarded large commercial contracts in projects (in various parts of the world), such firms could adopt a number of possible safeguards, available to help them minimise the risks (especially of being involved in fraud and corruption).

Such safeguards should be designed and, if they operate effectively, function to ensure that: (1) a reasonable and commercial relationship is put in place with the borrower organising the contracts; and (2) the business entity and its employees can limit the risks, dangers and ultimately the liabilities of engaging in a fraudulent or corrupt commercial relationship.

These safeguards, in no particular order, include the following:

8.1 Compliance

Many large companies have a compliance department; of those that don't, most still have a compliance function but it is operating through their legal or accounting functions. Compliance departments primarily are independent and try to ensure that the company is functioning within the laws of the country in which it is based and that the entity meets the regulatory burdens placed upon it. The head of such a function is usually titled the Chief Compliance Officer and may report directly to the company's chief executive officer, chief counsel and/or the Board of Directors.

Although such roles were more common in highly regulated sectors, especially in financial services, before 2000, such departments (and indeed the work they do) was less common in other industries. This changed in part as a result of events in the early 2000s (including in the USA, with the collapse of Enron, the related demise of Arthur Andersen and the resulting Sarbanes-Oxley Act) and resulted in a broader need for the work of compliance departments in different sectors.

D. Smith, *Promoting Integrity in the Work of International Organisations*,
Contributions to Finance and Accounting,
https://doi.org/10.1007/978-3-030-73916-4_8

Such departments seek to put in place internal controls, policies and procedures to ensure that the entity's workforce comply with applicable national laws and regulations, to conduct research on the appropriate laws and regulations when the company is working overseas, to keep it in line with strategic planning and that it stays on course with its goals or objectives.

Large corporations that often seek to participate in and take advantage of the opportunities provided by development projects (corporations that are smaller but mainly trade on the international markets do too) normally also have the benefit of a compliance or risk management unit along with a set of corporate policies (drawn up in part to mitigate the enforcement risks discussed above) to try to ensure that no-one from the company inadvertently breaks the law (local law or the law applicable to the home country of the company's head office) or offers to pay or does in fact pay bribes.

Purpose The purpose of the compliance work is to try to avoid potentially compromising or awkward situations and thereby to stop the entity breaking the law, thereby seeking to avoid the significant costs and liabilities, even including a damaging criminal prosecution/conviction, as well as to safeguard the entity's (potentially extremely valuable) name/brand and reputation in the market, that is both nationally and internationally.

This includes assessing the legislation, regulations and risks of the environment (s) in which the entity is functioning, including political developments in a new or existing market, especially if there is a high risk of corruption or there are rising geo-political tensions.

The compliance function is usually seen by others in the corporation as the department that promotes (and acts with) integrity, a team that is 'doing the right thing' and developing effective procedures. In many entities, embedding ethics and compliance within the culture of the entity is seen as a positive step by employees, even if this contradicts the culture of the corporation as it has previously manifested itself. Nevertheless, a department that is acting (and is seen to act) promptly and independently to resolve the potentially wide range of compliance issues that the business may face can be viewed positively by employees. This is true especially when the chief compliance officer has an appropriate level of seniority, so as to ensure that they have the appropriate level of influence and stature.

Process Data analytics and technology are two of the ways to provide important regular monitoring or occasional insights that allow a business not only to be compliant by identifying and addressing potential issues but more broadly to measure the effectiveness of the compliance program.

Such technology may even be used to identify strange or peculiar patterns and issues that may reflect potential problems well before they become endemic and embedded in the entity's processes. Indeed if the entity is subject to takeover discussions, stock market or regulatory scrutiny or speculation as to its conduct, there may be a range of external parties examining and probing the entity (and its partners) in great detail.

If the entity has in fact been found to be lacking appropriate controls in certain situations (especially if this occurred in the recent past), changes made to the compliance function as part of its remediation may be under heightened scrutiny. The list of key requirements grows year upon year as experience and events continue to demonstrate corporate and procedural weaknesses and the changes that have been implemented and now have become necessary to plug the gap.

Ethics and Compliance There is occasionally some confusion in an organisation between the roles to be played by ethics and compliance teams - in some places these roles are combined, in other entities they are treated separately. As discussed above, compliance is a corporate framework put in place to try to ensure that a company complies with applicable laws and regulations (and its own policies and procedures), whereas a team focused on ethics has the separate (but overlapping) aim of getting the entity to do what is right and give staff guidance on ethical issues.

What 'the right thing' to do is in a particular situation may be difficult to identify and perhaps even more difficult to achieve given the various (and possibly competing) factors of, for example transparency, impartiality, integrity and professionalism—such a question goes beyond what the law actually requires and covers both the spirit (as far as it can be determined) and the letter of the law.[1]

In some situations, the focus on ethics could make the decision-making process easier, especially if the corporate entity has adopted a values-driven approach as opposed to attempting to enforce the rules, thereby resulting in a more meaningful company culture.[2] Equally, there are those who consider: 'Ethical leadership in a business benefits the bottom line' and that ethics is profitable.[3]

Generally There have been many items (including probably large numbers of books, blog articles and corporate manuals) written about what a compliance programme should consist of. The following is a concise list of key points that may be included, in particular to assist in reducing the risks of fraud and corruption

[1]See also FCPA Blog article: 'Understanding behavioral ethics can strengthen your compliance program' by Jeffrey Kaplan, October 21, 2019 who notes that: 'Behavioral ethics is a well-known field of social science which shows how — due to various cognitive biases — "we are not as ethical as we think" ... Behavioral compliance and ethics (which is less well known) attempts to use behavioral ethics insights to develop and maintain effective compliance programs ... That is, what is lacking in many business organizations is an understanding that strong C&E is truly necessary. After all, if we are as ethical as we think, then effective risk mitigation would be just a matter of finding the right punishment for an offense and the power of logical thinking would do the rest. Behavioral ethics teaches that that assumption is ill-founded'.

[2]See www.forbes.com article dated May 9, 2019: What's the Difference Between Compliance and Ethics? By Bruce Weinstein

[3]See the article 'Seven bold leaders reveal how ethical leadership is a boon to business' by Bruce Weinstein for Forbes, ethikos newsletter 22/10/2019 which refers to Global Ethics Day and states that the Carnegie Council for Ethics in International Affairs created this event in 2014 to provide an 'opportunity for organizations around the world to hold events on or around this day, exploring the meaning of ethics in international affairs'.

infecting the implementation of a contract, perhaps one that has been issued as part of an internationally financed project or related activities.

(i) **Code of Conduct/Standards:** Setting appropriate and clear standards for staff in key written documents (that are easily available) is important. Such documents should be written in simple (not too complicated or legalistic) language having identified and assessed the key risks to the business and by evaluating the entity's strategic priorities, current situation and ethical approach.

Such documents should include statements concerning anti-fraud/corruption, anti-money laundering (AML) and other financial sanctions, governance and risk management frameworks, requirements to undertake regular training, communication, particular issues when due diligence is undertaken for mergers, acquisitions, joint ventures, partnerships and other strategic developments.[4]

(ii) **Hotline**: The investigation function and/or the compliance function may also run a confidential hotline, to allow for the possible reporting of potential compliance breaches in this or other projects. The inquiries and due diligence enquiries that result from such reports may disclose elements of illegality and integrity violations that are suspected to have already occurred, may be ongoing and/or may occur in the future.

Indeed, such work undertaken by the compliance unit or a related corporate investigation function could possibly uncover elements of a multi-jurisdiction or multi-party corruption or fraud case and could certainly uncover issues or misconduct that would set integrity alarm bells ringing.

In MDBs and other international organisations, the investigation functions generally maintain a hotline function (as well as providing other ways to report an allegation, such as by email, letter, etc.) of fraud or corruption.

(iii) **Governance function**: as an independent function in the corporate entity with representation at senior management level, the entity needs to ensure that the compliance function and Chief Compliance Officer in particular, understands the nature of the business and the risks involved, as well as being clear about what conduct or types of conduct is permitted and what is not, and to ensure there is an appropriate or even inspirational 'tone from the top'. There also

---

[4]FCPA Blog article 'Warning: Flawed Codes of Conduct can create ethical complacency' by Caterina Bulgarella on August 12, 2019 which states that 'organizations can shape the context in which employees operate and, by so doing, help people do the right thing. To this end, two objectives deserve attention. First, the code's design elements that impact conduct risk should be fully identified and isolated. Second, there should be a clear framework on how each element can be used to reduce risk'. Also, FCPA Blog article entitled 'Do modern Codes of Conduct help cause and conceal unethical behavior?' also by Caterina Bulgarella, dated July 16, 2019 which notes that the US DOJ guidelines ask 'Is the compliance program well designed? Is it being implemented effectively? And does it work in practice?' Her analysis is that codes sometimes ignore 'pressing influential factors' (e.g., the applicability of the code to management and/or the Board of Directors and therefore does not get sufficient credibility in the 'tone from the top'). With clear language, codes can also promote diversity and inclusion and strengthen a 'code's overall ethos and impact'.

needs to be clear lines of communication and responsibility on important and relevant topics.

(iv) **Due diligence**: Most corporate compliance officers realise that it is necessary to conduct checks on key third parties of their supply chain. This may take the form of standardised checks (which should give acceptable answers) for multiple firms in various scenarios but may be more accurate and effective (and indeed revealing) if the due diligence is made to be more focused on the individual entity in question, together with background research on its markets, integrity history and even geography.

The larger and more active the compliance team, the more proactive they could be. Consequently the team may be required to conduct some (or numerous, wide-ranging) due diligence enquiries and background checks concerning the individuals and entities already involved (and therefore some or all the risks already to be found) in the project(s)/contracts they are working on at the current time.

In addition, the due diligence work by the compliance team may also raise some possible future integrity risks ('what if X happens?' or 'what if Y develops?') which the entity may need to consider and respond to.

(v) **Training**: The investigation function (or where this doesn't exist as a separate unit, the compliance function) should ensure that all employees (or at least those working in operations) are brought up-to-speed in recognising possible red flags of fraud and corrupt behaviour and understanding the risks that may present themselves. Case-studies are particularly useful for educational purposes in demonstrating the risks that may be present; lessons learned about how to deal with or address them are similarly valuable for demonstrating appropriate remedial measures.

(vi) **Compliance programme**: Most large companies have published their ethics and compliance programmes online. Anyone who is interested can normally learn what goals the company has set, what its major integrity policies are and how it hopes to achieve them (and even perhaps which problems it hopes to avoid).

However from an internal perspective, there may also be some controls that are less visible (and possibly deliberately more secretive) that may be available and accessible if the need arises. Whilst most employees would expect transparency, there may also be the need for measures and tools that are less well-known, such as corporate AI-enhanced monitoring tools.

(vii) **Data**: when conducting due diligence research and analysis, it is important to ensure the accuracy of the data being used—in other words that the data is the most accurate and up-to-date that is available and that the technology and processes being used to conduct the search will identify appropriate situations that require answers so that appropriate (i.e. properly informed and quick) decisions can be taken.

Law Enforcement Guidance The guidance provided by the US DoJ and UK SFO say different things about what may be considered to be important elements of anti-corruption compliance programmes, in particular about the corporate assessment of the risks it faces, the role of middle/senior management and corporate investigations.

As an international firm may be affected by both, the design and implementation of the entity's controls will need to ensure that it: (a) prevents whatever significant problems may possibly arise; and, (b) if not, then at least their internal rules can save them from being prosecuted and convicted.[5] These are the requirements:

(i) **US Guidance**: The US Department of Justice has given guidance on how it will assess a company's compliance programme. One key factor will be the effectiveness of the compliance team and the work it does. This could be important for example in distinguishing between a prosecution or some other resolution if the company could potentially be investigated and prosecuted for alleged criminal conduct.[6]

    The document is called 'Evaluation of Corporate Compliance Programs' and is dated April 2019.

(ii) **UK Guidance**: The UK's SFO have also provided guidance in a document entitled the UK Bribery Act 2010 Guidance, issued in 2012.[7]

    Revised guidance issued by the then Director, Sir David Green QC, identifies a number of principles for a company to demonstrate that it has a defence if it is charged (for example with bribery of a public official; bribery of a foreign public official; soliciting or acceptance of a bribe as public official; embezzlement, misappropriation, or another diversion by a public official of property entrusted

[5]FCPA blog article: Compliance: Practice Alert: Key differences in UK Bribery Act guidance versus FCPA guidance By Sam Tate, May 20, 2019.

[6]www.justice.gov/criminal-fraud/page/file/937501/download.

[7]This has since been updated, see FCPA Blog article: 'SFO publishes new 'internal' guidance for evaluating compliance programs' by Aziz Rahman on January 21, 2020 in which he notes: 'the new document ... outlines the stages at which the SFO will examine a company's compliance: at the time of the alleged offending, when a decision is being made on whether to charge the company and, in some cases, in the future when introducing and maintaining an effective compliance program as a condition of avoiding prosecution. The new guidance pays close attention to the six principles detailed in the Bribery Act guidance published in 2011 by the Ministry of Justice. So it goes on in some detail about the importance of proportionate procedures, top-level commitment, risk assessment, due diligence, communication and training and monitoring and review....There is very little in what the SFO has just put out that can be classed as solid advice that companies can apply to their workplaces ... there is little that is new or noteworthy ... compliance cannot be done on a one-size-fits-all basis, due to the variations in companies' size and structure, the nature of their business and the risks they face. That is why any guidance on such an important issue is always welcome. It is hard, however, to muster much enthusiasm for what the SFO has just produced … the U.S. Department of Justice's updated guidance Evaluation of Corporate Compliance Programs from 2019, it emphasises that a compliance program will only be genuinely effective if compliance personnel are empowered in a company. Its message essentially boils down to the importance of a compliance program being well designed ... implemented effectively and in good faith and it working in practice'.

to the public official; and aiding or abetting of or conspiracy in the bribery-related offences listed above) with failing to prevent bribery.[8]

The SFO states that there is no presumption in favour of civil settlements in any circumstances[9] and that the (revised) guidance restates the primary role of the SFO as investigator and prosecutor of serious and complex fraud or corruption, that their approach is consistent with other UK prosecuting bodies and that the guidelines 'take forward OECD recommendations'.[10]

The guidance starts by encouraging firms to do business with integrity,[11] noting that such firms 'are better positioned to reduce risks and capitalise on commercial opportunities'. Such business is "more sustainable ... over the long-term" and it minimises 'the risk of prosecution'.[12]

The principles that firms can adopt concern the following topics:

- Adequate Procedures;
- Not making Facilitation Payments, 'regardless of size or frequency':[13] and,
- Business Expenditure (such as promotional gifts or hospitality) should be bona fide, not bribes that 'are sometimes disguised as legitimate business expenditure'.[14]

Key Functions At a minimum, a corporate compliance team should ensure that it can provide (or assist others in providing), the following key elements:

- Establish standards for staff conduct (if necessary, write and/or ensure the enforcement of the corporate Code of Conduct for staff);
- Operate a hotline;
- Ensure clear lines of management and governance;
- Conduct analysis and due diligence on internal processes, especially those that are vulnerable or those processes at high risk of being affected by fraud or corruption;
- Training—compliance and fraud awareness training/education should be available in the company and for certain staff may be thought should be compulsory;
- Undertake digital analysis and conduct regulatory checks; and
- Create and publish corporate compliance material (also possibly for ethics).

More generally, attitudes to compliance can vary between the following two extremes:

(1) as a positive corporate influence, motivated to do the right thing, implement innovative solutions to issues before they become endemic and embedded

---

[8]www.sfo.gov.uk/publications/guidance-policy-and-protocols/bribery-act-guidance/.

[9]Under Q&A 'Why were revisions published?'.

[10]Point 3 under Q&A 'Why were revisions published?'.

[11]www.u4.no/publications/the-relationship-between-business-integrity-and-commercial-success.

[12]3rd para, www.sfo.gov.uk/publications/guidance-policy-and-protocols/bribery-act-guidance/.

[13]www.sfo.gov.uk/publications/guidance-policy-and-protocols/bribery-act-guidance/.

[14]www.sfo.gov.uk/publications/guidance-policy-and-protocols/bribery-act-guidance/.

problems, has the position, character, personality and stature to be effective, is honest, transparent and cost effective in avoiding criminal, civil and regulatory headaches and embeds ethics and integrity into the company's culture;[15] or
(2) a dull exercise of box-ticking that does not enable the successful realisation of commercial objectives nor does it significantly reduce the risks or enhance the company's commercial objectives because the Chief Compliance Officer is too remote, proposes approaches that sound (and are in fact) different from that reflected in the entity's values and does not speak the organisation's business language.[16]

Given that law enforcement in the US and the UK (and elsewhere) are now examining, perhaps like never before, the extent to which an event of fraud or bribery has occurred, the key question is whether what happened was proposed, discussed and/or organised within or outside of the entity's rules and procedures and whether the entity's codes, rules and procedures are effective.[17]

To demonstrate this, it is important through testing, monitoring and data analysis, perhaps even through proactive testing not just the entity's own operating environment and staff, but the various external environments that may impact its trade relationships and the actions of staff of partners such as joint ventures, agents, intermediaries and key third parties in the supply or production chain. Equally it is necessary to consider (and even plan for) the possibility of sanctions for a breach such as debarment, loss of licences, operational disruption, reputational damage and financial impact.

---

[15]Article in Ethikos Weekly—Editor's Picks (Volume 32, Number 6 dated November 1, 2018) entitled: "'That's not fair': Why you need more than rules to have an ethical culture" by Nicole Y. Corn in which she notes 'As a compliance officer, we have an obligation to not only create and manage a compliance program, but to participate in creating an ethical culture beyond enforcing the rules or being an example for ethical behavior...One is that a code of conduct must be more than just a document with legalese that most employees do not understand ... Employees should be able to understand it, know where to find it, and who to contact if they have a compliance question...'

[16]FCPA Blog article: "What an effective Compliance Officer look like in 2019 and beyond?" by Annabel Reoch and Tom Barrett on January 16, 2019.

[17]See FCPA Blog article: 'Why every compliance program needs check-ins' by Richard Bistrong, October 23, 2019 in which he notes: 'I made my objectives and hence my bonus; I wasn't thinking of the wider ethical implications of my conduct — on society, on innocent employees and customers, and most regretfully, on my family and my own health ... The Department of Justice, for example, in its recent release of "Evaluation of Corporate Compliance Programs', addresses the importance of accessibility, availability and frequency of compliance messaging, measurement and communications. And in our world of technology, that goes well beyond annual on-line training and annual certifications. As we often hear, 'there's an app for that'.

8.2 More Ethical Companies

Some companies have taken the approach of trying to reduce the risks they are facing by focusing in particular on governance, compliance and ethics. To do this, companies should try to ensure that the rules they are operating under are clear and well communicated to all staff. A growing trend seems to involve greater reliance on ethics, not just reliance on the law, to inform the decisions to 'do the right thing'.

The website of 'The 2019 World's Most Ethical Companies' states:

> In 2019, 128 companies are recognised for exemplifying and advancing corporate citizenship, transparency and the standards of integrity.
>
> The honorees span 21 countries and 50 industries and includes 16 first-time honorees and eight companies that have been named to the list every year since 2007.[18]

In 2019 the list of most ethical companies was chosen by the Ethisphere® Institute which claims on its website to be:

> . . . the global leader in defining and advancing the standards of ethical business practices that fuel corporate character, marketplace trust and business success (and) . . . have a deep expertise in measuring and defining core ethics standards using data-driven insights that help companies . . . believe integrity and transparency impact the public trust and the bottom line of any organization.[19]

The list of companies includes, amongst the full list, the following well-known companies: Accenture, Best Buy, Capgemini, Dell, Dun and Bradstreet, H&M, Hasbro, Hewlett-Packard Enterprise, Hilton, Illy, Kellogg's, L'Oreal, Mars Incorporated, Microsoft, Natura, Nokia, Sony, Tata Steel, Texas Instruments, T-Mobile, Visa and Volvo.[20]

Under the title of 'Advancing Business Integrity for Competitive Advantage':

> Ethisphere brings together leading global companies to define and codify best practices for ethics and compliance; and helps to advance business performance through data-driven assessments, benchmarking, and guidance.[21]

Specifically in relation to Ethics and Compliance, a company can 'gain insights into the effectiveness of your compliance program, learn how it compares to leading practices and chart a path to improvement'.[22]

Specifically in relation to preventing corruption and 'Your Anti-Corruption Program':

---

[18]www.worldsmostethicalcompanies.com/honorees/.

[19]www.worldsmostethicalcompanies.com/advisory-panel/.

[20]www.worldsmostethicalcompanies.com/honorees/.

[21]www.ethisphere.com/?__hstc=244362458.cf8cbd08fa1497e3c781d5dad92cf4de.1578751227784.1578751227784.1578751227784.1&__hssc=244362458.7.1578751227784&__hsfp=3493896350.

[22]www.ethisphere.com/what-we-do/program-assessments/.

Ethisphere's Anti-Corruption Assessment provides a practical way to assess the weaknesses and strengths of corruption controls across your company – or that of your third party partners – and implement a road map for improvement.[23]

The UN has developed 'the Global Compact', a corporate framework to encourage businesses to adopt sustainable and socially responsible policies. There are ten principles, which are as follows:

Corporate sustainability starts with a company's value system and a principles-based approach to doing business. This means operating in ways that, at a minimum, meet fundamental responsibilities in the areas of human rights, labour, environment and anti-corruption. Responsible businesses enact the same values and principles wherever they have a presence, and know that good practices in one area do not offset harm in another. By incorporating the Ten Principles of the UN Global Compact into strategies, policies and procedures, and establishing a culture of integrity, companies are not only upholding their basic responsibilities to people and planet, but also setting the stage for long-term success.

The Ten Principles of the United Nations Global Compact are derived from: the Universal Declaration of Human Rights, the International Labour Organization's Declaration on Fundamental Principles and Rights at Work, the Rio Declaration on Environment and Development, and the United Nations Convention Against Corruption.

Principle 1: Businesses should support and respect the protection of internationally proclaimed human rights; and

Principle 2: make sure that they are not complicit in human rights abuses.

Labour

Principle 3: Businesses should uphold the freedom of association and the effective recognition of the right to collective bargaining;

Principle 4: the elimination of all forms of forced and compulsory labour;

Principle 5: the effective abolition of child labour; and

Principle 6: the elimination of discrimination in respect of employment and occupation.

Environment

Principle 7: Businesses should support a precautionary approach to environmental challenges;

Principle 8: undertake initiatives to promote greater environmental responsibility;

Principle 9: encourage the development and diffusion of environmentally friendly technologies.

Anti-Corruption

Principle 10: Businesses should work against corruption in all its forms, including extortion and bribery.

At the UN Global Compact, we aim to mobilise a global movement of sustainable companies and stakeholders to create the world we want. That's our vision.

To make this happen, the UN Global Compact supports companies to:

1. Do business responsibly by aligning their strategies and operations with Ten Principles on human rights, labour, environment and anti-corruption; and
2. Take strategic actions to advance broader societal goals, such as the UN Sustainable Development Goals, with an emphasis on collaboration and innovation.[24]

---

[23]See: www.worldsmostethicalcompanies.com/honorees/?fwp_number_of_employees=0.00%2C469000.00.

[24]www.unglobalcompact.org.

8.3 Whistleblowers

Apart from seeking to ensure that misconduct does not recur (especially if they are involved in it) and to reduce their future criminal liability, a whistleblower may also be motivated by taking responsibility to address problems that have arisen, self-security/preservation and/or in some cases even a desire to receive a reward.

In certain jurisdictions, this latter situation may be the case and the whistleblower can remain anonymous (or at least their name(s) will not be disclosed to interested third parties); in others, a whistleblower may run the risk of significant media attention, possibly resulting in physical or economic threats, challenges and/or legal actions, especially if their name is not kept confidential.[25]

There have been a number of positive developments on whistleblower protection in recent times—originally, it was left to individual EU Member States to identify and put in place mechanisms to support and protect whistleblowers but this was not found to work particularly effectively. Indeed, in some places, there was limited or no protection at all.

As a result of the varying levels of protection provided in different EU states, the European Commission decided to act. Consequently, whistleblowers will receive European Union-wide protection for the first time under rules agreed by the Member States in 2018/19. Based on common procedures at EU level, the Member States will in the future provide legal guarantees to those who have exposed corruption, tax evasion and other crimes.

The rules are designed for whistleblowers to receive protection when they report irregularities at the companies or public bodies where they work. Legal protection would be guaranteed when whistleblowers disclose illicit activities (including fraud and corruption) through internal channels or to public authorities. In addition, the new EU law will shield whistleblowers from retaliation.

[25]See FCPA Blog article entitled: "A 'speak up' culture can still be hard to find" by Richard L. Cassin, October 22, 2019 in which he notes that: 'Nearly a third of employees in Singapore were aware of misconduct at work during the past year but many of them didn't report it to management . . . according to a new survey released by the Institute of Business Ethics. Of those employees who were aware of misconduct at work and decided not to speak up, the main reason was because they didn't believe corrective action would be taken (41 percent). Awareness of misconduct was higher among Singapore employees than Swiss (16 percent) or UK respondents (12 percent), the IBE said . . . The Institute of Business Ethics (a London-based NGO founded in 1986) started surveying British employees in 2005 . . . IBE director Philippa Foster Back said: 'The results of the Ethics at Work survey in Singapore show the impact managers have on employee behavior, with a third saying they felt pressured by their bosses to compromise ethical standards'. 'However, it also shows the positive impact of effective speak-up procedures on employees. If organizations demonstrate their commitment to addressing concerns, employees will be more inclined to speak up about misconduct', she said'.

8.3.1 EU Protection of Whistleblowers

The EU directive[26] officially entered into force on 16.12.2019. It protects whistleblowers who report a violation of EU law including, for example, legal violations such as tax fraud, money laundering, or data protection violations. The Directive provides protection to all employees (including trainees, volunteers, and self-employed workers) and requires companies with more than 50 employees to take measures to: (a) protect whistleblowers; and (b) to establish confidential whistleblower channels and clear reporting processes.

Whistleblowers should make their initial report through internal channels. Depending on the circumstances, a whistleblower may subsequently contact a competent national authority or the competent EU institution, body, office or agency. In addition, whistleblowers can report the misconduct to the public and the media if, for example, no appropriate action is taken after the initial report to the company or the authorities, or if there is an immediate or obvious threat to the public interest.

All forms of retaliation (including dismissal or intimidation) are outlawed against whistleblowers and their supporters (colleagues, family members , etc.). Additionally, they are given access to legal, financial, and psychological support.[27]

So far as companies are concerned, apart from trying to ensure that they are acting legally, companies should prepare for the new law by putting in place whistleblower reporting mechanisms, internal hotlines, etc.

From the company's point of view, and in terms of the possible alternatives, it is desirable to try to first obtain the information internally. It is then possible to review the issues, respond as quickly as possible and potentially address the misconduct. This is especially useful as this can occur before the public becomes aware of it. Consequently, prompt and effective handling of information can help avoid reputational damage and/or financial risks.

The various options for making internal reporting as simple, easy and secure as possible (to locate as well as to use the process in a multinational company) will be examined by most companies in order to try to motivate whistleblowers to report to internal departments first—internal reporting channels such as letterboxes, email, ombudsmen, telephone hotlines and digital whistleblowing systems will all be under consideration. Experts are increasingly recommending digital whistleblowing systems, based on the security and anonymity they offer.[28]

This law is in contrast to the US where the desire of a person to be a whistleblower, in part, can be driven by the possibility of receiving a large reward—a number of significant payments have recently been made to whistleblowers.

---

[26]EU Directive 2019/1937.

[27]www.eqs.com/solutions/products/whistleblowing-system/eu-whistleblower-protection/#c27801.

[28]www.eqs.com/solutions/products/whistleblowing-system/eu-whistleblower-protection/#c25121.

8.3.2 US Securities and Exchange Commission (SEC)

The US SEC has an 'Office of the Whistleblower'[29] and can make payment to a whistleblower if they have voluntarily provided original, credible and timely information. In other words, the whistleblower will receive a payment of between 10% to 30% of the money collected when the monetary sanctions exceed $1 million, on the higher end of the range if they provide 'indispensable assistance that strengthens the agency's ability to protect investors and the capital markets'.

Indeed, the SEC has awarded in the range of US$385 million to 65 individual whistleblowers (as of July 2019) since it made the first award in 2012. Whistleblowers can be eligible for an award when they voluntarily provide the SEC with information that leads to a successful enforcement action.

The awards to whistleblowers are paid out of the penalties collected by the SEC from violators of securities law. By law, the SEC protects the confidentiality of whistleblowers and doesn't disclose information that could reveal a whistleblower's identity.

Recent payments were made by the US SEC to two whistleblowers in the same case—US$13 million and US$37 million (the SEC's third-biggest award). The SEC's payment of US$37 million award was based on the fact that the disclosure by the whistleblower included 'smoking gun' evidence.

The SEC's largest award to a whistleblower is US$50 million. This sum was paid to two former Merrill Lynch employees in March 2018 (a third former Merrill Lynch employee in the same case was also awarded US$33 million). The second highest award was US$39 million paid to a single whistleblower in September 2018.

To receive a payment, you don't have to be American. In July 2019, the SEC made an award to an overseas whistleblower of US$500,000. The SEC said that the prompt reporting by the whistleblower had helped the agency bring a successful enforcement action but did not give any further details about the company's violations or the whistleblower.

Indeed, the SEC has made awards to at least four 'overseas' whistleblowers including:

- US$30 million in 2014 (and at the time it was the largest award under the programme);
- In 2017, US$4.1 million was awarded for providing information about 'a widespread, multi-year securities law violation' to a foreign national working outside the United States; and
- US$4 million was paid to a whistleblower for 'extensive assistance' that led to a successful enforcement action in 2018.[30]

[29] www.sec.gov/whistleblower.

[30] FCPA blog article: SEC rewards 'overseas' whistleblower, By Richard L. Cassin, Tuesday, July 23, 2019.

The SEC has also recently made an award of more than US$4.5 million and said that the whistleblower's information had led to successful enforcement actions. It is believed that the whistleblower's tip triggered the company to launch an internal investigation and even to report the whistleblower's allegations to the SEC and another agency.

This was partly related to the firm earlier having faced FCPA charges that were settled with the US DoJ and SEC as part of a deferred prosecution agreement, one element of which caused the firm to hire an independent compliance monitor for 3 years. Although the monitor had already finished by the time of the recent allegations, the firm notified him anyway.

The SEC for the first time used a provision in the whistleblower regulations to give credit to the whistleblower for reporting the allegations to the company first and then to the SEC.[31]

8.3.3 US Commodity Futures Trading Commission (CFTC) Awards

The US Commodity Futures Trading Commission or CFTC regulates the US derivatives markets, including futures, options, and swaps. Its enforcement division investigates violations of the Commodity Exchange Act and CFTC Regulations, such as fraud, market manipulation and illegal trading practices.

The SEC is not the only US regulator to make payments to whistleblowers. The CFTC also has a Whistleblower Office that has made a number of such payments and announced in March 2019 that it was making an award of more than US$2 million to an individual whistleblower for original information that led to a successful CFTC enforcement action. The payment was based on the fact that the whistleblower had provided critical information by undertaking independent analysis of market data.

The US CFTC also protects the confidentiality of whistleblowers by law and does not disclose information that might (directly or indirectly) reveal a whistleblower's identity. Under the CFTC's Whistleblower Program,[32] people who voluntarily report violations of the Commodity Exchange Act may receive a payment if the information leads to a successful CFTC enforcement action resulting in sanctions of more than US$1 million. Whistleblowers are then eligible to receive between 10% and 30% of the monetary sanctions collected from the violator(s).

The CFTC has also recently made a combined award of US$2 million to two whistleblowers that were described as 'model' for providing the agency with 'significant information' that led to an investigation. One was given an award for 'identifying key relationships and explaining complex financial arrangements'. In

---

[31] FCPA blog article: SEC awards whistleblower $4.5 million By Richard L. Cassin, May 27, 2019.

[32] www.whistleblower.gov or www.cftc.gov.

addition, both whistleblowers provided interviews and documents to the CFTC that were 'highly informative'.[33]

8.4 Auditing/Accountancy

There are some situations in which a professional, with relevant knowledge and experience of the business in question such as an accountant or auditor, may prevent integrity violations. They would do this by their involvement in the professional work stream, analyzing data and spotting inconsistencies or red flags that may reflect wrongdoing.

The larger the company is, the more likely it is that there is an active and fully functional audit and accounting department, operating to try to ensure that, amongst other things:

- bills and invoices are accurate;
- corrupt payments are not being made, directly or indirectly;
- funds are not being misused or stolen; and
- internationally recognised professional standards are being observed.

In some of the larger and more complex projects, international firms with relevant experience may be brought on board to assist with the bureaucratic and organisational aspects.

Auditing of large projects can of course raise questions—some are questions of a cultural nature (why things are done or organised in a certain way, etc.) but also sometimes questions of a more fundamental and basic nature (e.g. where is this money going, why is X getting paid for items supplied by Y, etc.). However, external (or even internal) auditors are not always in a particularly useful position to reliably analyse information about alleged misconduct and to gather appropriate evidence.

The Association of Certified Fraud Examiners found in 2018 that 53% of occupational fraud is detected by employees. This is a high figure of discovery when compared to internal and external audits which reportedly only identified fraud in 15% and 4% of the time, respectively. This relatively low (and somewhat surprising) figure may be, in part, due to the fact that much of the fraud, like corruption and bribery schemes, occurs 'off-the-books' and is therefore not recorded, is usually undocumented and therefore not obvious to spot. Of course, a close examination of financial records, a physical inventory and other relevant data sources may nevertheless reflect some peculiarities and/or provide some indications.

This sort of detailed review and analysis of data can be undertaken by accountants and other professionals with relevant knowledge, skills and experience such as former law enforcement professionals, lawyers (such as former prosecutors),

---

[33]FCPA blog article: CFTC jointly awards two 'model' whistleblowers $2 million By Harry Cassin, July 1, 2019.

computer experts, investigators with forensic auditing knowledge and experience and researchers. If they have a wide range of complementary knowledge, skills and experience, such a team has the best chance of preventing, detecting/finding and resolving fraud and other misconduct.

Occasionally, prevention can take the basic but sometimes effective form of ensuring that there are sufficient local boots-on-the-ground to observe, identify and, if necessary and appropriate, intervene. Of course, once a problem has been identified, it becomes necessary to exhibit a range of different skills to undertake interviews, review the project (and sometimes other) books and records, conduct research on databases that have been used to store and record the details, gather relevant and important evidence and perhaps even communicate with local, national and/or international media.

One of the possible dangers is that companies rely only on accountants or auditors to detect and avoid involvement in any integrity misconduct. Relying only on auditors is not always successful because there is a range of other professionals with various different skills, experiences and mindsets that can identify and address such problems more quickly and effectively—auditors generally seek to ensure the accuracy of financial statements and this has an overlap with (but is not the same function as) seeking to identify, uncover and avoid fraud and corruption.[34]

Fraud and, to a lesser extent, corruption is of a nature that is unlikely to be detected through audits. Documents can be falsified, accounts can be adapted or altered so that the recording of transactions can appear normal and routine review is unlikely to uncover any major abnormality.

Also, if there are any off-the-books transactions (which are typical in fraud or corruption cases), they may only be uncovered by conducting a site visit, talking to third-parties who may know more about the inter-relationships of the people involved and/or be involved themselves.

Alternatively, if the books are accurate in their recording of transactional data (e.g. that there are shell companies involved or payments are being made to

[34]The audit and accountancy firm Grant Thornton is under scrutiny following the collapse of the British café chain Patisserie Valerie, which went into administration in early 2019 when a £40 million hole was uncovered in its balance sheet. The hole was allegedly caused by an internal fraud and the company's former finance director has been arrested on suspicion of fraud. However, the chief executive (David Dunckley) of the company's (independent) auditor Grant Thornton said that it was not the 'role of accountants' to uncover fraud. This is extremely difficult to understand given their role, purpose and virtually unlimited access to internal accounting data and records. Moreover, regulators such as the US SEC seek to rely on the audit function as a key tool to manage the risk of fraud on investors, especially in the light of Enron, Tyco, Adelphia and WorldCom accounting scandals. Indeed, the Sarbanes-Oxley Act is US legislation brought in to increase the responsibility of auditors to try to prevent accounting fraud in companies listed on the stock market. See FCPA blog article: Are auditors abdicating responsibility, or simply following the rules? By Martin Kenney, March 8, 2019.

jurisdictions not directly connected to the project), this may provoke some suspicions of corruption.[35]

8.5 ISO 37001 Anti-Bribery Management Systems[36]

The International Organisation for Standardisation (ISO) develops and publishes globally respected International Standards. They have developed a certification of anti-bribery management systems adopted and implemented by companies which is identified as ISO 37001.

There are a variety of public and private sector uses for the anti-bribery practices and procedures they have developed - it is certainly one way for an entity to mitigate the risk of becoming involved in bribery.

An organisation can also pass the requirement to be certified to ISO 37001 standard onto their partners—this improves their supply lines, potentially makes them more reliable and indeed passes the costs (in terms of time and administration as well as financial) of becoming certified to the third parties themselves. In certain sectors, relying on such a standard is distinctive, may become a prerequisite and could even become a contractual requirement.

Use of this standard is currently patchy but in the medium to long term, reliance on the standard may become an increasingly attractive prospect, especially to those that are involved in multinational operations. It would also provide a useful, standardised tool for public bodies to assess the quality of the anti-bribery programmes of potential counterparts, even potentially to make it a requirement for bidders in a procurement process.

There may be advantages to relying on such a standard, especially in countries with a historically high corruption risk. As an offshoot, a requirement to obtain such a certification may also be added as part of an anti-bribery settlement in cases brought by regulators and prosecutors.

Indeed, adoption of the standard and appropriate certification can be one credible way in which organisations help rebuild and restore trust, and thereby manage the fallout from a post-bribery situation. Examples of this could include the US colleges that have been implicated in corruption affecting admissions and athletic scholarships in Operation Varsity Blues.[37]

However, it is critical that the ISO 37001 standard provides a credible tool and imposes useful and worthwhile anti-bribery systems on an entity, in particular that the accreditation process is rigorous and independent.

---

[35]FCPA blog article: The risk of relying on auditors to find fraud, By Jeffrey M. Klink and Tracy Pastrick, March 20, 2019.

[36]See the website: www.iso.org.

[37]FCPA blog article: Attention colleges: ISO 37001 can help By Worth MacMurray, March 18, 2019—A 'rigorous audit of (a college's) anti-bribery management system, conducted by an accredited independent certifying body' will greatly assist. Also FCPA blog article: ISO 37001: Not all certifications are created equal By Vera Cherepanova, April 3, 2019.

8.6 Reputation

Corporate entities have a wide array of approaches to maintaining their reputation. Whilst most are, on the face of it, keen to maintain a good image, some entities don't try too hard to impress independent observers of the market as long as the company continues to generate significant income through high quantities of contracts/work and, if it is quoted on a stock market, potential investors are not negative in assessing the value of the firm.

Entities that do promote a positive (sometimes even squeaky clean) image would, on some occasions, turn down or not participate in the procurement process, so as not to have the opportunity of winning a contract and with it the potential risk incurring criticism or a black mark for the way in which it won the procurement process or negotiated the contract.

On the issue of reputation, see also the sections in Chap. 9 about honesty and trust.

8.7 Liability: Internal Controls

To reduce the liability risks, effective internal controls are required. Increasingly these are in part dependent on IT and artificial intelligence to analyse and detect (and even possibly correct) systemic weaknesses. This makes it more difficult for an employee or group of them that has bad intentions and wants to lead the entity astray.

What are effective internal controls? They are a system of internal accounting and other procedures and controls to provide assurances that:

1. transactions are generally or specifically authorised;
2. transactions are recorded: (i) to permit preparation of financial statements in conformity with generally accepted accounting principles; and (ii) to maintain accountability for assets;
3. access to and use of assets is generally pre-authorised; and
4. the use, acquisition and disposal of assets is recorded and regularly compared and any differences are resolved.

As the current SFO Director, Lisa Osofsky, has a background in a compliance consultancy, this may result in greater compliance awareness. It is the first time that an SFO Director has practical knowledge and personal experience of compliance and it may therefore become an important topic for discussion in settlement talks and other discussions with firms (and their lawyers) that are based in or connected to the UK jurisdiction and facing SFO action.

See also: (1) the section in Chap. 7 above; and (2) the section in this chapter above, dealing with the assessment by the US DoJ and UK SFO of the suspect company's compliance work to determine whether it is appropriate to prosecute the firm. In particular, did the corruption or fraud occur despite there being effective company rules and procedures?

Chapter 9
Other Possible Safeguards

There are a number of other factors that can result in a project not being deliberately mis-managed or becoming a victim of fraud or corruption. Some of them are as follows:

9.1 Honesty

At a basic, human level, the perceived and actual honesty of those involved in a project can play an important factor in whether the project is successfully implemented. This is true of people working for an agency, the civil service or government organisation, as well as for the firms and corporations participating by undertaking works or supplying goods or services in a project.[1]

Most of the large corporations have internal staff (lawyers, accountants and compliance officers) and external third parties (auditors and accounting firms, law firms advising on a particular transaction, etc.) who are involved in assessing/reviewing the performance on the project. This may require a review of the books and records of a transaction or series of transactions which should normally disclose unusual or odd payments. This is the situation unless individuals with sufficient authority decide to utilise personal emails and other forms of communication (telephone calls, etc.) in order to try to hide or camouflage the agreement to conduct fraudulent practices or pay/receive bribes, collusive discussions and ultimately agreements with competitive entities (who may thereafter become informal partners) or discussions about illegal payments and when they are expected, etc.

[1]See FCPA blog article dated April 17, 2019: Management Can Own Honesty or Deceit. So Pick One by Richard Bistrong. Also FCPA blog article dated February 27, 2009: Pride's Disclosure Tells the Story by Richard Cassin.

D. Smith, *Promoting Integrity in the Work of International Organisations*,
Contributions to Finance and Accounting,
https://doi.org/10.1007/978-3-030-73916-4_9

Honesty is something that can sometimes be relied upon in a larger group of people (one person or a small number of people do not normally like to be identified by the wider group as dishonest or acting illegally) but when a large group exists, it can be also depend on the leader or senior group's mentality and qualifications. In some circumstances, desires of the senior people—ministers, CEOs and the senior project managers can seriously jeopardise the way in which a project is implemented.

In some cases, ignorance, cultural naivety or a lack of awareness on the part of senior managers can be rapidly and effectively transformed by training which then enables them (and the people working in their team) to understand the implications of certain types of behaviour and even identify red flags of fraud and corruption.

There are also laws in most countries seeking to outlaw deceptive activities such as misrepresentations or false claims about products/services and seeking deliberate overpayment. If people choose to engage in dishonest conduct on a large scale, of course, they normally run the risk of breaching legislation—either at the time of the misconduct or later when they (for whatever reason) no longer have such a significant influence over decisions to investigate and prosecute.

Moreover, there may be reviews, inquiries and investigations by interested parties (public sector bodies, private sector agencies and potentially also law enforcement bodies). Such work will be focused on what has happened (including to the funds) and whether the contracts in the project were properly and appropriately awarded and managed.

Indeed, depending on who is looking into the alleged dishonesty or misconduct, there may be questions about the intent of the persons who were involved at an earlier stage and whether a criminal offence may have been committed.

9.2 Accountability

Part of the general desire for honesty is not only that taxpayer's funds have been used but also about the need to account for their (proper) use(s). There are a number of ways in which such accountability can be obtained, including publicity through the use of the media and the internet to provide important information to the public. The progress of a project can be much more easily monitored if plans, progress and key developments are publicised—such as times, dates and places for planned works to be carried out and amounts to be paid.

Indeed, once the sums of money due to the beneficiaries in a project are clearly notified (even publicised), it can prevent skimming, as in the case of an education project where the funds loaned were paid to the central government ministry but different layers of administration were involved in the distribution of the funds. Certain small amounts could be (and previously had been) siphoned off by the various levels but clear publication of the sums expected to be paid to and received by the ultimate beneficiary (eg. US$X to Y school for purchase of new Z textbooks) in the media meant this was significantly reduced and those who did take a percentage off were required to account for what was taken and why.

One way this accountability can be obtained in major projects is by using 'open contracting'—this organisation says on its website:[2]

Open Contracting Partnership

We connect governments, civil society and business to open up and monitor public contracting through data, disclosure and engagement so that the huge sums of money involved are spent honestly, fairly, and effectively.

We also have two new inspiring stories about innovators in Latin America who are using open contracting to solve specific social problems and improve government accountability:

In Honduras, open contracting is shaping public-private partnerships, project design and participation in the country's growing but risky public infrastructure sector, thanks to our partners at CoST - the Infrastructure Transparency Initiative.

In Chile, civil society groups and government are analyzing open data to scrutinise competition in procurement spending worth US$ 11 billion, monitor corruption red flags, and improve integrity in the health and construction sectors.

A major new report by the UK's Information Commissioner looks at the 'transparency gap' in outsourcing of UK services to private companies.

52 countries are now required to publish their oil, gas and mining contracts by 2021, as part of updates to the Extractive Industries Transparency Initiative (EITI) Standard.

Nearly 300 Open Data Day events took place worldwide, including many that explored open contracting in Bolivia, Colombia, Costa Rica, Guatemala, Mexico, Nigeria and elsewhere.

Of course, if senior management is deliberately and knowingly involved in wrongdoing, as in the US case involving the German medical equipment company Fresenius, that can set a very negative example/tone and undermine many other efforts, including by project/operations, legal, compliance and/or accountancy staff, to try to ensure that the company is operating legally.

Unfortunately, the misconduct in Fresenius continued over an extended period of time (from 2007 to 2016[3]), involved top management making corrupt agreements, employees being ordered to destroy records and workers in the firm's field offices being told to delete files from computers and alter or destroy documents. Moreover, the wrongdoing took place in many different places (Angola, Turkey, Spain, China, Serbia, Bosnia, Saudi Arabia, Morocco and Mexico as well as countries in the West African region).

This was not a small, bespoke US manufacturing or engineering firm accidentally involved in such fraud—Fresenius Medical Care is headquartered in Germany and is the world's largest provider of dialysis equipment and services. The company has agreed to a settlement with the US DOJ and SEC that cost $231 million to resolve FCPA violations in at least 17 countries.[4]

[2]www.open-contracting.org.

[3]www.reuters.com/article/amp/idUSKCN1RA1X7 and www.justice.gov/opa/pr/fresenius-medical-care-agrees-pay-231-million-criminal-penalties-and-disgorgement-resolve.

[4]See FCPA blog article: At Fresenius, management owned the graft By Richard L. Cassin, dated April 4, 2019 and www.justice.gov/opa/pr/fresenius-medical-care-agrees-pay-231-million-criminal-penalties-and-disgorgement-resolve.

Accountability in society can apply just as much to individuals as to the commercial entities and in a regulatory way.[5] More broadly, accountability that impacts a project or situation can occur in different ways, can have different causes and different results/outcomes. Probing by investigative journalists can be based on a range of facts, evidence and/or rumours. More recently, accountability has resulted from disclosures made to journalists by anonymous sources of large quantities of confidential material such as the Panama Papers.[6]

Indeed, the Panama Papers according to Wikipedia: 'were created by (and taken from) the Panamanian law firm and corporate service provider Mossack Fonseca'. Indeed, although offshore business entities are sometimes legal, according to Wikipedia: 'journalists found that some of the shell corporations created by Mossack Fonseca were used for illegal purposes, including fraud and tax evasion . . .'

The disclosure came from an anonymous person but nicknamed 'John Doe'. The disclosure provided a huge quantity of documents to a German journalist (Bastian Obermayer from the newspaper Süddeutsche Zeitung). The documents were then shared with the International Consortium of Investigative Journalists (ICIJ). The documents were eventually posted on the ICIJ website. News stories were first published on April 3, 2016, along with 150 of the documents themselves. There was even a film made about the Panama Papers called The Laundromat (see the list of films at Appendix A).[7]

---

[5]See the following report from BBC news (www.bbc.com):

Panama Papers: Germany 'pays millions' for leaked data, 5 July 2017: Germany has paid millions of euros for the so-called Panama Papers revealing offshore tax evasion, reports say. The Federal Crime Office (BKA) said it would put the multi-million-file inventory into electronic form to allow for detailed evaluation. It did not confirm the sum, but government sources told German media 5 m euros (£4.4m; $5.7m) had been paid. The documents leaked last year exposed rich and powerful people, who had used tax havens to hide their wealth. The leaks put heads of state, businessmen and celebrities under pressure, with some resigning over the revelations. . . .

[6]See the following reports from BBC news:

Nawaz Sharif: Ex-PM leaves Pakistan for medical treatment, 19 November 2019: . . . Sharif was prime minister from 1990 to 1993, then again from 1997 to 1999, and finally from 2013 to 2017. He is also one of the country's richest industrialists. In 2018 - following the Panama Papers leak - he was found guilty of corruption, relating to his family's ownership of upmarket London apartments. He was given a 10-year prison sentence, but was released 2 months later when the court suspended the sentences, pending a final judgement. But in December 2018 he was jailed for corruption again, this time for seven years, in relation to his family's ownership of steel mills in Saudi Arabia. He denies wrongdoing and accuses the military of conspiring to end his political career; and,

Panama Papers: Voices from Iceland as PM resigns 5 April 2016: Sigmundur Gunnlaugsson has resigned as prime minister of Iceland after leaks from Panama law firm Mossack Fonseca showed he owned an offshore company with his wife. Mr Gunnlaugsson, his wife and other Icelandic ministers were named in the Panama Papers. He had said no rules had been broken but was accused of concealing millions of dollars worth of family assets.

[7]Indeed, there are a number of reports/articles on these and related issues, including the following FCPA Blog articles: (1) Shruti Shah on the Panama Papers: A year of gains for transparency, but gaps remain, Shruti Shah on April 12, 2017; (2) Mossack Fonseca arrests reignite Panama Papers scandal, Martin Kenney on March 7, 2017; (3) Panama Papers: RBS, NatWest disclose FCA

Although the Panama Papers was the largest and most significant disclosure of recent times, there have been a number of similar disclosures of confidential material including the disclosures called Bahamas Leaks, Mauritius Leaks, Paradise Papers, Swiss Leaks and Wikileaks.[8]

9.3 Trust

To the extent that this has not already been covered above under 'Honesty' (more focused on reliability of character, ability, strength, or truth of someone or an entity), this is a separate entry. In some situations, project staff are likely to be able to rely on, or trust, an entity or individual and vice versa.

Such trust is likely to be based on experience and past conduct that has previously been experienced in a potentially difficult situation; trust may be generated by a person/people or an organisation, especially if such positive behaviour has been experienced on a difficult previous occasion or even on a number of different occasions or in a range of different circumstances.

The question that persists is whether other people working in the same organisation will perform or respond to difficulties that emerge in the same way as their colleagues have previously done. Trust is derived from and is a function of personal relationships, not necessarily of institutions. To see the negative side of such behaviour, one doesn't have to look much further than the largest Ponzi scheme in world history and the largest financial fraud in US history (US$64.8 bn estimate) run by Bernie Madoff who betrayed many of the 4800 people that had trusted him to invest their funds, some of them giving him their life savings. Perhaps they trusted him based on who he was, what he said or what he did but words can be deceptive—specific actions, context, intent and general behaviour also matter in such an environment.[9]

Organisations don't generally build trust per se—they can only facilitate, or hinder, interpersonal trust. Instead it is up to the employees themselves, different from the role and claims of the organisation, that can help and facilitate those personal experiences. This is also true of sustainability—being a good 'green'

inquiry, Richard L. Cassin on May 10, 2016; (4) Shruti Shah on the U.S. response to the Panama Papers: A step in the right direction but more action is needed, Shruti Shah on May 9, 2016; (5) Shruti Shah: The Panama Papers and the United States, Shruti Shah April 15, 2016; (6) Bill Waite on the Panama Papers: It's time for some crisis management, Bill Waite on April 14, 2016.

[8]There was a further disclosure recently, as noted in the FCPA Blog article: Five takeaways from the Luanda Leaks by Alison Taylor on January 28, 2020 where she noted: '... Last week brought the latest revelatory data dump: The Luanda Leaks have provided damaging new insight into business dealings and corporate relationships of Isobel dos Santos, the daughter of Angola's former president. . .'

[9]The 2017 movie about Madoff, called The Wizard of Lies, reflects these deceptions. It is included in the list of films at Appendix A.

organisation is great for appearances but are the motives and claims genuine? Should people trust your company more than others in the market? It is not possible to regulate or technologise your way to personal trustworthiness—the decision to trust someone, especially if that person is being relied on as an expert or professional advisor, is ultimately a personal one.

Doug Conant, the former CEO of Campbell Soup, is reported to have created the **Conant Flywheel**, with 'inspiring trust' as the outcome of six drivers. It is noteworthy because it emphasises the personal nature of trust, and the critical personal role of leaders in creating it.[10]

> . . . trust . . . is the foundational element of elite performance; (the principles) . . . are a powerful, self-reinforcing tool for **transforming individuals and organizations** with everlasting momentum. . . .
>
> Trust is the axis upon which our entire suite of leadership behaviours depends. Your actions must be anchored in trust or the flywheel ceases to function properly and the momentum comes to a halt . . . you must continually inspire trust at every step along the way.

Some bullet points to inspire trust include:

- Uphold high ethical standards.
- Model the behaviour you expect from others.
- Acknowledge mistakes.[11]

Trust Across America is another U.S.-based organisation looking at trust. It has developed the FACTS Framework, which measures corporate trustworthiness.[12] Trust Across America's Trust Alliance has also created TAP, the following 12-point guide to organisational guidelines:

> **Truth**: We are honest and humble. We put the truth ahead of personal or professional gain.
>
> **Accountability:** We hold one another accountable, we each take responsibility without regard to level or role.
>
> **Purpose:** We engage our stakeholders to build shared purpose. We avoid short term wins that undermine future success.
>
> **Integrity**: We do what we say, our everyday actions and talk are consistent.
>
> **Notice**: We seek out and listen to diverse perspectives. Every voice can matter.
>
> **Talent**: We reward moral character. We hire and promote in alignment with our purpose and values.
>
> **Openness:** We are open and ready to learn. We can be vulnerable and not have all the answers.
>
> **Transparency**: We reject hidden agendas, we are transparent wherever and whenever possible.
>
> **Respect:** We respect each other, we encourage questioning and create a 'zero fear' environment where innovation can thrive.
>
> **Understanding**: We celebrate our successes, we acknowledge and examine our failures with empathy, and learn from both.
>
> **Safety**: We call out unethical behaviour or corrupt practices, we make it safe to be honest with no fear of reprisal.

---

[10]https://conantleadership.com/conantleadershipflywheel/.

[11]https://conantleadership.com/conantleadershipflywheel/.

[12]See their website: www.trustacrossamerica.com.

> **Tracking**: We define and score our performance against our value and values. We measure both.[13]

These principles could also be used by leaders in various situations, including one where leaders are seeking to create or re-establish trust in an organisation after a situation involving their company's fraud or corruption has been revealed. There are links to various materials from the website, including 3 books entitled: 'Trust Inc: Strategies For Building Your Company's Most Valuable Asset', 'Trust Inc: A Guide For Boards and C-Suites' and 'Trust Inc: 52 Weeks of Activities and Inspirations for Building Workplace Trust'.

Apart from those discussed above, other trust models also exist to measure trust at the individual, team and organisational level—various books and Ebooks are available specifically focussed on trust.

In addition, the EU announced the publication of a:

> **Trust Model Guidance document** to help businesses and public administrations to make an informed decision on the trust model to operate when using the Connecting Europe Facility (CEF) eDelivery Building Block.
>
> This document is a key resource to facilitate the choice of the best fitting trust model for projects aiming to use CEF eDelivery. It lists organisations' general requirements and the assessment of the different trust models is based on expert opinion and industry good practices.
>
> A **trust model** is a collection of rules that ensure the legitimacy of the digital certificates used by the CEF eDelivery components. Digital certificates enable the identification of the organisations using eDelivery and are instrumental for the authenticity, confidentiality, integrity and non-repudiation of the information. Different trust models are available based on different trust anchor models and different rules to create, manage, distribute, store and revoke the digital certificates.
>
> A **trust anchor** represents an authoritative entity via a public key and associated data. The public key is used to verify digital signatures, and the associated data is used to constrain the types of information for which the trust anchor is authoritative. A relying party uses trust anchors to determine if a digitally signed object is valid by verifying a digital signature using the trust anchor's public key, and by enforcing the constraints expressed in the associated data for the trust anchor....
>
> This document considers four alternative trust models that can be used in any implementation of CEF eDelivery:
>
> - **Dedicated Domain PKI**: in this model, digital certificates are associated with a single trust anchor. In this case, the trust anchor serves a single domain i.e. it is a dedicated anchor.
> - **Shared Domain PKI**: in this model, digital certificates are associated with a single trust anchor. In this case, the trust anchor serves multiple domains i.e. it is a shared anchor.
> - **Mutual exchange**: this model relies on digital certificates from different trust anchors. As there is no single trust anchor, organisations use the trust anchor of their choice (typically, according to a set of well-defined criteria).
> - **Domain trusted lists**: this model relies on a list containing the trusted certificates and/or trust anchors complying with a common domain policy. As a result, organisations are free to choose their preferred trust anchor from that list.

[13]www.trustacrossamericas.com/tap-into-trust.shtml. Their motto is: Trust starts with trustworthy leadership. It must be built into the culture.

This document relates to the Security Controls guidance document also available on CEF Digital 2018.[14]

An organisation with high levels of trust is one where the staff behave in trusting and trustworthy ways towards each other and towards all of the stakeholders. Perhaps trust can be considered as being driven and experienced at the personal level and the role of the organisation is to help those personal experiences become trust-positive?

This (positive) approach is different to the sort of situation in which employees must have found themselves at Fresenius Medical Care,[15] where senior management not only participated in corruption in a range of jurisdictions but also gave orders to employees to camouflage it or cover it up by destroying documents. The corporate objectives and targets must have appeared very distorted, despite the number, type and seniority of the company people involved and the geographical range of places affected (Europe, Africa, Asia and the Middle East).

In a wider context, a company leader needs to contemplate what the employees are going to be inspired by, how they might feel and react when they are put in such an unethical situation or when the corporate objectives are radically different from their own, personal ones. This may be exacerbated by senior staff ordering juniors to delete documents and alter computer records.

In the worst case scenario, corporate trust (and therefore, integrity) can be severely jeopardised if self-survival and the need to comply with orders takes precedence. This difficult situation may become even more challenging for the employee if he/she is based in a remote office with a big time difference and/or long distances from the corporate HQ as well as the employee being removed from many of the other support mechanisms.

Such challenging situations may not be very unusual in a large or growing company but knowing where the boundaries are, what the risks are and whether the deal is sufficiently important enough to justify that they can 'bend' the corporate rules is key. In many situations, the fundamental question is 'Whose interests are being served?'

Reducing the risks by improving corporate trust may assist in resolving such issues. It may also assist to combine and ensure active conduct and compliance in the operational divisions to reduce the potential friction of competition between what some employees may see (and treat) as corporate objectives.[16]

One critical question when something bad happens (or more accurately is discovered), is how can you regain trust? Normally, this takes one of two routes: seek to

[14]https://ec.europa.eu/cefdigital/wiki/display/CEFDIGITAL/2018/09/11/Publication+of+Trust+Models+Guidance%3A+learn+what%27s+the+best+option+for+your+project.

[15]As discussed above pp. 86–87; www.reuters.com/article/amp/idUSKCN1RA1X7 and www.justice.gov/opa/pr/fresenius-medical-care-agrees-pay-231-million-criminal-penalties-and-disgorgement-resolve.

[16]FCPA blog article: Management can own honesty or deceit. So pick one, by Richard Bistrong, dated April 17, 2019.

openly and candidly reveal that it has happened and repair the ethical breach, or attempt to bury the scandal and move on without instituting serious organisational change.[17]

9.4 Detailed Reviews by the Financier

In circumstances where there are some very high risks to the successful implementation and completion of a project, the international organisation(s) funding it can utilise an in-depth review of the project (or series of linked projects) to undertake a detailed study of the implementation, management and... of a project to determine whether it has been implemented as agreed or whether there are red flags of fraudulent or corrupt misconduct having impacted it. These reviews may also identify and develop preventive measures to mitigate risks of fraud and corruption, improve the management of projects (either this specific one or projects more generally), enhance project implementation, and replicate lessons learned for future projects.

The names of these reviews change according to the institutions and may even have some substantive differences, but essentially the reviews will have a detailed review of work that has been done on the project (as far as the project has already been implemented) and look for warning signs that may indicate broader or more systematic problems. These reviews are undertaken by investigators with assistance from accountancy firms and if necessary independent specialists in the subject matter of the project(s) concerned.

Such reviews are called a number of things, including as follows:

- Detailed Implementation Review ('DIR') at the World Bank;[18]
- At the EIB[19] and WFP,[20] such a review is called a Proactive Integrity Review ('PIR');
- Project Procurement-Related Reviews (PPRR) at the Asian Development Bank.[21]

[17]'A look at regaining the public's trust, once it's lost' by Sascha Maturszak, Ethikos newsletter dated 22/10/2019. She notes that 'Several examples of both options can be seen in recent corporate history. For instance, Swedish company Telia Co, AB is working hard to change its culture. On the other side, the repeated ethical problems surrounding consumer privacy at Facebook, despite a consent decree with the United States government and multiple public breaches, shows how a company with enough clout – and hubris – can attempt to overcome unethical behavior without truly changing anything about its business model'.

[18]http://siteresources.worldbank.org/INTDOII/Resources/DIR.pdf.

[19]https://www.eib.org/attachments/general/combatting_fraud_and_corruption_en.pdf.

[20]https://docs.wfp.org/api/documents/WFP-0000038444/download/.

[21]www.adb.org/site/integrity/reports-project-procurement-related-review.

Also, some of the organisations have other, similar checks on certain key aspects that will affect how the project is being managed:

- EBRD: procurement reviews; and
- AfDB: Independent Procurement Review (IPR).

If significant problems are identified, executing/implementing agencies will be informed and indeed will be expected to develop an action plan to implement the recommendations. Follow-up checks can then be conducted to monitor how well the problematic areas are being dealt with.

For more on this subject, see Chap. 11.

9.5 Possible Investigation/Sanctioning by Financier

As mentioned briefly in Chap. 7, the lending institution(s) can undertake an investigation. If the project has attracted large international organisations to participate with high value contracts at stake in a country where corruption is a major risk, that may increase the possibility that fraud or corruption has occurred or could in the future occur and that it may be investigated.

Indeed, if there is sufficient evidence that has been (or can in the future be) gathered of integrity violations or other illegal conduct, this may result in prosecutions in the same jurisdiction of the project and/or may also result in other legal cases in other jurisdictions impacted by, for example, banking systems, manufacturing of items for international delivery or location of the headquarters of the company or companies responsible. Equally, if sufficient evidence of the fraud or corruption is gathered by the financing institution, it may also result in a case for debarment of those responsible.[22]

There is further discussion of these topics in Chaps. 12 and 13.

9.6 Related Law Enforcement Action

If funds are being generated illegally by individuals or corporate entities and paid to spouses, partners, etc., these funds and the use of them may become the target for law enforcement, as the following examples from the UK indicate:

- **UK Suspicious Activity Reports (SARs):** In 2019, the UK's National Crime Agency received a record number of suspicious activity reports, or SARs (478,437, up 3%) between April 2018 and March 2019. These reports were

[22]See the descriptions of the various systems used by the MDBs including World Bank: www.worldbank.org/en/about/unit/sanctions-system; EIB: www.eib.org/en/about/accountability/anti-fraud/exclusion/index.htm; and EBRD: www.ebrd.com/ineligible-entities.html.

flagging potential money laundering, terrorist financing and other suspicious financial activity. However, only one in three reports relating to money laundering resulted in a criminal investigation.

Also, there were 34,543 reports from institutions requesting a 'defence against money laundering' from the agency, which allowed them to handle potentially suspicious property transactions without breaking the law (a 53% increase on the previous year).[23]

- **UK's Recovery of Criminal Assets and Unexplained Wealth Orders (CROs and UWOs)**: In England and Wales, Civil Recovery Orders (CROs), can be obtained under Part 5 of the Proceeds of Crime Act 2002. Recoveries in this way, however, have been perceived as slow and difficult. Despite that, in 2018 a notable CRO of £4.4 million ($5.7 million) was recorded against diplomats involved in the 'Chad Oil' deal and a further significant CRO was made in relation to alleged corruption in Uzbekistan.

In addition, 2018 marked the first use of a new tool in the UK; Unexplained Wealth Orders (UWOs).[24] UWOs were introduced by section 1 of the Criminal Finances Act 2017 and require an individual to explain to a court their interest in an asset (including a property), such as providing information on how the property was obtained.

Getting off to a quick start, UWOs were used three times in 2018, including a contested UWO against a Mrs. Zamira Hajiyeva (the wife of a jailed state banker in Azerbaijan) during which it was revealed that she had reportedly spent £16 million ($20.5 million) in Harrods for over 10 years.[25]

> Zamira Hajiyev was the subject of the first two UWOs, which were obtained by the National Crime Agency (NCA) against two properties worth a total of at least £22 million.
>
> Her husband, Jahangir Hajiyev, was the chairman of the International Bank of Azerbaijan and is serving a 15-year sentence in the country for fraud and embezzlement.[26]

9.7 National Law Enforcement Agencies

There are a number of risks when a corporate entity or an individual decides to engage in negative behaviour or misconduct and then proceeds to engage in such misconduct (of one type or another) that amounts to criminal conduct or behaviour. If: (1) the issues involved are significant in the context of the project; (2) the

[23] More details at: www.ft.com.

[24] https://edition.cnn.com/2018/10/10/uk/uk-wealth-order-hajiyeva-intl/index.html. www.gov.uk/government/publications/circular-0032018-criminal-finances-act-unexplained-wealth-orders/circular-0032018-unexplained-wealth-orders.

[25] https://edition.cnn.com/2018/10/10/uk/uk-wealth-order-hajiyeva-intl/index.html.

[26] www.telegraph.co.uk/news/2019/12/12/mcmafia-orders-designed-used-against-sainsburys-rbs-heads-court/amp/.

misconduct by individuals is potentially or actually serious; or (3) there are large sums of money involved or at stake, then it is likely that one (or more) law enforcement agency(ies) (and if more than one, from the same or different countries) will receive a complaint and be asked to examine the matters more closely.

If the complaint concerns dishonesty or significant errors in the conduct of one of the contractors or consultants involved in the project, the law enforcement body may start a criminal investigation and have to work through the issues or allegations by gathering evidence using the manpower and other resources that are available to them.

In some cases, the criminality may be thought to have occurred in part overseas and so Mutual Legal Assistance[27] powers and the ability to gather evidence (documents, notes, telephone records, diaries, etc.) will be an important factor in whether there is sufficient evidence to justify charging individuals with specific offences.

If the criminality has occurred in another jurisdiction, largely overseas, there may be strategic decisions taken about notifications being sent to those other places, not requesting assistance to gather evidence but giving the other agency (agencies) control over the conduct of the investigation.

As can be seen from frequent reports in the media, there have been many reports of convictions for fraud and corruption, as well as reports identifying suspicious transactions, reports of people charged with criminal offences, applying for bail and then standing trial or reaching an agreed resolution with a prosecutor. In a summary of some recent reports, the following section identifies how wide ranging fraud and corruption can be and how it applies to many sectors and different subjects.

For further information on the US FBI and Department of Justice's work in this area, see further Chap. 15.

Regarding the UK:

UK Code for Crown Prosecutors

> In the UK, the decision to charge is made by prosecutors under the Code for Crown Prosecutors. The prosecutor will need to consider the scope of the criminal conduct that has been investigated, the scope and range of the investigation, the nature, extent and sufficiency of the evidence available to prove the conduct, the public interest in commencing a prosecution and the number of suspects under investigation.
>
> No matter how serious or sensitive it may be, a case where there is insufficiently reliable evidence must not be allowed to proceed; if there is sufficient, admissible and reliable evidence and there is realistic prospect of conviction against each suspect on each charge, such cases will be pursued. It means that an objective, impartial and reasonable jury or bench of magistrates (or a judge hearing a case alone), properly directed and acting in accordance with the law, is more likely than not to convict the defendant of the charge alleged.[28]

[27] As was discussed in the document entitled Mutual Legal Assistance in Asia and the Pacific - Experiences in 31 Jurisdictions at: www.oecd.org/corruption/ADB-OECD-Mutual-Legal-Assistance-Corruption-2017.pdf.

[28] https://www.cps.gov.uk/publication/code-crown-prosecutors.

Losses Due to Fraud

In the UK, central and local governments combined lose over £20.6 billion a year from fraudulent activity and more than £300 billion of government spending is vulnerable to attack every year.

Law enforcement agencies such as the SFO,[29] the National Crime Agency[30] or City of London Police[31] will usually issue reports and press releases of major developments/decisions and there will be press reports of the actions taken to account for the type, nature and extent of the work they are doing and also as a deterrent, to minimise those who are tempted to engage in criminal misconduct.

More generally, improving cross-jurisdictional liaison and information sharing can assist those organisations to build capabilities, to investigate significant fraud or corruption allegations and to advise others on the possible ways to fill the gaps that have appeared.

Bribery Act 2010 Royal assent was given to the Bribery Act in 2010[32] and the first contested corporate trial under the Act occurred shortly afterwards; the first successful prosecution of a company for failure to prevent bribery under section 7 of that Act also occurred recently.

Parliament: A parliamentary committee recommended that financial crimes, like fraud and money laundering, should be subject to the tougher laws that apply to bribery. A report by a Lords committee said the UK's Bribery Act was a 'model piece of legislation'.

In its report, the Select Committee concludes that the Bribery Act is an excellent piece of legislation, creating offences that are '*clear and all-embracing*'. In particular, the offence of corporate failure to prevent bribery is regarded as effective and enables those in positions of influence in a company to ensure that the company operates ethically.[33]

UK's Serious Fraud Office (SFO) The SFO[34] is responsible for the investigation and prosecution of serious and/or complex fraud, including corruption, in the UK. In 2018–2019 the SFO's annual budget stood at £53.6 million (US$68 million) and usually has a pipeline of about 60 large fraud cases at any point in time. It does so using a multi-disciplinary team of investigators (from Police Fraud Squads, HM Customs and Excise, Inland Revenue, the Stock Market and other financial market regulators, etc.), lawyers, accountants and others.

To meet the criminal burden of proof is difficult in any case that relies on witnesses and other potential evidence (with all the problems that go with it) but this is especially true in complex fraud cases. In addition, the SFO investigates frauds that are not only complex, but that may be politically, financially or internationally sensitive.

[29]www.sfo.gov.uk.

[30]www.nationalcrimeagency.gov.uk.

[31]www.cityoflondon.police.uk.

[32]www.legislation.gov.uk/ukpga/2010/23/contents.

[33]www.natlawreview.com/article/house-lords-bribery-act-2010-committee-publishes-post-legislative-scrutiny.

[34]www.sfo.gov.uk.

The way in which a case is investigated by the SFO (with investigative lawyers working together with Police Officers, accountants and other financial investigators) is an exception to the normal practice in the UK, in which crime is generally investigated by a police force or government department (such as Inland Revenue or HM Customs and Excise) and the evidence passed to the Crown Prosecution Service (CPS) to decide whether to prosecute.

If the investigation results in sufficient evidence of the criminality being obtained that supports a realistic prospect of conviction and if a prosecution is considered to be in the public interest under the Code for Crown Prosecutors,[35] charges will normally be brought against those responsible.

Self Reporting The SFO seeks to encourage companies to come forward when the company themselves (or those acting for them) uncover wrongdoing. The Director of the SFO, Lisa Osofsky, said the SFO would provide companies and their legal advisers 'with added transparency about what they might expect if they decide to self-report fraud or corruption'.[36]

Companies that do decide to report themselves to the SFO are more likely to be considered for a deferred prosecution agreement (DPA), thereby avoiding being prosecuted. A DPA would likely include other penalties such as paying a fine, an overhaul of their compliance measures and/or a monitoring programme.[37]

Deferred Prosecution Agreements (DPAs) DPAs have only been available under English law since February 2014. This is different to the USA, where such agreements are longstanding and common. In the UK, there has often only been one DPA per year.

As an alternative to pursuing charges through a criminal trial, the Director of the SFO may consider inviting a company to enter into negotiations for a Deferred Prosecution Agreement. The SFO's first DPA was with Standard Bank in 2015.[38] With Lisa Osofsky, the current SFO Director, it is possible that in future years that there will be many more DPAs.

(i) **Rolls-Royce**: the company, which makes engines and generators for the aerospace, defence, marine, and energy sectors reached an $800 million global settlement in early 2017 with UK, US, and Brazilian authorities.

The company entered into deferred prosecution agreements with the US DOJ and UK SFO. In the UK enforcement action, Rolls-Royce admitted paying bribes or failing to prevent bribery in China, India, Indonesia, Malaysia, Nigeria, Russia, and Thailand over a lengthy period (from 1989 to 2013). The SFO said in the statement

[35]https://www.cps.gov.uk/publication/code-crown-prosecutors.

[36]www.ft.com/content/553fdc32-5639-11e9-91f9-b6515a54c5b1.

[37]www.sfo.gov.uk/publications/guidance-policy-and-protocols/corporate-self-reporting/.

[38]Subsequently DPAs were agreed with Sarclad Ltd in 2016 and significantly with Rolls-Royce and Tesco in 2017. In 2019, a DPA was agreed with Serco Geografix Ltd.

'there will be no prosecution of individuals associated with the company'.[39] It said Rolls-Royce 'is continuing to comply with the terms of the Deferred Prosecution Agreement including in relation to its compliance program'.[40]

In the United States, the DOJ charged a number of individuals, including former Rolls-Royce employees, for their roles in overseas bribery; four pleaded guilty.[41]

(ii) **Tesco**: In early 2019, three former members of Tesco's senior management (Carl Rogberg, Christopher Bush and John Scouler) were acquitted in a case brought by the SFO (after a 2 year investigation) for fraud and false accounting. The case arose after income was attributed to the wrong time period and Tesco's profit was overstated by approximately £250m.[42]

A few months before the trial, Tesco Stores Ltd had entered into a Deferred Prosecution Agreement (DPA) with the SFO. The DPA included a 'Statement of Facts' that named the three individuals alleged to have committed the fraud, stated that they had committed fraud and false accounting and detailed the manner in which that was done. Although the fact of Tesco's DPA was made public, publication of the Statement of Facts was delayed until the conclusion of the trial because it was prejudicial to the individuals.

Before the DPA could be published, the three individuals tried to have their names removed from the Statement of Facts. Later, the trial judge ruled at their trial that, based on the evidence produced, there was no case to answer.

> The DPA allowed Tesco to escape criminal prosecution in return for a £129m fine and £85m compensation for investors...The DPA says that the three men were 'aware of and dishonestly perpetuated the misstatement [of figures]' leading up to market statements in August and September 2014, 'thereby falsifying or concurring in the falsification of accounts or records made for an accounting purpose'.[43]

However, the court supervising the DPA found that it had no jurisdiction to change the DPA or amend the Statement of Facts under the statutory scheme and the DPA could be published as it was.

This is a strange combination of outcomes. If similar situations are to be avoided in the future:

---

[39] www.sfo.gov.uk/2019/02/22/sfo-closes-glaxosmithkline-investigation-and-investigation-into-rolls-royce-individuals/.

[40] In an article entitled: Guilty Pleas in the United States arising from investigations into Rolls-Royce's former Energy Division dated 8 November 2017 at: www.sfo.gov.uk/2017/11/08/guilty-pleas-united-states-arising-investigations-rolls-royces-former-energy-division/.

[41] On November 7, 2017, a US DoJ statement entitled: Five Individuals Charged in Foreign Bribery Scheme Involving Rolls-Royce Plc and Its US Subsidiary was published on their website at: www.justice.gov/opa/pr/five-individuals-charged-foreign-bribery-scheme-involving-rolls-royce-plc-and-its-us.

[42] www.bbc.com/news/amp/business-46468228.

[43] Report dated 23/01/2019 in the Financial Times, www.ft.com/content/b6c2b688-1f29-11e9-b126-46fc3ad87c65.

- companies may need to undertake their own investigation in parallel to the SFO (and to access all evidence and material gathered by the SFO);
- the court supervising the DPA may need to review the trial evidence;
- individuals could be anonymised unless there is a conviction; and/or
- there could be a review process designed to protect the reputation of individuals (eg. by allowing the content of a DPA to be revised where it is incorrect).

(iii) **GSK**: The UK's Serious Fraud Office announced on 22 February 2019 that it closed a bribery investigation into the sales practices of UK-based GlaxoSmithKline (GSK) PLC—the SFO stated that '... following a detailed review of the available evidence and an assessment of the public interest there will be no prosecution in this case.'[44] In a response filed with the London Stock Exchange, GSK said it was 'pleased that the SFO have closed their investigation' and that no further action was required.[45]

However, in 2016, GSK had paid the US Securities and Exchange Commission US$20 million to settle FCPA violations in China. The SEC found that GSK subsidiaries there spent millions of dollars on pay-to-prescribe schemes for several years in order to increase drug sales. The FCPA offences spanned at least 2010 to 2013 and involved gifts, improper travel and entertainment with no or little educational purpose, shopping excursions, family and home visits, and cash, the SEC said. GSK agreed to pay the US$20 million civil penalty without admitting or denying the SEC's findings. The DOJ didn't prosecute GSK for the China FCPA offences.

In addition, a court in Changsha, China had also fined GSK $490 million following a conviction for bribery. GSK's former head of China operations, Mark Reilly, was given a suspended 3-year prison sentence and then deported. Other China nationals working as GSK executives were sentenced to between 2 and 4 years in prison. The authorities in China accused GSK of paying $482 million in bribes to health officials and doctors to boost sales.[46]

In addition the US Department of Justice (DoJ) and the Federal Bureau of Investigation (FBI) and the cases they investigate are discussed later. Some cases may also require the assistance of INTERPOL, not in the investigation of international fraud or corruption that can affect or impact a number of other countries, but in the circulation and enforcement of arrest warrants once the evidence of the criminal wrong-doing has been gathered and a decision to charge has been made.

---

[44]www.sfo.gov.uk/2019/02/22/sfo-closes-glaxosmithkline-investigation-and-investigation-into-rolls-royce-individuals/.

[45]www.wsj.com/amp/articles/u-k-closes-corruption-probes-of-glaxosmithkline-rolls-royce-individuals-11550872708.

[46]See also FCPA Blog article: China fines GSK $490 million for bribery by Richard Cassin on September 19, 2014.

(iv) **Guralp Systems Ltd (GSL)**

Guralp Systems Ltd is a small, UK-based company which designs and sells seismological equipment—instruments that are used for detecting nuclear weapons tests, structural monitoring of dams and public utilities, and earthquake early warning systems.

From October to December 2019, three former GSL employees (Dr. Cansun Guralp who was the founder, Andrew Bell and Natalie Pearce) were on trial for conspiracy to make corrupt payments to an official in South Korea. A jury at Southwark Crown Court in London, UK acquitted them. The day the trial ended, the Serious Fraud Office also published the Deferred Prosecution Agreement that it had earlier (on October 22, 2019 after the trial started) agreed with the company.

According to the DPA, GSL made payments totaling US$1 million to South Korean public official, Dr. Heon-Cheol Chi, who worked at the government funded Korea Institute of Geoscience and Mineral Resources (KIGAM), supervised by a government ministry and certifies seismic instruments used by public bodies.

Corrupt payments by GSL made to Dr. Chi were disguised as 'technical advice fees'. Dr. Chi used his position at KIGAM to influence the award of contracts to GSL over a period from 2002 to 2015 (i.e. a period covered by both old corruption laws and the new Bribery Act in the UK). In July 2017, Dr. Chi was convicted in the United States on one count of laundering the proceeds of bribes. The fact that Dr. Chi was convicted (of laundering the bribes paid by GSL) and the individuals charged in the UK settled a civil case brought by the company against them, makes the jury acquittal of the individuals particularly disappointing for the SFO.

The Guralp DPA

> GSL accepted the charges of conspiracy to make corrupt payments and failure to prevent bribery and agreed to pay a total of £2,069,861.[47] However, it is the first DPA where the company paid no financial penalty, only the disgorgement of £2 m (US$2.6 million) profit and with no timetable for its payment but with a deadline for payment of the total by the 'fifth anniversary of the date of the agreement'.

The Director of the Serious Fraud Office, Lisa Osofsky, said: 'The Deferred Prosecution Agreement with Güralp Systems Ltd ensures that the company will pay the price for the wrongdoing that occurred under its roof. The DPA is a result of Güralp Systems Ltd's timely self-reporting and full cooperation, and holds the company to account whilst also promoting positive changes in corporate culture'.[48]

Also, the DPA allows for the terms of the DPA to be amended if GSL cannot fully repay. The judgement acknowledges that 'it is very unusual for a DPA to be approved on the basis that its terms may not be met', but the circumstances of GSL's finances were unusual enough.

---

[47] https://www.sfo.gov.uk/cases/guralp-systems-.

[48] https://www.sfo.gov.uk/2019/12/20/three-individuals-acquitted-as-sfo-confirms-dpa-with-guralp-systems-ltd/.

In fact, GSL self-reported the suspected bribery to both the SFO and the US DOJ in 2015, after a new executive chairman took over at the company and ordered an internal investigation. In August 2018, the DOJ issued a letter of declination to Guralp 'notwithstanding evidence of violations of the FCPA arising from GSL's payments to Chi.' The US DoJ appears to have ceded primacy to the SFO in this investigation.

Implications After the acquittals of individuals in relation to wrongdoing in this (GSL) case and the Tesco case (discussed above, and another case involving Sarclad), the procedure of agreeing a DPA will once again be under great scrutiny. Does the acquittal of individuals reduce or totally undermine the incentive for companies to self-report? Is it fair for individuals to be personally named in a published Statements of Facts when they have been acquitted at trial by a jury? As a result of these cases, the SFO will need to try to identify why it is so difficult to attain jury convictions - perhaps evidence presented to juries needs to be more effective, including evidence showing why such cases are important and corruption is so damaging?[49]

INTERPOL INTERPOL is an inter-governmental organisation that shares data on crimes and criminals and provides technical and operational support to national police forces. In particular, the international police organisation coordinates international arrest warrants from the General Secretariat based in headquarters in Lyon, France and through their National Central Bureau offices located in each country. They use a communication system (I-24/7) that is a secure network.

INTERPOL's website says the following about financial crime:[50]

> Theft, fraud, deception, blackmail, corruption, money-laundering... The possibilities for making money illicitly are seemingly endless. To so-called white collar criminals, the risks appear low and the returns high.
>
> Financial crime ranges from basic theft or fraud committed by ill-intentioned individuals to large-scale operations masterminded by organised criminals with a foot on every continent. These are serious criminal activities whose importance should not be minimised as, over and beyond their social and economic impact, they are often closely linked to violent crime and even terrorism.
>
> We are all impacted by financial crime which has taken on a whole new dimension with the rapid advancement of digital technology.
>
> Criminal gangs operate transnationally to avoid detection, and stolen funds cross many physical and virtual borders before they reach their final destination. This is where our global police networks play an essential role.

[49]See also FCPA Blog article: 'Guralp receives UK DPA, individuals acquitted' by Susan Hawley, dated December 23, 2019 who noted that: 'This is the third DPA in the UK where individuals charged with the wrongdoing that formed the basis of the DPA have been acquitted by a court. The SFO is absolutely right to pursue individual prosecutions where it has entered into a DPA. However, this latest set of acquittals will raise serious questions for the SFO about whether its prosecutorial strategy is working and once again, about how effective the UK's Deferred Prosecution Agreement regime is'.

[50]www.interpol.int/en/Crimes/Financial-crime.

Furthermore, INTERPOL can:

> ... play a dual role in tackling financial crime, combining our everyday support to member countries with organising targeted operations and joint investigations. The nature of financial crime means we often work in collaboration with organisations outside the law enforcement community.
>
> Our daily work involves processing requests and messages received from member countries who are seeking support. We carry out checks against our databases to provide information that can support the national police force in charge of the case investigation and identify links with other cases.[51]

Unfortunately the first Chinese President of INTERPOL pleaded guilty in 2019 to taking US$2 million in bribes between 2005 and 2017. Meng Hongwei admitted helping companies 'make illegal gains' and resigned as INTERPOL president in October 2018 (after having served two of his 4-year Presidency).[52]

9.8 EPPO/OLAF

EPPO The possibility that legal action will be taken and a prosecution can result from any integrity violations that also amount to criminal offences will increase with the creation of the European Public Prosecutor's Office (EPPO). Their jurisdiction extends to issues affecting the budget or financial interests of the European Union in the 22 member states (not Sweden, Hungary, Poland, Ireland or Denmark) that are signed up. This includes funds provided by EIB, ECB or the European Commission.

The EPPO is envisaged to take up its functions by the end of 2020. Important steps have already been taken to implement the Regulation establishing the EPPO, including implementing measures for the selection and appointment of the European Chief Prosecutor and European Prosecutors, the development of the Case Management System, and other logistical, administrative and financial matters.

The corruption prosecutor from Romania, Ms. Laura Codruta Kövesi, was appointed to the position of European Chief Prosecutor.[53] She will be an independent and form a decentralised prosecution office of the European Union, based in Luxembourg, with the competence to investigate, prosecute and bring to judgment crimes against the EU budget, such as fraud, corruption or serious cross-border VAT fraud.[54]

Currently, only national authorities can investigate and prosecute fraud against the EU budget. But their powers stop at national borders. Existing EU-bodies such as

---

[51] www.interpol.int/en/Crimes/Financial-crime/Our-role-in-fighting-financial-crime.

[52] FCPA blog: Former Interpol chief admits taking $2 million in bribes By Richard L. Cassin, dated June 20, 2019.

[53] www.europarl.europa.eu.

[54] www.ec.europa.eu.

Eurojust, Europol and the EU's anti-fraud office (OLAF) lack the necessary powers to carry out criminal investigations and prosecution.

OLAF OLAF investigates fraud against the EU budget and corruption and serious misconduct within European institutions.[55] Like the European Commission, it is based in Brussels, Belgium.

OLAF has developed an Anti-Fraud Strategy, the overall objective of which is to improve the prevention and detection of fraud, as well as to improve the conditions for its investigation, whilst achieving an adequate level of reparation and deterrence.

Private entities, Member States and ultimately the European Union itself face an ever-increasing range of challenges within the financial crime arena. As a result, there is a growing focus on making greater use of intelligence and methods that help prevent fraud rather than responding to it.[56]

9.9 Better Study of (and Training on) Fraud and Corruption

There are a number of institutions that have developed courses for students to study fraud and corruption; there are many others who include such topics but do not focus on them.

Two places that have developed specific courses are:

(1) the **International Anti-Corruption Academy** (**IACA**[57] based in Vienna, Austria) which has developed amongst other things, a Masters course in anti-corruption, compliance and collective action that is specially designed for practitioners involved with the business sector. It consists of six modules, each including an intensive in-class session, as well as a practical final project or thesis.

and

(2) the **Basel Institute on Governance**[58] (based in Basel, Switzerland). Gretta Fenner, their Managing Director noted that corruption continues to occupy newspaper headlines around the world. In elections, voters seem to support political outsiders and this trend links to a desire not to support the existing political elite, which is perceived as corrupt. She says that corruption can directly affect life, politically, economically and socially.

---

[55] www.ec.europa.eu/anti-fraud/home.

[56] https://ec.europa.eu/anti-fraud/policy/preventing-fraud_en.

[57] www.iaca.int.

[58] www.baselgovernance.org.

In addition to academic studies, there are a large number of trainers and consultants who can provide short, practical training sessions on compliance, due diligence, fraud risks, outcomes of misconduct and related subjects.

One example would be training provided for compliance officers on the use of a risk-based approach to the hiring and use of third-parties by the company.

Most of the places also have useful websites that can be accessed—on some there are training modules and activities and/or databases to gather information.

For example, the Basel Institute on Governance has a website which contains materials that might be useful, such as:

- Free e-learning courses for investigators;[59] and
- AML index - assessment of ML/FT country risk.[60]

There are a number of other useful training materials that also are publicly available.[61]

9.10 Trade Agreements

In some cases, the nature and form of trade between countries can be pre-determined. For example, the anti-corruption provisions in Chapter 27 of the Trade Agreement between United States-Mexico-Canada (USMCA) could be important. Indeed the anti-corruption provisions are one of the major differences between the newly negotiated pact and its predecessor, the North American Free Trade Agreement (NAFTA). However, it is important to note that the contents of Chapter 27 will only come into effect when the USMCA is ratified by the three signatories.

The provisions in Chapter 27 would oblige the three parties (United States, Mexico, and Canada) to adopt or maintain anti-corruption measures whilst encouraging the promotion of anti-corruption organisations and campaigns, the training of public officials and cross-border cooperation among law enforcement authorities.

Chapter 27 of the agreement contains the most detailed set of anti-corruption provisions of any free trade agreement to which the United States is a party. In

[59] www.baselgovernance.org/asset-recovery/free-elearning-courses.

[60] www.baselgovernance.org/asset-recovery/basel-aml-index.

[61] Such as the one posted on the FCPA Blog: Second Mastercard-produced training video now Available to Everyone by Richard Bistrong on November 4, 2019 which notes: 'Mastercard has followed the success of its first compliance training video with a second release, this time about the perils of getting too close and comfortable with third-party suppliers, agents, and other intermediaries. "From Beach House to Blackmail: How Silence Isn't Golden" is real-life compliance training. It depicts actual events leading up to my own FCPA violations, eventual guilty plea, and sentencing to fourteen and a half months in federal prison...The first Mastercard-produced compliance training video, "Behind the Bribe," won numerous industry awards and has been hugely effective. Multinationals around the world have integrated "Behind the Bribe" into their online training libraries as part of their compliance training and awareness programs'.

practical terms, Chapter 27 of the USMCA's anti-corruption provisions can be divided into the following three categories, namely: (1) legislative measures—i.e., laws to criminalise corruption and bribery; (2) administrative measures—i.e., measures, not new legislation; and (3) promotional measures—i.e., measures that call for the three countries to promote awareness and the adoption of anti-corruption practices but with no specific action.[62]

[62]FCPA Blog article: 'Takeaways from the Anti-Corruption Chapter of the USMCA' by Collmann Griffin, Richard Mojica and Marc Alain Bohn, dated January 9, 2019.

Chapter 10
Warning Signs (or Red Flags) of Fraud and Corruption in Procurement

It is important to ensure that projects financed by international organisations are as robust as possible. Firstly, this is because the funds to be spent on the project may have to be repaid and should not be wasted. Secondly, the impact of fraud and corruption can ruin or destroy a project and negatively impact the lives of many people in various ways. 'Red flags' are warnings in documents or during inspections that things are not quite right.

The World Bank Integrity Vice Presidency (INT) produced a brochure which summarises the warning signs of fraud and corruption that could impact a project. It is 'designed for task teams and other practitioners working on development projects to help them identify the most common warning signs or 'red flags' of fraud and corruption in procurement'.[1] The text is as follows:

> There are multiple warning signs that can help identify the risk of fraud, corruption, collusion or coercion in procurement. If you spot any of these warning signs (also known as 'red flags') in a World Bank Group (WBG) funded project, there may be reason for concern. For complaints related to possible fraud or corruption on WBG-funded projects please contact the Integrity Vice Presidency (INT) using the online form provided on the WBG public website: https://www.worldbank.org/integrity.

---

[1]The brochure was prepared by the Integrity Vice Presidency (INT) of the World Bank and they note special thanks to Enzo De Laurentiis, Chief Procurement Officer (OPCS) and Anna L. Wielogorska, Lead Procurement Specialist (EFI), whose contributions were fundamental in the preparation of the brochure. INT request that allegations: from the borrower or third parties making reference to fraudulent and corrupt practices; procurement complaints where fraud or corruption is suspected; or red flags of fraud and corruption found as part of due diligence activities or during project implementation; are reported. The brochure can be found at: https://documents.worldbank.org/en/publication/documents-reports/documentdetail/223241573576857116/warning-signs-of-fraud-and-corruption-in-procurement.

D. Smith, *Promoting Integrity in the Work of International Organisations*,
Contributions to Finance and Accounting,
https://doi.org/10.1007/978-3-030-73916-4_10

1. Complaints

Complaints may come from different sources, but the World Bank Group (WBG) takes all complaints seriously. Bidders, Bank staff, Project officials or disgruntled employees of winning companies may lodge complaints which can help prevent and identify fraud and corruption. For example, a complaint might be related to procurement, such as narrow technical specifications that only one bidder can meet, potentially indicative of bid rigging or collusion.

2. Many Small Contracts

Sometimes large bidding packages are split up to enable many small local firms to compete for contracts. However, sometimes contract splitting is done to avoid competition from larger firms, thereby creating opportunities for fraud, corruption or collusion, because the smaller packages do not usually justify a high level of scrutiny. Whatever the purpose, multiple smaller packages can create a lot more administrative work and can put serious strain on a project.

3. Overpricing

Investigations have shown that the money used for bribes often comes from overpricing of contracts through quite simple frauds, so ensuring value for money can help reduce integrity risks. For example:

- An international contractor hires a local agent to assist with marketing, but the agent uses the fees to pay bribes on behalf of the firm.
- Office equipment is ordered at a price that seems reasonable, but the seller provides substandard or used equipment and the illicit profit is used to bribe project personnel.
- The rent of the project office is very expensive, but some of the rent is channelled back to high level officials for preferential treatment to an associated firm.

4. Bidding Patterns

A group of companies working together to rig bids is sometimes referred to as a 'collusive ring'. Collusive rings can preselect (or 'designate') a winner, and the whole bidding process is made to look competitive by the companies secretly cooperating. The designated winner might prepare the bids of the other bidders in the collusive ring, and even dictate the prices they will bid.

In other cases, the designated winner might use fake companies, or its own subsidiaries or affiliates, to submit bids that will lose in the evaluation process. Collusion can significantly inflate costs above reasonable estimates and if left unchallenged it can undermine competition and disrupt whole markets.

- Companies might not want to waste a lot of time preparing bids that will lose, so a lot of copying often happens and a close review of bid documents can often reveal unlikely similarities between bids, such as identical formatting or identical grammatical and spelling mistakes. In some cases, the same people might appear in key positions in competing bids.
- Other examples of warning signs can include unusual similarities among bid estimates (for example competing bids differ by an exact percentage); unexplained inflated bid prices, (i.e. total bid price or components of the bid seem unjustifiably higher than the cost estimate); a large proportion of identical unit prices for the same items included in bids submitted by different bidders; or unusually large last-minute discounts.

- Some signs of abuse can only be spotted across several bids, for example: when a losing bidder(s) becomes a subcontractor to its 'competitor(s)' or when there is an apparent 'rotation' of winning bidders, where firms in a collusive ring take turns in winning contracts.

5. Suspicious Bidders

A fake or 'shell' company is a company that exists in name only and usually has no formal registration number, no substantial assets, no permanent business facilities or employees. Some investigations have found fake firms that were set up by project personnel.

- Many fake companies can be identified through simple checks such as searching for a company website, checking for the company name in the telephone directory or checking the legal existence through corporate registries.
- If no information can be found on a company in these searches, then something is probably wrong.
- Prospective employers should carry out specific reference checks with entities that have been listed as previous employers: call them and follow up with an email where appropriate.

6. Viable Bids Rejected

When bids are rejected without good reasons, this can indicate that someone is trying to rig the bidding process. A company might be bribing an official to put pressure on the Bid Evaluation Committee to alter the scoring or find excuses for bid rejection. Sometimes the pressure is from a higher ranking official, on behalf of a friend or relative.

Value for money is important and the lowest bids are not always the best, so it is important that all bids are evaluated carefully and fairly. No viable bid should be rejected from a bidding process without good reason nor should less technically qualified bids be accepted or weaknesses in less qualified bids be overlooked.

7. Many Awards to One Company

There can be something seriously wrong when a company wins many contracts unless it has some very clear market advantage. This could be a problem of weak competition, or perhaps the client prefers one company over the others because of previous experience, but such situations need to be very closely reviewed—especially if there is a request for an exception to the approved procurement plan to allow that single bidder to gain multiple contracts within one project.

If the bidding process seems repeatedly skewed towards one company or the same bidder loses repeatedly, this could be due to fraud, corruption, collusion or even coercion.

8. Changes in Contract Terms and Value

Significant changes to a contract can be justified post award, but these changes always require careful review. Aspects that can be abused might include: amount or type of services; contract value; number of units for a specific component or aspect, and; increased unit costs. In some cases, the price increases without real justification.

In other cases, the cost stays the same, but the agreed quality or quantity of outputs is lowered. In one scheme an element is dropped on which the winning bidder had bid much lower than others, knowing well in advance that the element would ultimately not have to be provided. All too often a 'change order' or 'variation order' or 'contract amendment' or 'addendum' is just considered as normal practice and not scrutinised. This can result in inefficiencies as well as opportunities for fraud or corruption. Be particularly concerned where a single contract attracts multiple unplanned changes or extensions.

9. 'Bait and Switch'

Bidding processes can take a long time to complete, and a firm might have to make changes to its staff, equipment or facilities in the interim. Sometimes, however, a firm might enter a bid under false pretenses, promising things that it knows it cannot deliver. This is fraud.

For example, a consultancy firm might promise a certain team knowing that those people will not really be available to carry out the contract. This kind of fraud, often referred to as 'bait and switch', may occur soon after contract signing suggesting that the intent to substitute was known beforehand. The client often feels obliged to continue the contract, especially if a rebid or reselection would be subject to high level reviews or take a long time.

10. Unclear or Subverted Processes

Except in emergency situations, bidding processes should follow planned, or pre- agreed steps. Extremely fast or slow processes in one or more of these steps can indicate wrong-doing. Examples of serious warning signs might include a long or intentional delay in the evaluation of the bids, or where overall delays are so extreme that bid guarantees need to be extended multiple times.

For government teams, it is good practice to have the steps of the procurement process carefully defined in terms of number of days for each, as well as clear allocations of roles and responsibilities, so that routine checks can be made as the process progresses.

11. Poor Quality of Works or Services

All contracts need to avoid creating undue risks such as those related to health, safety and environmental damage. These types of risks often emerge in situations affected by fraud, corruption, collusion or coercion. Investigations have provided many instances of such risks linked to poor quality resulting from fraud and corruption, e.g. when a contractor pays bribes to win a contract, and then tries to recover the costs by delivering lower-quality than specified in the terms of the contract.

Good contract management is essential to mitigate the risk of fraud and corruption. From contract award to completion, it is important to have effective monitoring in place, with appropriate checks on quality and quantity. Determining the right award decision also needs to be cognizant of abnormally low pricing, where a bid price is so low that it is questionable whether the contractor or supplier can deliver the contract for the price quoted. In such situations, contractors may seek to cut costs, health, safety, environmental and/or quality standards, or make claims to recover their costs and profit margins.

The World Bank issued guidance on identifying and dealing with abnormally low bids available at www.worldbank.org/procurement.

Chapter 11
Proactive Reviews

Proactive reviews are distinguishable from a formal investigation but investigative offices from some international organisations can and do find it useful to undertake both. They are not normally undertaken because of an allegation, more on the basis that the project to be reviewed is of a relatively high risk but has not been the subject of an allegation.

11.1 Proactive Reviews by the Six MDBs

EIB says that a Proactive Integrity Review (PIR) is a:

> risk assessment methodology to identify operations which are vulnerable to (as yet unreported) fraud or corruption. These operations are then the focus of a Proactive Integrity Review.
>
> The PIR is a forensic, anti-fraud review. Projects which are subject to PIRs tend to be highly complex or implemented in a difficult environment. Both factors increase the risk of exposure to fraud and corruption. The process then looks for and identifies'red flags', possible indicators of fraud and/or corruption.This approach improves the preventive capability of the EIB Group and increases deterrence against abuse of EIB finance.[1]

Indeed, EIB has developed a Fraud Risk Scoring Model (FRSM) that was:

> ... developed in 2017 following a detailed review of the financial and operational data available within the EIB, as well as external data sources. In the FRSM, all active EIB operations are scored against approximately 30 risk factors designed to identify red flags relating to project performance, counterparts or location.
>
> Via data visualisation software, FRSM selects a sample of high-scoring EIB operations for further study and analysis (desktop review). IG/IN verifies the system-generated scores

[1]www.eib.org/attachments/general/combatting_fraud_and_corruption_en.pdf.

D. Smith, *Promoting Integrity in the Work of International Organisations*,
Contributions to Finance and Accounting,
https://doi.org/10.1007/978-3-030-73916-4_11

and identifies the most suitable operations, from an integrity risk perspective, for an in-depth, on-site Proactive Integrity Review.[2]

Consequently, EIB IG/IN undertakes PIRs by taking:

> A small sample of EIB projects (two to three per year), preselected through the FRSM, are then subject to a Proactive Integrity Review (PIR) – a forensic anti-fraud audit. PIRs enable IG/IN to examine an EIB Group-financed project to ensure that the Group's funds are being used for their intended purposes and, in doing so, to assess the project's vulnerability to prohibited conduct. PIRs also identify gaps in areas of higher risk and recommend remedial action. In each case, IG/IN determines if there is a need for a follow-up investigation. The PIR fieldwork is performed on the borrowers/promoters' premises and on the project site. In addition, surveyors and subject-matter experts are contracted by IG/IN to verify the ultimate quality and quantity of the works and goods delivered.
>
> The PIR is the final result of the risk assessment and desktop review process. However, a PIR can also be launched independently by IG/IN on a given EIB Group operation or at the request of other EIB Group services and/or management.[3]

ADB ADB undertake Proactive Integrity Review (PIR), formerly known as Project Procurement-Related Review (PPRR), and they state:

> reports are intended to help executing agencies, implementing agencies, and ADB to identify and develop preventive measures to mitigate risks of fraud and corruption, improve project management, enhance project implementation, and replicate lessons learned for future projects.
>
> Executing/implementing agencies are expected to develop an action plan to implement PIR recommendations, which will be monitored by the Office of Anticorruption and Integrity through follow-up reviews.[4]

The ADB's PIR reports are available for the public too.

IDB IDB conducts Integrity Risk Reviews of operational projects and activities.[5] These are reviews of operations already in execution, conducted by the investigation office (OII) in close coordination with the project team and look at: (1) internal controls of the project implementation unit; (2) procurement; (3) asset verification; and (4) financial management.

World Bank Similar reviews are undertaken by other operational departments (audit, financial management, procurement, etc.) in other MDBs such as World Bank, whose INT used to conduct Detailed Implementation Reviews (DIRs)[6] and now contribute to Joint In-Depth Fiduciary Reviews. The WB INT FY 19 annual report notes:

> In FY19, INT, in collaboration with Operations, undertook two Joint In-Depth Fiduciary Reviews (JIFR) of an education project in the South Asia region. One of the JIFRs was completed whilst the other is ongoing. A total of US$ 156.5 million in transactions was sampled. The JIFR validated 60% of the sample but identified serious record-keeping

[2] www.eib.org/en/publications/fraud-investigations-activity-report-2018.

[3] www.eib.org/en/publications/fraud-investigations-activity-report-2018.

[4] https://www.adb.org/site/integrity/reports-project-procurement-related-review.

[5] See page 14 of their 2018 Annual Report.

[6] http://siteresources.worldbank.org/INTDOII/Resources/DIR.pdf.

weaknesses in US$ 21.9 million of transactions which were inadequately documented. The JIFR also identified potential procurement fraud indicators as well as instances of apparent procedural non-compliance. Relevant JIFR findings resulted in mitigation measures that have been incorporated into the design of a follow-on project in the same sector and country. The fraud and corruption risk mitigation measures are regularly monitored, and additional fiduciary measures are being considered in the new project.[7]

Also on page 19 of the same report, the WB INT noted:

In-Depth Reviews in FCV (Fragility, Conflict and Violence) Countries

An In-Depth Review is a multi-disciplinary tool that can be used to holistically and effectively address integrity risks in projects ... an In-Depth Review is performed collaboratively by INT and ... may draw on a range of relevant expertise, including... financial management and procurement specialists.

In FY19, INT continued and increased its involvement with In-Depth Reviews of projects in FCV countries. FCV contexts involve particular fiduciary risks, such as lower institutional capacity, the extensive use of cash payments due to large unbanked populations, the use of local implementation partners that often have limited track records or ties to public officials, security risks that limit the ability to supervise projects and reduce the likelihood of complaints, the possible over-reliance on third-party monitors, and limited local internal and external audit capacity. In-Depth Reviews can be particularly useful in FCV contexts in enhancing existing fiduciary control frameworks, identifying risk-mitigation measures, and acting as a deterrent to the misuse of WBG funds. In line with the WBG strategic focus on FCV, INT is committed to continuing its support of WBG teams operating in these contexts in FY20 and beyond.[8]

AFDB AfDB (Integrity and Anti-Corruption Department, IACD) undertakes 'Proactive prevention through risk assessments, sensitisation programmes, due diligence, and other activities'.[9]

CII More broadly, in 2019 the Conference of International Investigators (CII),[10] in which staff from investigation offices of most international organisations participate (i.e. not just the six MDBs but including them), approved General Principles for Proactive Integrity Risk or Fraud Detection Activities for such reviews by the investigation service of any international organisation that seeks to undertake them.[11]

There are a range of objectives for such reviews, including:

- to seek to prevent and detect corrupt, fraudulent, coercive and collusive practices;
- to check whether the project (or particular aspects of it) are being/have been implemented according to the agreed terms;

---

[7] www.documents.worldbank.org/curated/en/782941570732184391/World-Bank-Group-Sanctions-System-Annual-Report-FY19.

[8] http://documents.worldbank.org/curated/en/782941570732184391/World-Bank-Group-Sanctions-System-Annual-Report-FY19.

[9] https://www.afdb.org/en/about-us/organisational-structure/integrity-and-anti-corruption.

[10] The CII has its own website at: www.conf-int-investigators.org.

[11] www.conf-int-investigators.org/cii-guidelines/.

- to seek to determine whether the funds have been used for the proper (ie. intended) purposes;
- to prevent or reduce negative publicity; and
- to provide recommendations on how the project could be more effectively implemented or possible improvements to internal controls to mitigate any opportunities for fraud, corruption or abuse in future projects.

Joint Reviews Reviews normally are conducted by a team from a single organisation, normally in consultation with the organisation's business operations staff or as a result of a management request or a risk assessment exercise or even at their request if they suspect the borrower has misused the funds or that, despite the borrower's best efforts, the project is being badly implemented.

Such reviews can also be undertaken jointly with other financiers and/or the control functions of organisations that have contributed funds for use in the project. Although this has not happened frequently, this seems like an area of possible expansion, given the increasing trend of co-financing and the likely resource implications.

Not Just Suppliers The scope and range of such reviews can be wide. For example, EIB has used the PIRs not just to test the quality, efficiency and effectiveness of suppliers chosen through procurement in the infrastructure projects selected for review (e.g. transport projects such as laying a new road or railway/tram construction) but also has looked at Financial Intermediaries that have been the recipient of a loan to see if the on-lending criteria (e.g. for smaller loans to SMEs) were adhered to.[12] Based on these findings, the EIB concluded that a number of the sub-loans granted were ineligible and requested a partial prepayment of the loans to the relevant FI. In addition, a remediation plan has been implemented at the EIB to strengthen the controls over the allocations.

World Bank INT DIR in India Health Projects The World Bank INT used to undertake large-scale DIRs such as the DIR on the Indian Health Sector in 2006-7.[13] This was a particularly large and detailed exercise that found some serious deficiencies in five WB-funded health projects (including the Food and Drink Capacity Building Project, the Second National AIDS Control Project and the Malaria Control Project). The report that was generated after the review was completed is in two volumes and also contains a series of photos to demonstrate some of the situations that the reviewers discovered.[14]

The Report's Executive Summary states that:

> 'The India DIR found significant indicators of fraud and corruption in all five projects. These indicators appear to have affected, to varying extents, the projects' implementation and

[12] See page 11 - 12 of EIB's Anti-Fraud Activity Report 2017 at: https://www.eib.org/attachments/general/reports/ig_fraud_investigations_activity_report_2017_en.pdf.

[13] www.siteresources.worldbank.org/EXTDOII/Resources/WB250_Web_Vol1_012408.pdf.

[14] Photos are always useful to demonstrate the issues identified - the pages of photos are called 'Photo Gallery' in the Report, such as pp. 139–165 and p. 277 in Volume 1 and p.410 in Volume 2.

outputs. The DIR found indicators of fraudulent and corrupt practices related to procurement such as collusive behaviours, bid rigging, bribery, and manipulated bid prices. It also found indicators of fraudulent and corrupt practices related to project implementation, including deficient civil works certified as complete; broken or damaged equipment certified as compliant with specifications; and under-delivery of services from contractual obligations. Moreover, the DIR observed inadequate project financial, audit, and internal controls systems. These findings will result in a number of Bank investigations into specific cases of possible fraud and corruption'.[15]

Financial Intermediaries Whilst financial intermediaries are often regulated financial organisations themselves (in some cases, the intermediaries are commercial banks or could also be public promotional or development banks), through the use of proactive reviews into such beneficiaries EIB has identified that a number of them are either victims of fraud schemes or that the intermediary's themselves are operating fraudulently. Therefore EIB has identified a number of red flags (or indicators) of the misuse of the funds.

Examples of the sort of control issues that have been discovered are:

- Weaknesses of internal control systems;
- Weak AML/CFT policies, no PEP policy or the absence of a compliance officer/function;
- Inadequate monitoring of related parties and PEPs;
- Some Public Promotional Banks are not regulated by the local Banking Agency; and
- Political committees of government ministers override previous negative credit decisions without adequate business rationale or justification.[16]

Indeed, the EIB IG/IN also notes[17] (in the entries about PIRs in the yearly Activity Reports) that, having reviewed the loan files and inspected the credit and loan approval process, they also conducted on-site visits of the respective projects and Financial Beneficiaries. In the sample of operations reviewed, irregularities and schemes identified including:

- Weaknesses of internal control systems, deficient 'know your customer' and anti-money laundering due diligence; and inadequate monitoring of related parties and politically exposed persons (PEPs);
- Indications of money laundering or false accounting;
- Irregularities with regard to the purpose of the allocations; and,

[15]Text from page 1 of the Report's Executive Summary, www.siteresources.worldbank.org/EXTDOII/Resources/WB250_Web_Vol1_012408.pdf.

[16]www.eib.org/en/publications/fraud-investigations-activity-report-2017.

[17]Such as the 2018 Report at: www.eib.org/en/publications/fraud-investigations-activity-report-2018.

- Final Beneficiaries acting as front companies set up to obtain funds to the benefit of other, related entities which by themselves would not have been eligible (e.g. for SME funding).

11.2 Other Organisations

This has been quite a recent growth area and other international organisations have also started to conduct proactive work—they consider that it can be very useful in trying to achieve the organisation's goals as well as aiding prevention and deterrence.

For example, the World Food Programme have published the following text on its website:

> **Legal Basis**
>
> The Office of the Inspector General may undertake Proactive Integrity Reviews on specific operational issues that may indicate risk of fraud, corruption, collusion and other wrongdoings.[18]

And the WFP notes, under the heading 'Definition', that a PIR is:

> . . . a proactive tool that examines WFP business processes or operations, including procurement and logistics activities and WFP financed projects, to ensure that WFP funds and assets are being utilised for their intended purposes and, in doing so, to assess their susceptibility to fraud, corruption, collusion, coercion, and/or other wrongdoings.[19]

According to the WFP, under the heading 'Objectives':[20]

> PIR should be distinguished as separate and distinct from existing audit, investigation or inspection activities. PIR seeks to fill the gaps in assurance that may exist due to the different operational standards and scope of OIG's investigation, audit and inspection functions.
>
> - A PIR is <u>not an investigation</u>, which determines whether specific allegations can be substantiated;
> - A PIR is <u>not an audit</u>, which is designed to provide assurance on the design and operating effectiveness of governance, risk management and internal controls;
> - A PIR is <u>not an inspection</u>, which has the objective to provide objective information to management about field offices, units in Headquarters and processes with no predetermined focus on fraud risk.[21]

Indeed, WFP states, under the heading 'Objectives - CONTINUED', that a PIR has broad objectives:

- to indicate whether a business process or operation might suffer from fraud or corruption ('red flags')

[18]https://docs.wfp.org/api/documents/WFP-0000038442/download/.

[19]https://docs.wfp.org/api/documents/WFP-0000038442/download/.

[20]https://docs.wfp.org/api/documents/WFP-0000038442/download/.

[21]https://docs.wfp.org/api/documents/WFP-0000038442/download/.

- to assess how large that problem may be and to identify areas for follow-up and intervention.
- to identify appropriate mitigation measures[22]

WFP also notes under 'Objectives - CONTINUED' that:

- ... the PIR may also identify possible weaknesses in project and programme design, implementation and control as well as in the WFP's current control instruments.[23]

Under the heading 'Implementation - Key Issues', WFP gives the following further information about how they conduct a PIR:

- ***Risk Identification***: Red flags range from facts that directly indicate fraudulent or corrupt activities (e.g. witness admissions), to facts that indicate a high likelihood of fraudulent or corrupt activities (e.g. bidders sharing one address), or facts that suggest an increased risk for such activities (e.g. poor control environment)
- ***Fieldwork:*** Therefore, and in order to ascertain the probability of fraud, PIR may involve conducting clarification interviews with key WFP, vendor and Cooperating Partners staff, in-depth review of individual expenditures, use of forensic accounting techniques, analytical review of data, and sampling/inspection of delivered product involving Expert Specialists, as required.[24]

Also under the heading 'Implementation – CONTINUED', WFP note:

Risk Mitigation: The PIR is a useful tool to provide appropriate fraud risk mitigation measures by the Management Unit or Process at an early stage, thus complementing the traditional channel of acting only upon the receipt of complaints.

Instigation of a PIR: PIRs respond to specific concerns, as referred by WFP management or flagged by audit work or raised by external entities, which may indicate risk of fraud, corruption, collusion, coercion and/or other wrongdoings. It can also be instigated following a specific fraud risk exposure scoping (or assessment).

Investigations of fraud and corruption: From a PIR, WFP Management can refer indications of potential fraud or red flags to OIG for investigation after a review of the real nature of the issues/risk. Separate and independent of the PIR, OIG can open an investigation if an allegation is made during the execution of a PIR, in line with OIG investigations guidelines. Any prima facie evidence of fraud (not simply a red flag) prompts the opening of an investigation by OIG following a notification to the relevant level of management.[25]

WFP also state under 'Implementation – CONTINUED':

[22] https://docs.wfp.org/api/documents/WFP-0000038442/download/.

[23] https://docs.wfp.org/api/documents/WFP-0000038442/download/.

[24] https://docs.wfp.org/api/documents/WFP-0000038442/download/.

[25] https://docs.wfp.org/api/documents/WFP-0000038442/download/.

- Recommendations: WFP business entities have the responsibility to take ownership of PIR findings.
- Reporting Results: To WFP Management, EB through OIG Annual Report and Briefing (March 6 FY 2016)[26]

At WFP, the management and the business entities in WFP are informed of the PIR result and findings—no doubt, they will also have a chance to learn the lessons and adapt their policies and procedures to prevent and deter fraud and corruption accordingly. On another slide, WFP notes:

> PIR - An increasing trend
>
> Proactive data monitoring and analysis processes such as PIRs were recently identified by the Association of Certified Fraud Examiners (ACFE) as the most effective control mechanism at limiting the duration and cost of fraud schemes. Organisations that implemented proactive control instruments similar to the PIRs experienced a reduction in their losses of up to 60 percent and decreased the duration of the schemes up to 50 percent when compared to organisations that did not.
>
> EIB – Proactive Integrity Review of EIB funded projects
>
> Asian DB - Project Procurement-Related Reviews
>
> WB – Detailed Implementation Review
>
> UNDP – Proactive Investigations but based on fraud risk assessment
>
> The objectives being sought are similar in nature, but there are slightly different procedural approaches due to different organisational structure and mandates.[27]

In the third slide entitled 'PIR - Actions and Next Steps', WFP note that:

> ***Results of the 5 PIR's***
>
> Key Results include the following:
>
> - 5 significant WFP operations 'stress tested' for fraud risk;
> - Compliance and control issues reviewed and number of recommendations for WFP Management action identified (e.g. Syria procurement PIR 12 recommendations).
> - 4 OIG investigations already launched as a result of PIR's by OIG and 6 more are under review/investigation. Limited referrals for investigation from WFP Management with the exception of CAR Country Office
> - WFP Management units are responsible for the risk mitigation measures identified. OIG follow up reviews on Jordan/Lebanon/Syria Procurement ongoing in Q1.[28]

UNDP In addition to WFP, the investigation office of the United Nations Development Programme (UNDP OAI) also undertakes Proactive Investigations (based on a fraud risk assessment exercise). The results of these reviews are not published. As a result, the 'what, where and how they are done' remains publicly unclear. Both UNDP's Anti-Fraud policy and OAI's Investigation Guidelines[29] mention 'proactive investigations' and the fact that OAI can do them.

---

[26]https://docs.wfp.org/api/documents/WFP-0000038442/download/.

[27]https://docs.wfp.org/api/documents/WFP-0000038442/download/.

[28]https://docs.wfp.org/api/documents/WFP-0000038442/download/.

[29]https://www.undp.org/content/undp/en/home/accountability/audit/office-of-audit-and-investigation.html.

Other UN Investigation Offices Some of them have the mandate to conduct such reviews but do so either occasionally or are gearing up to undertake them, such as UN OPS[30] and UNICEF. In other cases, resources are fully stretched investigating the existing caseload without looking to undertake these types of reviews which could identify other cases requiring investigation.

CII As noted above, the Conference of International Investigators (CII, in which investigation office staff from most international organisations participate), in 2019 approved General Principles on proactive investigations. Consequently, such reviews may be used by an increasing number of investigation services to review the projects and activities of (especially the outputs and other deliverables provided by) international organisations.[31]

11.3 Generally

Such proactive activity can help to reveal otherwise hidden risks and red flags of fraud and corruption. The identification of such risks can reveal red flags such as those that range from facts that directly indicate fraudulent or corrupt activities (such as witness admissions or contradictory facts obtained from different documents with the same author), to facts that indicate a high likelihood of fraudulent or corrupt activities (e.g. apparently competing bidders sharing one address, phone number and email, or using consecutively numbered bank guarantees), or to facts suggesting higher risks (e.g. poor control environment).

In the sense that these reviews regularly uncover issues that have not previously been identified or reported as an allegation to start an investigation, they are very useful and helpful at seeking to ensure that funds are not misused and the risks of fraud and corruption impacting the project are minimised, normally at an early stage. However, the reviews can be quite resource intensive and, depending on the circumstances, may require significant organisation.

In particular, field work is necessary, as a review is not just based on a 'desk review'—in order to ascertain the likelihood of fraud, those conducting the review may conduct interviews with key staff, vendors/suppliers and partners, in-depth review of certain documents such as expenditures, use of forensic accounting techniques, analytical review of data and sampling/inspection of delivered product.

---

[30] See the discussion of them in their Charter and 2018 Annual Report.

[31] The guidelines are all published on the website: www.conf-int-investigators.org.

11.4 Risk Identification and Mitigation

Generally, these reviews can be a very useful tool for investigative offices as it can identify the risks or weaknesses in controls, in some cases before any fraud or corruption has actually materialised.

As a result, appropriate fraud risk mitigation measures or different/new controls can be recommended for implementation at an early stage. This complements the traditional channel of acting only upon the receipt of a complaint, when a fraud is likely to have occurred already and thus adding value in terms of prevention.

11.5 Investigation to Follow

As noted above (in the text quoted from the WB INT Executive Summary and the WFP slides), the results of a review in terms of indications of potential fraud, corruption or red flags of other misconduct may be sent for a follow-up investigation.

Having said that, an investigation could be started in parallel if an allegation is made during the conduct of a review. Indeed, any prima facie evidence of a fraud having been committed (not simply a red flag indicator) may prompt the opening of an investigation at any point, irrespective of what other work is being carried out in parallel.

Review Effectiveness Proactive data monitoring and analysis processes such as PIRs were recently identified by the Association of Certified Fraud Examiners (ACFE) as the most effective control mechanism at limiting the duration and cost of fraud schemes.

Indeed, organisations that implemented proactive controls similar to PIRs are said to have experienced a reduction in their losses of up to 60% and decreased the duration of the schemes up to 50% in comparison with those organisations that did not.[32]

Naming As noted above by the WFP, the reviews are given different names by different organisations:

- EIB and WFP—Proactive Integrity Reviews;
- ADB—Project Procurement-Related Reviews;
- WB—Detailed Implementation Review; and
- UNDP—Proactive Investigations but based on fraud risk assessment

The objective(s) being sought by the different organisations that conduct such reviews are similar in nature, but there are sometimes slightly different procedural approaches due to the different organisational structures and mandates of those

[32]See the ACFE 2018 Report to the Nations at www.acfe.com/report-to-the-nations/2018/default.aspx.

undertaking them. Nevertheless, important features are that the beneficiary's use of the funds, operational modalities, governance, products and applicable control framework are generally reviewed in detail. When gaps are spotted, appropriate recommendations are identified for implementation or adoption.

Generally These initiatives tend to fly in the face of a concern that auditors generally find it difficult to uncover or identify fraud. In general, the detailed reviews of the type and nature that have been discussed in this Chapter are conducted by auditors and others, although generally they do so with a more investigative (curious, sceptical) mindset and using a more investigative methodology.

Also, they are conducted proactively, based on risk analysis (indicating a high risk situation) or concerns that have been raised or identified. As the text quoted from the WB INT DIR above reflects, such reviews can and do identify issues in connection with fraud, corruption and the misuse of funds.[33]

[33]FCPA Blog article by Jeffrey Klink and Tracy Pastrick dated March 20, 2019 entitled 'The Risk of Relying on Auditors to Find Fraud' which notes that 'Shell companies are formed in minutes, and a cursory review of the Panama Papers show how these entities are used to defraud others. Failure to perform due diligence is often the flaw in the internal control process and site visits are often the only means available to assess whether a company is real or a fake. The audit process typically does not utilise site visits or other extensive field research to assess whether one or five hundred shell companies are defrauding a client' and '... it is important to use the right resource to ferret out fraud. Unless specifically requested to perform a forensic audit to look for fraud, an audit performed by an auditor in the ordinary course of business is unlikely to uncover such misconduct'.

Chapter 12
Investigations

Most, if not all, of the MDBs and other international organisations provide (in the documentation for or about the project and/or financing agreement) that the organisation can, if necessary, conduct an investigation into the project or use of the funds.

12.1 Allegations

Such an investigation may result for a number of reasons, such as:

- an allegation (that is credible and provable) is made directly to the organisation that is financing the project about fraud, corruption or misuse of funds or about the conduct of its staff;
- a local law enforcement agency is conducting an investigation into criminal misconduct arising out of circumstances linked to or affecting the project; or
- other negative reports or experiences such as those experienced by third party monitors, local press or other interested or affected parties.

The ability to conduct an investigation includes the right to inspect the site or sites of the project.

In most cases, allegations sent to an organisation are subject to an initial review and assessment in a case intake process first. Those allegations that are false, made-up or are unprovable will be closed and only those that appear to be credible, provable and affecting a project financed by the organisation or the conduct of specific staff members would be allocated to investigators for further work.

Complaints or allegations that fall outside of the organisation's jurisdiction may be redirected to other areas of the organisation or may even be passed on to the organisation that is, in fact, financing the project, as appropriate

D. Smith, *Promoting Integrity in the Work of International Organisations*,
Contributions to Finance and Accounting,
https://doi.org/10.1007/978-3-030-73916-4_12

In essence, an assessment seeks to determine whether: the complaint relates to a sanctionable practice in a project financed by the organisation, the reported allegation has credibility and the matter is of sufficient gravity to require an investigation.

In some organisations, the allegations that meet these initial requirements, may be subject to a priority assessment. There may be limited resources available and consequently only those allegations of a higher priority will be investigated. Of course, part of this assessment includes the possible reputational risk to the organisation, the amount of funds involved and quality of the information that may be available.

12.2 Prevention/Lessons Learned

Even if the receipt of the allegation does not lead to an investigation being started, it may be the case that the risks of fraud and corruption in the future in the project can be reduced by acting on and responding to certain issues that have been identified in the complaint.

Equally, it is possible to share with business units of the organisation at this point (if not earlier) the findings and recommendations from previous similar cases if the allegation concerns the same risk(s), country, sector or companies involved.

Outreach efforts to the internal operations team working on the project may also assist and improve communication lines as well as seeking to ensure that the project team are trained on fraud and corruption risks, can recognise red flags if/when they appear and know who to contact in case of issues in the future.

12.3 External Investigation

The aim of an investigation is to try to prove (or disprove) that Prohibited Conduct has occurred. Of course, there may be instances where in reality such conduct has occurred but in practice there is insufficient or no evidence to prove it, so the basic principle of the Presumption of Innocence would apply.

The key purpose of the investigation is to attempt to gather a minimum amount (reasonably sufficient) of evidence to substantiate the allegation that Prohibited Conduct has occurred (or whatever other misconduct issue(s) have emerged).

12.4 Internal Investigation

The integrity of the institution's own staff and operations is of equal, if not greater, importance—to maintain its credibility, an international institution needs to ensure that allegations of internal misconduct are dealt with promptly and effectively. This includes not just allegations against regular staff members but also against others working in or for the organisation, such as consultants, corporate vendors and suppliers (who, if proved to have engaged in Prohibited Conduct, could be sanctioned by exclusion).

In some organisations, investigators are expected to deal with a combination of both external and internal cases, whereas in other places, there is a dedicated Internal Investigation team. Any cases of misconduct that are proved against staff members are normally dealt with under the institution's own internal disciplinary system; any cases against external vendors or suppliers may be dealt with under the sanctions mechanism.

It is important to ensure that: (1) not only does the institution promote and encourage the reporting, detection and prevention of misconduct; but that (2) when cases arise, they are dealt with (not just in terms of the investigation but also in terms of completion of disciplinary process) promptly and expeditiously.

Examples of allegations against staff within the Internal Investigations Unit's investigative mandate given by the World Bank on its website include:

- the abuse of position for personal gain,
- misuse of Bank funds or trust funds,
- embezzlement,
- fraud, corruption and collusion, involving either Bank operations or in the administration of Bank business, and
- conflicts of interest or lesser included acts of misconduct.[1]

For international organisations, there are additional administrative requirements upon staff recruited from other countries (and their families) such as work permits, visas, yearly tax declarations and a range of birth/marriage/death requirements for resident relatives. A breach of any of the laws of the host country is potentially problematic and could result in a criminal conviction.

12.5 All Investigations

The investigation process used by an international organisation would usually involve some sort of initial review of the type and nature of the complaint or allegation and, if it is confirmed as a case that requires further attention, will be allocated to an investigator for more detailed investigation work. This further investigation work includes the review of relevant documents, interviews of witnesses knowledgeable about the project and circumstances affecting it, inspections and spot-checks and interviews under caution of the suspect(s).

As a result, the process used by an investigator from an international organisation to try to uncover the facts and determine whether misconduct has occurred as alleged

[1] www.worldbank.org/en/about/unit/integrity-vice-presidency#2.

or otherwise, is not significantly different from an investigation conducted by officers from a domestic law enforcement agency who are undertaking an investigation into alleged criminal conduct. Both types of investigations would generally include: (1) meeting and interviewing witnesses who may have relevant information and/or documents; (2) the review of documents; (3) inspections of the site(s) and/or companies/equipment affected; and (4) interviews of the suspect(s), sometimes with legal representation.

The main differences of course are that: (1) there are no judicially approved search and arrest warrants available to the investigators from international organisations, for example in the situation where a suspect has refused (or is believed not to have provided) relevant but potentially incriminating documents when asked; and (2) suspect interviews taking place under caution, with a consequence in a criminal trial if it can be proved that the suspect has lied under oath.

Whether or not the investigators in an international organisation have gathered evidence to substantiate a case, a final investigation report (which discusses the key issues) would normally be produced, see below.

12.6 Investigation Principles

Investigations for an international organisation are undertaken by professional investigators in line with clear and reasonable principles. The IFI Uniform Framework[2] was one of the first documents to reflect general principles on how an investigation carried out by an MDB investigation office should be undertaken. These general principles were accepted and signed up to in 2006 by the six large MDBs and have also been used and adopted by the investigation offices of many other international organisations.

Indeed, the general principles for undertaking an investigation have been expanded for (and accepted by) a wider range of international organisations including OLAF and organisations from the UN that participate in the Conference of International Investigators (CII).[3] The CII website notes the significant value of harmonising investigation practices amongst international organisations and:

> In recognition of the necessity of continuing to improve investigative practices, the participating investigative offices have ... produced these revised Principles and Guidelines for Investigations.
>
> These Principles and Guidelines are intended to be used as guidance in the conduct of investigations subject to the regulations, rules, policies and the privileges and immunities applicable in each organisation ... and are not intended to bind the Organisations or confer,

[2] https://www.eib.org/en/about/documents/ifi-anti-corruption-task-force-uniform-framework.htm. Also available at: https://www.afdb.org/fileadmin/uploads/afdb/Documents/Generic-Documents/Uniform_Framework_for_Combatting_Fraud_and_Corruption.pdf and https://www.adb.org/publications/uniform-framework-preventing-and-combating-fraud-and-corruption.

[3] http://www.conf-int-investigators.org/uniform-guidelines-for-investigations/.

impose or imply any duties, obligations or rights actionable in a court of law or in administrative proceedings on the Organisations.[4]

These investigation guidelines cover the following topics:

- Definitions
- Rights and Obligations-witnesses and subjects
- Sources of Complaints
- Receipt of Complaint
- Preliminary Evaluation
- Case Prioritisation
- Investigative Activity
- Investigative Findings
- Referrals to National Authorities

12.7 Standard of Proof

Since an investigation by an international organisation is administrative in nature, the standard of proof is the 'balance of probabilities' and, as a result, it is lower than the criminal standard of 'beyond a reasonable doubt' (that folks who enjoy reading court dramas appreciate!).

Consequently, if the investigators obtain sufficient evidence to this level (on the balance of probabilities), it will be considered that the allegation has been substantiated; the reverse is also true, namely that an allegation will be considered unsubstantiated if insufficient evidence is available.

If there is evidence to contradict the allegation, the allegation is considered as disproved or unfounded.

12.8 Final Reports

Normally, a Final Case Report (or final investigation case report) is produced at the conclusion of the investigation, whether or not sufficient evidence to substantiate the allegation has been gathered. The report would normally summarise the process (es) undertaken, the people and corporate entities approached, the interviews conducted, the documents obtained (and where from) and record the findings that can be drawn from the available evidence (in comparison with the original allegation

[4]http://www.conf-int-investigators.org/uniform-guidelines-for-investigations/.

and other misconduct which may have appeared to have occurred during the investigation).[5]

In some cases, irrespective of the direct follow-up with the person(s)/entity(ies) concerned that the evidence allows, there may be important lessons to be learned by the institution, so a separate report may be produced and circulated internally, so that the lessons (and policy implications) can be shared with colleagues.

Apart from the detailed report that is used internally (for a number of potential purposes), there are various ways in which an international organisation can communicate with the outside world about the findings of an investigation.

One way used by the World Bank INT is to publish a redacted report on its website. Copies of the report may have already been provided to operational colleagues and/or to the Board of Executive Directors in advance of such publication. The publication of the report may only take place after any related criminal proceedings and/or sanctions process have been completed.[6]

12.9 Sanctions

If the investigation has gathered evidence that proves that there was Prohibited Conduct or some other form of misconduct (either as originally alleged or otherwise as identified during or as a result of the investigation, such as obstruction), the individual(s) and/or entity(ies) responsible are likely to be the subject of a sanctions process by an MDB. This aspect will be covered in greater detail in the following chapter.

---

[5]Apart from each organisation's templates for investigation documents, such as reports, memos, case notes, etc., there are other materials available on-line, such as these at i-sight which is a Canadian website that gives a contact address in Ottawa, Canada. For example, they list publications such as: (i) 12 Tips for Writing an Effective Investigation Report (ii) Top 10 Investigation Report Must Haves and (iii) Investigation Report Writing. The website notes: 'In fact, a comprehensive investigation report can serve as crucial evidence in litigation, showing that a thorough investigation was undertaken and that the process and outcome were fully documented. In cases of employee misconduct, fraud, bribery and corruption, the investigation report shows that the company took the behaviour seriously and acted appropriately, demonstrating a culture of ethics and a commitment to compliance. Courts have been known to be more lenient with companies when their investigation reporting is thorough and timely.

Our resources library contains a plethora of tools to help you hone your investigation reporting skills and establish effective documentation procedures'. https://i-sight.com/collections/investigation-reporting/.

[6]https://www.worldbank.org/en/about/unit/integrity-vice-presidency/redacted-investigation-reports.

12.10 Referrals

If the investigation has gathered evidence that tends to indicate that there was criminal misconduct (either as originally alleged or otherwise), the individual (s) and/or entity(ies) responsible can also be the subject of a referral report by the international organisation to the Police or other national law enforcement agency (such as a dedicated anti-corruption organisation) based in that country.

A referral report is usually a new document created specifically to allow the international organisation to send the allegation(s) (usually if the allegation was proven but sometimes when they are difficult to prove but are very serious) and evidence if available, to a relevant national law enforcement agency. The referral is normally made if evidence has been gathered that indicates that the laws of a member country have been broken.

In some cases that involve a number of countries (e.g. international companies using a supplier from a second country to defraud or pay bribes to project officials in a third country—who may even be using offshore bank accounts in a number of other countries to gather corrupt payments), there may be a referral to more than one place, especially if there are a number of law enforcement agencies with jurisdiction to investigate, for example in corruption cases.

12.10.1 Europe-Based EIB Prohibited Conduct

'The European Investment Bank Group (EIB Group) has a zero tolerance of Prohibited Conduct whether occurring in connection with projects and activities financed by the EIB Group or perpetrated by its own staff. The EIB Group consists of the European Investment Bank (EIB or the Bank) and the European Investment Fund (EIF)'.

The Fraud Investigations Division is an independent office within the EIB Group and is the sole office mandated to investigate Prohibited Conduct within EIB Group.

Prohibited Conduct includes fraud, corruption, collusion, coercion, obstruction, money laundering and financing of terrorism affecting the EIB Group's operations and activities.

The Fraud Investigations Division aims to protect the EIB Group's finances and reputation through six core activities:

- Assessment and, where necessary, investigation of allegations
- Policy work aiming at ensuring the existence of a robust anti-fraud policy framework at the EIB Group and incorporating the lessons learned from the investigations into policies and practices
- Proactive Integrity Reviews (PIRs) to identify actual fraud or potential vulnerabilities
- Fraud awareness training for all EIB Group staff
- Raising awareness of Prohibited Conduct-related issues in the public and private sectors
- Analysis and information gathering to support the above five activities

The EIB Group encourages everyone to report promptly to the Fraud Investigations Division suspicions of Prohibited Conduct in EIB Group-financed operations or activities. Investigations are primarily triggered by reporting of suspicions. External reports from parties or persons involved in EIB Group projects and activities are therefore of important value for the EIB Group.[7]

12.10.2 EBRD

Their website notes:

> Investigating fraud, corruption and misconduct
>
> The Office of the Chief Compliance Officer is responsible for procedures governing the ethical behaviour of Bank officials, employees and consultants, and it conducts investigations on alleged staff misconduct. It also sets the standards of integrity that the Bank expects of its business partners.
>
> The EBRD combats corruption and fraud, as well as misconduct of Bank officials, employees and consultants, or any other activity, which might compromise the integrity of the Bank and its partners.[8]

12.10.3 OLAF

The European Anti-Fraud Office (or OLAF to use its acronym in French) conducts administrative (i.e. non-criminal) investigations into 'fraud against the EU budget, corruption and serious misconduct within the European institutions and develops anti-fraud policy for the European Commission' in particular to protect the financial interests of the EU.[9]

They are based in Brussels, Belgium and they conduct investigations in EU countries and beyond (including potentially a country that is receiving EU funds in Asia, Africa, the Caribbean, the Middle East or Central/Southern America). OLAF also works cooperatively with national investigation and prosecution agencies in Europe and beyond, as well as the EPPO in future.

12.10.4 EPPO

The European Public Prosecutor's Office is a new development on the European law enforcement landscape, designed to provide a consistent approach to 'tackling large-scale cross-border crime against the EU budget' such as 'fraud, corruption and serious cross-border VAT fraud'. They will conduct criminal investigations.

---

[7] https://www.eib.org/en/about/accountability/anti-fraud/index.htm The Investigation Procedures are also available at:

https://www.eib.org/en/publications/anti-fraud-procedures.htm.

[8] https://www.ebrd.com/who-we-are/our-values/investigating-fraud-and-corruption.html.

[9] https://ec.europa.eu/anti-fraud/home_en.

It will start operating in 2020, will be based in Luxembourg and will be the first EU decentralised prosecution office. Until it has had a number of cases, the way in which it will work and cooperate with law enforcement agencies in the EU (as well as its interaction with the European Commission and in particular with OLAF) is not easy to predict.

The EPPO website notes:

> The European Public Prosecutor's Office will be an independent and decentralised prosecution office of the European Union, with the competence to investigate, prosecute and bring to judgement crimes against the EU budget... At this stage, there are 22 participating EU countries.
>
> Currently, only national authorities can investigate and prosecute fraud against the EU budget. But their powers stop at national borders. Existing EU-bodies such as Eurojust, Europol and the EU's anti-fraud office (OLAF) lack the necessary powers to carry out criminal investigations and prosecutions.[10]

MDBs Globally

The MDB Cross-Debarment website notes:

> Cross debarment is an agreement between:
> - the African Development Bank Group,
> - Asian Development Bank,
> - European Bank for Reconstruction and Development,
> - Inter-American Development Bank and
> - the World Bank Group (referred to as Multilateral Development Banks)
>
> to mutually enforce each other's debarment actions, with respect to the four harmonised sanctionable practices, i.e., corruption, fraud, coercion, and collusion.
>
> These Multilateral Development Banks (MDBs) signed the 'Agreement on Mutual Enforcement of Debarment Decisions' on 9 April 2010. The agreement became effective for the MDBs on the following dates:
> - Asian Development Bank—9 June 2010
> - European Bank for Reconstruction and Development—9 June 2010
> - World Bank—19 July 2010
> - Inter-American Development Bank—9 May 2011
> - African Development Bank—11 July 2012
>
> An innovative coordinated global initiative, cross debarment creates a formidable additional deterrent to firms and individuals engaged in fraud and corruption in MDB-financed development projects, and possibly provides an incentive for firms to clean up their operations.[11]

[10] www.ec.europa.eu/info/law/cross-border-cases/judicial-cooperation/networks-and-bodies-supporting-judicial-cooperation/european-public-prosecutors-office_en.

[11] http://crossdebarment.org/oai001p.nsf/Home.xsp.

12.10.5 WB INT

The WB website notes:

> The Integrity Vice Presidency (INT) is an independent unit within the World Bank Group that investigates and pursues sanctions related to allegations of fraud and corruption in World Bank Group-financed projects. INT supports the main business units of the World Bank Group and external stakeholders, mitigating fraud and corruption risks through sharing investigative findings, advice, prevention and outreach efforts.[12]

12.10.6 WB Sanctions

The WB website notes:

> The World Bank Group's Sanctions System
>
> Tackling Corruption Through a Two-Tier Administrative Sanctions Process
>
> Promoting good governance and tackling corruption are critical to achieving sustainable development and poverty reduction. Diversion of funds from development projects through corruption impairs the ability of governments, donors, and the World Bank to achieve the goals of reducing poverty, attracting investment, and encouraging good governance.[13]

12.10.7 IDB

The IDB website notes:

> The Office of Institutional Integrity (OII) plays a key role in the IDB Group's integrity efforts. OII as an integral part of the Sanctions System is responsible for investigating allegations of fraud and corruption in IDB Group-financed activities, and taking efforts to prevent them. Annually, OII and the Sanctions System report their activities in their annual report.
>
> In its investigations, OII follows the Principles and Guidelines for Investigations, incorporated in the Uniform Framework for Preventing and Combating Fraud and Corruption adopted by the International Financial Institutions Anti-Corruption Task Force.
>
> OII's prevention activities aim to identify, assess and mitigate integrity and reputational risks on IDB Group-financed activities. To this end, OII extracts lessons learned from investigations and conducts training activities to improve the IDB Group's knowledge regarding identification of integrity risk or prohibited practices. OII also develops and enforces policies and mechanisms to strengthen the overall integrity of IDB Group-financed activities.
>
> The Office reports its ongoing activities and significant findings to the Bank's senior management and the Audit Committee of the Board of Executive Directors.[14]

---

[12]https://www.worldbank.org/en/about/unit/integrity-vice-presidency.

[13]https://www.worldbank.org/en/about/unit/sanctions-system.

[14]https://www.iadb.org/en/about-us/departments/oii.

12.10.8 ADB

The ADB website notes:

> Investigations help safeguard development funds and prevent integrity problems from recurring.
>
> The Office of Anticorruption and Integrity (OAI) screens complaints to ensure they relate to an integrity violation and involve ADB-related activities.
>
> OAI considers whether or not the complaints are:
>
> - within OAI's mandate—relate to activities that OAI is authorised to investigate;
> - credible—there is a reasonable possibility that a violation has occurred;
> - verifiable—practicable options exist to obtain sufficient evidence to determine the truth of the allegations on the balance of probabilities; and
> - material—the matter is of sufficient importance to justify the projected requirements of the investigation and any remedial action.
>
> Complaints that meet all four criteria are converted into full investigations. Otherwise, the complaint is closed.
>
> OAI's Integrity Principles and Guidelines require that its investigative findings are presented to subjects of an investigation whenever possible. Subjects may prepare an explanation of the facts and circumstances from their perspective and in their own words. This explanation is presented to ADB's Integrity Oversight Committee (IOC) for consideration. As the investigation process is administrative in nature, ADB's procedures do not provide for personal appearances or representations at IOC meetings.[15]

12.10.9 AfDB

The AfDB website notes:

> Integrity and Anti-Corruption
>
> The African Development Bank Group views corruption, fraud and other sanctionable practices as highly inimical to the achievement of its mandate. In order to spur sustainable economic development and social progress on the continent, AfDB endorses a multi-pronged approach to combating these harmful practices. Consequently, IACD uses proactive measures including risk assessments and sensitisation programmes to deter sanctionable practices and prevent their occurrence in internal corporate procurement issues and operations financed by the Bank Group.
>
> Mandate
>
> The Integrity and Anti-Corruption Department has the overriding mandate to carry out independent investigations into allegations of corruption, fraud and other sanctionable practices in Bank Group Financed Operations. 'Bank Group Financed Operations' are internal corporate procurement issues and operations financed by the Bank Group. The Department also develops preventive measures to proactively reduce the potential for corruption, fraud, misconduct and other sanctionable practices within Bank Group Financed Operations. IACD's operational responsibilities further include risk assessments and employment of surveillance measures towards investigations.

[15] https://www.adb.org/site/integrity/investigations.

IACD was established in November 2005 and became operational in June 2006. In order to further strengthen the Bank's anti-corruption agenda, the Board of Directors approved the restructuring of the Department on the 5th of July 2012. IACD's mandate is reflected in its independence, authority, access and operations provided in its terms of reference.[16]

12.10.10 Other Global organisations

12.10.10.1 UN OIOS

The OIOS website notes:

> The Office of Internal Oversight Services (OIOS) is the internal oversight body of the United Nations (UN).
>
> The Office assists the Secretary-General in fulfilling his oversight responsibilities in respect of the resources and staff of the Organisation through the provision of audit, investigation, inspection and evaluation services.
>
> OIOS helps the UN become more efficient, effective and relevant, delivering on timely, reliable, objective information about the biggest risks and challenges facing the Organisation through our functional divisions.[17]

12.10.10.2 UN Development Programme

The UNDP website notes:

> Investigations
>
> As part of UNDP's strategy to strengthen the accountability framework for the Organisation and to provide opportunities for bringing to light any misconduct, wrongdoing by any individuals working for or doing business with UNDP, the Office of Audit and Investigations (OAI) has established an Investigations Hotline and other measures to ensure that persons wishing to report fraud may do so, free of charge, using a number of different options.[18]

12.10.10.3 The Global Fund

The Global Fund website notes:

> The Office of the Inspector General safeguards the assets, investments, reputation and sustainability of the Global Fund by ensuring that it takes the right action to accelerate the end of AIDS, tuberculosis and malaria as epidemics.
>
> Through audits, investigations and consultancy work, the Office of the Inspector General promotes good practice, reduces risk and reports on abuse.

---

[16] https://www.afdb.org/en/about-us/organisational-structure/integrity-and-anti-corruption.

[17] https://oios.un.org.

[18] https://www.undp.org/content/undp/en/home/accountability/audit/office-of-audit-and-investigation.html.

The scope of work for the Office of the Inspector General includes all systems, processes, operations, functions and activities of the Global Fund and of the programmes it supports. The Inspector General has the authority to:

- Access all books and records maintained by the Global Fund
- Access all books and records relating to grants funded by the Global Fund, whether maintained by grant recipients or Local Fund Agents
- Access the sites where these records are kept and where the programmes are implemented, as permitted under applicable arrangements
- Seek any information required from any personnel involved in the Global Fund's projects and require such personnel to cooperate with any reasonable request made by the Office of the Inspector General
- Obtain independent professional advice and secure the involvement in its activities of outside persons with relevant experience and expertise, if and when determined necessary

The Office of the Inspector General is independent of the Global Fund Secretariat and reports directly to the Board through its Audit and Finance Committee.[19]

12.10.10.4 Conference of International Investigators

The CII website notes:

> The Conference of International Investigators (CII) is a forum for investigators of international organisations to exchange ideas, discuss integrity issues, address challenges in fighting fraud and corruption, receive new developments and share leading practices.
>
> Established in 1999 by and for investigators of international organisations, the CII encourages and enables collegiality and close cooperation among investigative offices of participating organisations. It provides support and guidance to investigators and their offices through its annual conferences and published materials.[20]

12.11 Working with Local Law Enforcement

As noted above,[21] the investigation may gather evidence of a criminal offence having been committed. If so, the individual(s) and/or entity(ies) responsible could be the subject of a referral report by the international organisation to the Police or other national law enforcement agency based in that country.

The importance of effective interaction between international organisations such as the MDBs and national authorities was identified and commented upon by the Canadian Supreme Court in 2016 in the case of *World Bank v Wallace* as follows:

> Corruption is a significant obstacle to international development. It undermines confidence in public institutions, diverts funds from those who are in great need of financial support, and violates business integrity. Corruption often transcends borders. In order to tackle this global problem, worldwide cooperation is needed. When international financial organisations, such as the World Bank Group, share information gathered from informants across the world with

[19]https://www.theglobalfund.org/en/oig/.

[20]http://www.conf-int-investigators.org.

[21]Page 122.

the law enforcement agencies of the member states, they help achieve what neither could do on their own.

In order to provide a framework within which such interaction with a local law enforcement agency (or agencies if the matter is referred to more than one country) can take place, formal documents such as a Memorandum of Understanding (or MoUs for short) are agreed and signed with the agency. EIB has agreed to a number of such documents and published them on its website.

12.12 Examples of Prohibited Conduct Affecting an International Organisation

The following is a list of some types of misconduct that may affect, dramatically or on a more limited basis, the nature and implementation of projects financed by international organisations:

- False (larger) measurements given for newly built buildings so as to over bill for construction, materials, supplies of decoration (tiles, paint, wallpaper etc.) or for a road or rail line (possibly built through a remote area, and therefore perhaps less likely to be spotted or checked);
- False documents being supplied when copies of the project documents are requested, for example changing the amounts, dates of delivery, size, number or type of equipment;
- False corporate documents supplied in procurement processes such as the type or number of machinery to be supplied, the cost of supplies, the CVs of people who claim to be available to participate in the team etc.;
- Collusion among bidders to agree and thereby rig key data in what should be competitive bids (such as prices, dates or quantities);
- False accounting and/or misleading data being provided or supplied in a loan application or other critical financial documents;
- The number of employees (for example, 30,000 'ghost' Government employees uncovered a few years ago in Mozambique);[22]
- Procurement processes being dominated by the corporate entities (or their intermediaries/agents) to indicate that they are willing to make the highest bribe payments rather than the most competitive and lowest priced bids.

Of course, this sort of behaviour is not just limited to impacting large, publicly financed projects funded by international organisations. The provision of false or misleading data, frauds on consumers and/or the organiser/payor of a newly constructed house/office/school/hospital/ medical clinic, corruption affecting the choice of competing bidders and collusion between supposed competitors to fix key issues (such as prices, delivery dates, amounts or quantities, types of supplies)

[22]See earlier reference, on page 39 and footnote 67, www.bbc.com/news/amp/world-africa-46520946.

can happen in public or private projects, to projects of small or large value and in a range of sectors (health, education, transportation, etc.), anywhere around the world.

Unfortunately, fraud, corruption, collusion or other forms of misconduct can materialise in any project (whether it is in the public or private sector) and irrespective of the levels of national salaries/incomes, the freedom of the press, power and influence of other types of media or the influence and effectiveness and rigour of the application of the rule of law.

12.13 Broader Examples of Misconduct

Of course, fraud and corruption (and other forms of misconduct) do not just affect the projects financed by the MDBs or more broadly the work of international organisations. Fraud and corruption are criminal offences, are common global phenomena and therefore occur frequently in various domestic (as well as international) settings, industries, sectors, etc.

No doubt examples of cases in sectors you are particularly interested in (such as medicine, justice, education, health, construction, local and international politics, local and international trade)—some cases that are well known, others less so—can be obtained by searches on the internet.[23] Such cases demonstrate the ability to adapt and pursue illegal conduct (and the apparent financial and social benefits that accompany it), such is human behaviour.

Some examples of cases more directly impacting MDB's work (in projects around the world) follows in Chap. 14.[24]

[23]See FCPA Blog article: 'Ericsson jolts the FCPA top ten list by Richard L. Cassin, December 9, 2019' which includes a list of the top ten cases (in terms of value) and notes: 'Stockholm-based Ericsson cracked our top ten list Friday with a $1 billion mega-settlement that landed at number two . . . Non-U.S. companies continue to dominate the FCPA top ten, still holding nine of ten spots. The only US company currently on the list is KBR / Halliburton, now ranked ninth with its $579 million resolution from 2009 . . . With the addition of Ericsson there are now four mobile phone companies in the FCPA top ten. Two of them — Ericsson and Telia — are based in Sweden. Sweden, by the way, ranks as one of the world's cleanest countries. It's tied at number three on TI's latest Corruption Perceptions Index which measures perceived corruption at home. Apparently a country's rank on the CPI isn't always a good predictor of how companies from there will behave when they do business overseas.. . .'

[24]Page 148.

Chapter 13
Sanctions

Once evidence of misconduct has been gathered by investigators, the organisation, if it is an MDB, can seek to impose a range of sanctions/exclusion on those engaging in the integrity violations by commencing a sanctions case. The evidence has to implicate each person and/or entity named in the formal accusation (in some places called a Notice of Debarment or Exclusion). Each MDB has a Sanctions Committee which comprises a blend of senior managers from the institution and outsiders to ensure objectivity although some of the Committees only contain outsiders.

If the sanctions case is successful, the Committee decides that the fraud or corruption has been proven. Consequently, the level of punishment and degree of sanctions imposed on those found to have undertaken the misconduct, will be determined by the Committee depending on a number of factors including:

- the nature and seriousness of the misconduct;
- the length of time the conduct took place;
- the number of people and seniority of those involved; and
- the effect the conduct has had on the overall success and implementation of the project.

13.1 Purpose of Sanctions

Sanctions are applied with the intention to both:

(1) prevent and deter future misconduct in similar situations; and
(2) encourage rehabilitation of the sanctioned party(ies).

Partly, this double aim for the application of sanctions is driven by the facts of the case and the individual/entity's circumstances and response to them. Also important is the fact that the sanctioning decisions are likely to be publicised. This will result in

D. Smith, *Promoting Integrity in the Work of International Organisations*,
Contributions to Finance and Accounting,
https://doi.org/10.1007/978-3-030-73916-4_13

the entity (and individuals too if they are well known, senior corporate managers or notorious intermediaries/agents) needing to ensure that they have a publicly credible explanation of what happened and/or a response to the incident that minimises the damage to their public reputation and possible press coverage.

The institutions generally use five types of sanctions:

- fixed-term debarment or exclusion;
- debarment with conditional release;
- conditional non-debarment;
- letter of reprimand; and/or
- restitution.

The most common sanction applied by the MDBs is debarment with conditional release, which means that the entity will be excluded (or debarred) from receiving new contracts anywhere in the world for a minimum period of time. In addition, the sanctioned party may only be released after satisfying certain conditions, such as the effective implementation of a compliance program or the green light from a third party anti-corruption monitor.

Debarments exceeding 1 year extend across several other MDBs, namely ADB, AfDB Group, EBRD, and IDB Group (but not EIB), pursuant to the cross-debarment agreement[1] signed in 2010.

13.2 Process

The parties concerned will engage in a quasi-judicial process where the institution will demonstrate (by documents and evidence gathered during an investigation), the nature and extent of the misconduct. The affected parties are also entitled to submit evidence and pleadings, evidence to disprove the alleged misconduct or to mitigate the effects and explanatory pleadings. If the Sanctions Board (or other group, such as a Committee, controlling the proceedings) determines that the parties have engaged in fraudulent, corrupt, coercive, collusive, obstructive practices, or other integrity violations, appropriate sanctions will be applied.

The rules for the process, commonly known as a Sanctions Hearing, are sent to those accused of integrity violations and are published on their website. Normally representation for the company includes the senior manager(s) involved and a lawyer or lawyers for the company and the individuals concerned. In some cases, the evidence of an integrity violation is not challenged but other facts, not obvious from the evidence already gathered, is presented in mitigation and/or to explain the role of others in the misconduct.

In some cases the integrity violations will be uncovered by the company and will be 'self reported'. This may lead to further investigation by the institution(s) affected

[1]See the website www.crossdebarment.org.

and may ultimately lead to a Settlement Agreement or some other type of agreement with the institution concerned—the World Bank has in the past reached Voluntary Disclosure agreements that may be outside the scope of Cross Debarment but requires the company to undertake and disclose further investigation of their other contracts.

13.3 Different Systems

As can be seen below, there are a number of different administrative (quasi-judicial) systems for the processing of a sanctions case, depending on the institution. However most of the MDBs also feed into the cross debarment system (ie. cross recognition of a debarment decision) by the other MDBs), whereas EIB does not.[2]

13.3.1 World Bank

The sanctions system of the World Bank Group (including IDA, IFC and MIGA) is a two-tiered administrative process designed to protect the integrity of its operations and ensure that the development finance is used for its intended purpose(s).[3] This website notes that: 'promoting good governance and tackling corruption are critical to achieving sustainable development and poverty-reduction'.

At the first tier, cases of sanctionable conduct proposed by the WBG Integrity Vice Presidency (INT) and the evidence underpinning it, are reviewed by an Evaluation and Suspension Officer. If sanctions proceedings are started, the accused party(ies) is/are temporarily suspended from being awarded WBG-financed contracts.

The sanctioned individual/entity may nevertheless appeal to the second tier, the Sanctions Board. Such an appeal would provide a de novo review of the accusations and/or recommended sanction and a full hearing, if requested by the parties or called for by the Chair of the Sanctions Board. The Board has seven external (i.e. independent) members (jurists and development experts).

The World Bank's two-tier system is designed to provide due process to parties accused of misconduct before rendering any decision. The World Bank's system also includes parallel procedures for cases related to the different institutions, the International Finance Corporation (IFC) and the Multilateral Investment Guarantee Agency (MIGA).

The World Bank INT can also sign a settlement agreement.

---

[2]www.crossdebarment.org.

[3]www.worldbank.org/en/about/unit/sanctions-system.

A full list of firms and individuals currently debarred by the World Bank Group can be found on their website.[4] Their website notes that the World Bank Group debarred 48 firms and individuals during the Fiscal Year 2019. In addition, the World Bank recognised 33 cross-debarments from other participating MDBs.

The World Bank website also notes the following:

> In addition to evaluating allegations of fraud and corruption, INT works to prevent corruption in ongoing Bank Group projects. INT staff identified and worked to mitigate integrity risks in 152 projects, steps that made progress in safeguarding the equivalent of $28.9 billion in project commitments. The team also provided advisory services in 47 countries.
>
> Finally, INT's Integrity Compliance Office (ICO), which works with sanctioned firms and individuals to institute reforms in alignment with the Bank Group's Integrity Compliance Guidelines to reduce the possibilities for future misconduct, provided guidance to 93 parties. The ICO determined that 23 firms and individuals had met the conditions required to be released from sanction and are now eligible to participate in Bank Group-funded projects.[5]

13.3.2 European Bank for Reconstruction and Development (EBRD)

EBRD's Enforcement Policy and Procedures[6] provide that an individual or entity can be subject to sanctions proceedings if:

- They have engaged in any Prohibited Practice (as defined in Section II(46) of the Enforcement Policy and Procedures) in the context of an EBRD Project;
- They are subject to a Third Party Finding; or
- They are subject to a Debarment Decision by a Mutual Enforcement Institution.

EBRD also has a two tier sanctions process:

- the Enforcement Commissioner is the first-tier decision-maker of Enforcement Proceedings;[7]
- the second (and final) decision-maker is the EBRD's Enforcement Committee[8] which receives and determines appeals from the Enforcement Commissioner's Decisions and/or the Enforcement Commissioner's determinations, authorisations and non-authorisations issued. The Enforcement Committee consists of five members (with three external members and two internal members

[4]www.worldbank.org/debarr.

[5]www.worldbank.org/en/news/press-release/2019/10/10/world-bank-group-debarred-48-firms-and-individuals-during-fiscal-year-2019.

[6]www.ebrd.com/news/publications/policies/enforcement-policy-and-procedures.html.

[7]www.ebrd.com/who-we-are/our-values/enforcement-commissioner.html.

[8]www.ebrd.com/our-values/integrity-and-compliance/enforcement-committee.shtml.

appointed by the EBRD President from senior staff members). One of the external members shall act as the Chairperson of the Committee.[9]

Para 10.1 provides that the purpose of Enforcement Actions (and Disclosure Actions) are to 'assist a Respondent and its Affiliates to address deficiencies in control or compliance functions that may have contributed to the occurrence of a Prohibited Practice and/or to reduce the Bank's operational and reputational risks in the carrying out of Bank Projects with a Respondent and/or any of its Affiliates'.[10]

Para 10.2 provides that Enforcement Actions can result in a range of outcomes including:

> (iv) Debarment: a Respondent and certain of its Affiliates are declared ineligible, either indefinitely or for a stated period of time, to become a Bank Counterparty in any new Bank Project.
>
> (v) Conditional Non-Debarment: a Respondent and certain of its Affiliates are required to comply, within stated time periods, with certain remedial, preventative or other measures as a condition to avoid debarment. In the event the Respondent or certain of its Affiliates (if any) fail(s) to demonstrate its/their compliance with the prescribed conditions within the prescribed time periods, a debarment will automatically become effective for the period provided in the relevant decision.
>
> (vi) Debarment with Conditional Release: the Respondent and certain of its Affiliates are declared ineligible for a stated period of time subject to conditional reinstatement pursuant to which the period of debarment is reduced or terminated if the Respondent and its Affiliates (if any) demonstrate(s) compliance with specified conditions set forth in the relevant decision.
>
> (vii) Restitution: the Respondent is ordered to make restitution to another party or the Bank (with respect to the Bank Resources) in an amount representing the diverted funds or the economic benefit that the Respondent obtained as a result of having committed a Prohibited Practice.[11]

Para 13.1 deals with Settlements:

> (i) A Settlement Agreement is a signed agreement between the CCO[12] (or a person duly appointed by or on behalf of the CCO) acting on behalf of the Bank, and an individual or entity, whether prior to or after becoming a Respondent, which contains terms that include one or more Enforcement Actions.
>
> (ii) A Settlement Agreement shall contain an acknowledgement by all parties that are subject to it, including the CCO (or a person acting on her behalf), that the Respondent entered into it freely and fully informed of its terms.[13]

The list of EBRD debarments is on their website.[14]

---

[9]The current members of the committee are identified on the website: www.ebrd.com/our-values/integrity-and-compliance/enforcement-committee.shtml.

[10]www.ebrd.com/news/publications/policies/enforcement-policy-and-procedures.html.

[11]www.ebrd.com/news/publications/policies/enforcement-policy-and-procedures.html.

[12]CCO stands for Chief Compliance Officer.

[13]www.ebrd.com/news/publications/policies/enforcement-policy-and-procedures.html.

[14]www.ebrd.com/ineligible-entities.html.

13.3.3 Asian Development Bank

The ADB says that it will impose sanctions on parties that have engaged in fraudulent, corrupt, coercive, collusive, obstructive practices, or other integrity violations. As with the other four institutions that signed the Cross Debarment Agreement,[15] ADB will also cross debar parties that have been debarred by any of the other participating MDBs, namely EBRD, IADB, AfDB or WB.

The full list of entities sanctioned by the ADB is available to authorised users only. However, there is also a published sanctions list of those entities that are 'Sanctions violations, second and subsequent violations, debarred entities who are uncontactable, cross debarred entities' that is accessible through ADB's website.[16]

ADB also provides on their website summaries of ADB cases involving debarred entities.[17]

13.3.4 African Development Bank

The AfDB has a sanctioning system similar to those discussed above. Their Sanctions Procedures (dated November 2014)[18] provide for a two stage sanctions process: a Sanctions Commissioner and an Appeals Board. The Sanctions Commissioner, under section 5.7, '... shall review the finding of Sanctionable Practice(s)...in order to determine whether a preponderance of the evidence supports a finding that the Respondent has engaged in a Sanctionable Practice'.

The Appeals Board, under Section 10.1 of the Procedures, '... shall consider whether a preponderance of the evidence supports a finding that the Respondent engaged in a Sanctionable Practice'. If so, the Appeals Board shall prepare its findings and shall impose '... any of the sanctions referred to in Section 11' (in section 11(2), these sanctions are specified as: letter of reprimand, conditional non-debarment, debarment, debarment with conditional release, permanent debarment, restitution and/or remedy, or other sanction) without further appeal and with immediate effect.[19]

The list of AfDB debarments is on their website.[20]

---

[15] www.crossdebarment.org.

[16] www.adb.org/site/integrity/sanctions.

[17] www.adb.org/site/integrity/case-summaries.

[18] www.afdb.org/sites/default/files/2019/05/10/afdb_sanctions_procedures_-_november_2014.pdf.

[19] www.afdb.org/sites/default/files/2019/05/10/afdb_sanctions_procedures_-_november_2014.pdf.

[20] www.afdb.org/en/projects-operations/debarment-and-sanctions-procedures.

13.3.5 EIB

For legal reasons, EIB did not sign up to the Cross Debarment Agreement so it has its own independent sanctions mechanism with an Exclusion Committee, comprised of a blend of external experts and lawyers, etc., appointed by the President (who give a decision an objectivity) and senior EIB staff (who know the projects of the Bank and how they would have been affected).

EIB does not have the same immunities and privileges as the other MDBs. Indeed, EIB is subject to legal review and oversight by the European Court of Justice (ECJ). The ECJ is also based in Luxembourg, in fact it is currently situated across the road from EIB.

EIB has also signed a number of settlement agreements that are publicised on their website including settlement agreements signed with:

- Siemens;[21]
- Iberinco (part of the Iberdrola group of companies);[22] and
- VW.[23]

The EIB exclusions (debarments) are listed on their website.[24]

13.4 Cross Debarment Agreement

In accordance with the Cross Debarment Agreement signed in April 2010,[25] the five participating banks (even though potentially only one or two were financing the project in which the misconduct occurred and were therefore directly affected) may also cross debar the parties—in other words, parties that have been debarred by the institution(s) affected are also likely to be debarred by all of the participating MDBs.

To ensure a consistent approach, participating MDBs have agreed on harmonised principles for the appropriate sanctions to be applied and the way in which corporate groups will be treated. Each participating institution may incorporate these guidelines into their respective processes for considerations of the level and extent of the sanctions.

[21] https://www.eib.org/en/press/news/eib-and-siemens-settlement-agreement.

[22] https://www.eib.org/en/press/news/eib-and-iberinco-settlement-agreement-to-address-and-combat-fraud.

[23] https://www.eib.org/en/press/news/agreement-reached-between-the-european-investment-bank-and-volkswagen-ag-in-relation-to-eib-loan-antrieb-rdi.

[24] www.eib.org/en/about/accountability/anti-fraud/exclusion/index.htm.

[25] http://crossdebarment.org/oai001p.nsf/Content.xsp?documentId=EF42202683A26B524825789A00839502&action=openDocument&SessionID=CWO0W588ZO or https://lnadbg4.adb.org/oai001p.nsf/.

13.5 Level of Sanctions Applied

As stated in the agreement on Cross Debarment,[26] the base sanction for integrity violations is the debarment (or exclusion) from receiving new contracts (there is no effect on existing contracts which are, nevertheless, to be completed) for a period of 3-years but a period of debarment/exclusion for a greater or lesser period may be applied depending on the facts and circumstances (including the estimated damage and previous issues of misconduct in other projects) of the case.

Some entities on the list of debarments published by the World Bank have been permanently debarred, probably because the corporate entities were part of a fraudulent scheme in which shelf companies of no or little genuine substance were used and subsequently debarred.

13.6 Publication

As well as links published by some of the institutions (on their internet sites) to the list of names of debarred entities (debarred by that institution or recognised as being debarred by another institution under the Cross Debarment Agreement), some of the MDBs also publish a summary of the facts and findings of the case.

The fact that the lists of the names of sanctioned entities are published on the internet means they are relatively easy to find, not just by interested third parties (including local people monitoring the project and interested journalists) and potential business partners but by: (1) other project teams for enforcement purposes; and (2) regulators from the entity's home jurisdiction (in case a disclosure or statement on a stock market is thereby required).

13.7 Domestic Systems

There are a number of jurisdictions that have their own domestic sanctions system. Most of these systems are governed by administrative law, although criminal and/or civil law convictions could also play a role.

Indeed, suppliers or consultants that are subject to domestic exclusion proceedings can face major repercussions, including lengthy exclusions from public contracting, bad publicity, reputational damage and/or fines or additional penalties.[27]

[26] www.crossdebarment.org.

[27] FCPA Blog article: How can we understand the world's various debarment regimes? By Collin Swan, Eleanor Ross and Amanda McDowell, June 12, 2019.

Chapter 14
Notable Cases

There are a number of cases involving individuals and multinational companies (with a focus on international transactions) that have been pursued by law enforcement organisations in various countries in recent years. Depending on the location of the law enforcement agency concerned, the agency will have certain distinct legal provisions applying to the way in which the agency can conduct the investigation. This applies equally to the prosecution of the misconduct, that may be classified as corrupt or fraudulent by national legislation.

For example, the investigators from the UK's Serious Fraud Office can utilise section 2 powers to question (and request relevant documents from) witnesses and suspects about any of the issues which are under investigation, irrespective of sensitivity or commercial confidentiality. In terms of case management and charging offenders, the USA's Department of Justice and FBI may take a 'start at the bottom and work up as far as the criminality goes' approach which, if it works, can see senior managers and chief corporate officers implicated in criminal wrongdoing.

Fraudulent or corrupt schemes have impacted the projects funded by international organisations and can infect a wide range of situations—the following extracts concern large-scale, international (and in many cases, multi-jurisdictional) examples. The detailed text is deliberately replicated from other organisations' websites in fairness to all parties and to avoid any further possible legal challenges:

D. Smith, *Promoting Integrity in the Work of International Organisations*, Contributions to Finance and Accounting,
https://doi.org/10.1007/978-3-030-73916-4_14

14.1 Siemens

14.1.1 Text from the Website of the US Department of Justice[1]

Siemens Aktiengesellschaft (Siemens AG), a German corporation, and three of its subsidiaries today pleaded guilty to violations of and charges related to the Foreign Corrupt Practices Act (FCPA), the US Department of Justice and US Securities and Exchange Commission announced.

At a hearing before US District Judge Richard J. Leon in the District of Columbia, Siemens AG pleaded guilty to a two-count information charging criminal violations of the FCPA's internal controls and books and records provisions. Siemens S.A.-Argentina (Siemens Argentina) pleaded guilty to a one-count information charging conspiracy to violate the books and records provisions of the FCPA. Siemens Bangladesh Limited (Siemens Bangladesh) and Siemens S.A.—Venezuela (Siemens Venezuela), each pleaded guilty to separate one-count informations charging conspiracy to violate the anti-bribery and books and records provisions of the FCPA. As part of the plea agreements, Siemens AG agreed to pay a $448.5 million fine; and Siemens Argentina, Bangladesh, and Venezuela each agreed to pay a $500,000 fine, for a combined total criminal fine of $450 million.

According to court documents, beginning in the mid-1990s, Siemens AG engaged in systematic efforts to falsify its corporate books and records and knowingly failed to implement and circumvent existing internal controls. As a result of Siemens AG's knowing failures in and circumvention of internal controls, from the time of its listing on the New York Stock Exchange on March 12, 2001, through approximately 2007, Siemens AG made payments totalling approximately $1.36 billion through various mechanisms. Of this amount, approximately $554.5 million was paid for unknown purposes, including approximately $341 million in direct payments to business consultants for unknown purposes. The remaining $805.5 million of this amount was intended in whole or in part as corrupt payments to foreign officials through the payment mechanisms, which included cash desks and slush funds.

From 2000 to 2002, four Siemens AG subsidiaries—Siemens S.A.S. of France (Siemens France), Siemens Sanayi ve Ticaret A.S. of Turkey (Siemens Turkey), Osram Middle East FZE (Osram Middle East) and Gas Turbine Technologies S.p.A. (GTT)—each wholly owned by Siemens AG or one of its subsidiaries, were awarded 42 contracts with a combined value of more than $80 million with the Ministries of Electricity and Oil of the government of the Republic of Iraq under the United Nations Oil for Food Program. To obtain these contracts, Siemens France, Siemens Turkey, Osram Middle East and GTT paid a total of at least $1,736,076 in kickbacks to the Iraqi government, and they collectively earned more $38 million in

[1]https://www.justice.gov/archive/opa/pr/2008/December/08-crm-1105.html.

profits on those 42 contracts. Siemens France, Siemens Turkey, Osram Middle East and GTT inflated the price of the contracts by approximately 10% before submitting them to the United Nations for approval and improperly characterised payments to purported business consultants, part of which were paid as kickbacks to the Iraqi government as 'commissions' to the business consultants. For the relevant years, the books and records of Siemens France, Siemens Turkey, Osram Middle East and GTT, including those containing false characterisations of the kickbacks paid to the Iraqi government, were part of the books and records of Siemens AG.

As the charging and plea documents reflect, beginning around September 1998 and continuing until 2007, Siemens Argentina made and caused to be made significant payments to various Argentine officials, both directly and indirectly, in exchange for favourable business treatment in connection with a $1 billion national identity card project. From the date that Siemens AG became listed on the New York Stock Exchange on March 12, 2001, through approximately January 2007, Siemens Argentina made approximately $31,263,000 in corrupt payments to various Argentine officials through purported consultants and other conduit entities, and improperly characterised those corrupt payments in its books and records as legitimate payments for 'consulting fees' or 'legal fees'. Siemens Argentina's books and records, including those containing the false characterisations of the corrupt payments, were part of the books and records of Siemens AG.

According to court documents, beginning around November 2001 and continuing until approximately May 2007, Siemens Venezuela admitted it made and caused to be made corrupt payments of at least $18,782,965 to various Venezuelan officials, indirectly through purported business consultants, in exchange for favourable business treatment in connection with two major metropolitan mass transit projects called Metro Valencia and Metro Maracaibo. Some of those payments were made using US bank accounts controlled by the purported business consultants.

In the charging and plea documents, Siemens Bangladesh admitted that from May 2001 to August 2006, it caused corrupt payments of at least $5,319,839 to be made through purported business consultants to various Bangladeshi officials in exchange for favourable treatment during the bidding process on a mobile telephone project. At least one payment to each of these purported consultants was paid from a US bank account.

14.1.2 Text from the US Department of Justice Website[2]

The former Technical Manager of the Major Projects division of Siemens Business Services GmbH & Co. OGH (SBS), a wholly owned subsidiary of Siemens Aktiengesellschaft (Siemens AG), pleaded guilty today to conspiring to pay tens

[2]https://www.justice.gov/opa/pr/former-siemens-executive-pleads-guilty-role-100-million-foreign-bribery-scheme.

of millions of dollars in bribes to Argentine government officials to secure, implement and enforce a $1 billion contract to create national identity cards.

Acting Assistant Attorney General John P. Cronan of the Justice Department's Criminal Division, US Attorney Geoffrey S. Berman of the Southern District of New York and Assistant Director in Charge Andrew W. Vale of the FBI's Washington, DC Field Office made the announcement.

> Eberhard Reichert, 78, of Munich, Germany, was employed by Siemens AG from 1964 until 2001. Beginning in approximately 1990, Reichert was the Technical Manager of the Major Projects division of SBS. Reichert pleaded guilty today in the Southern District of New York to one count of conspiring to violate the anti-bribery, internal controls and books and records provisions of the Foreign Corrupt Practices Act (FCPA) and to commit wire fraud. Reichert was arraigned last December on a three-count indictment filed in December 2011 charging him and seven other individuals. He will be sentenced by US District Judge Denise L. Cote of the Southern District of New York, who accepted his plea today.
>
> 'Far too often, companies pay bribes as part of their business plan, upsetting what should be a level playing field and harming companies that play by the rules', said Acting Assistant Attorney General Cronan. 'In this case, one of the largest public companies in the world paid staggeringly large bribes to officials at the uppermost levels of the government of Argentina to secure a billion-dollar contract. Eberhard Reichert's conviction demonstrates the Criminal Division's commitment to bringing both companies and corrupt individuals to justice, wherever they may reside and regardless of how long they may attempt to avoid arrest'.
>
> 'Eberhard Reichert tried to sidestep laws designed to root corruption out of the government contracting process', said US Attorney Berman. 'As he admitted in Manhattan federal court today, Reichert helped to conceal tens of millions of dollars in bribes that were paid to unfairly secure a lucrative contract from the Argentine government. Today's plea should be a warning to others that our office is committed to bringing corrupt criminals to justice, no matter how long they run from the law'.

In 1998, the government of Argentina awarded to a subsidiary of Siemens AG a contract worth approximately $1 billion to create state-of-the-art national identity cards (the Documento Nacional de Identidad or DNI project). The Argentine government terminated the DNI project in 2001. In connection with his guilty plea, Reichert admitted that he engaged in a decade-long scheme to pay tens of millions of dollars in bribes to Argentine government officials in connection with the DNI project, which was worth more than $1 billion to Siemens. Reichert admitted that he and his co-conspirators concealed the illicit payments through various means, including using shell companies associated with intermediaries to disguise and launder the funds.

Reichert also admitted that he used a $27 million contract between a Siemens entity and a company called MFast Consulting AG that purported to be for consulting services to conceal bribes to Argentine officials.

In 2008, Siemens AG, a German entity, pleaded guilty to violating the books and records provisions of the FCPA; Siemens Argentina pleaded guilty to conspiracy to violate the books and records provisions of the FCPA; and Siemens Bangladesh Limited and Siemens S.A.—Venezuela each pleaded guilty to conspiracy to violate the anti-bribery and books and records provisions of the FCPA. As part of the plea agreements, the Siemens companies paid a total of $450 million in criminal fines. The US Securities and Exchange Commission (SEC) also brought a civil case against Siemens AG alleging that it violated the anti-bribery, books and records and internal controls provisions of the FCPA. In resolving the SEC case, Siemens AG paid $350 million in disgorgement of wrongful profits. The Munich Public Prosecutor's Office also resolved similar charges with Siemens AG that resulted in a fine of $800 million. In August 2009, following these corporate resolutions with US and German authorities, Siemens AG withdrew its claim to the more than $200 million arbitration award.[3]

The following text is taken from the EIB website:[4]

EIB and Siemens Settlement Agreement, 15 March 2013

The European Investment Bank (EIB) and Siemens have entered into a Settlement Agreement that addresses alleged past violations of the EIB Anti-Fraud Policy in connection with projects financed by the EIB. The Agreement follows an investigation carried by the EIB with the support of the Siemens Group and OLAF on the past conduct of a Siemens' business unit in relation to a tender process.

The Settlement Agreement includes a commitment by Siemens that the concerned business unit will voluntarily refrain from bidding on EIB financed projects or enter into any relationship with the EIB as a tenderer, contractor, supplier, consultant or any other form, for a period of 18 months.

As part of this Settlement, Siemens also commits to provide funds, totaling EUR 13.5 million over 5 years, to international organisations, inter-governmental organisations, non-governmental organisations (NGO), business associations, and/or academic institutions that support projects or other initiatives that promote good governance and the fight against corruption. Details on the management of this fund, eligibility criteria and selection process will be published on Siemens and EIB's websites when available.

Furthermore, Siemens has agreed to closely cooperate and assist the EIB going forward in its efforts to investigate alleged prohibited conduct in any EIB-financed project. Both parties also agreed to exchange best practices in relation to compliance standards and the fight against fraud and corruption.

The following text is taken from the Siemens website[5]

---

[3]In addition to other proceedings, in November 2019 (fourteen years after a judicial inquiry was first launched) a Greek court found 22 people guilty including the former Siemens Hellas CEO Michalis Christoforakos. The case related to an estimated EUR70 m bribes paid by the German electronics giant and its local subsidiary to clinch a contract with telecom provider OTE, which was owned by the Greek state at the time, see www.greece.greekreporter.com.

[4]www.eib.org/en/press/news/eib-and-siemens-settlement-agreement.

[5]https://new.siemens.com/global/en/company/sustainability/compliance/collective-action.html.

14.1.2.1 Siemens Integrity Initiative

Collective Action – building alliances against corruption

In the face of the widespread and deep-rooted corruption problem that affects society in general, governments, their procuring entities and the private sector in equal measure, it seems highly unlikely that individual activities alone will be sufficient to bring about significant ethical changes and improve the transparency of business processes.

This is precisely where Collective Action methods become important: Collective Action enables corruption to be fought collectively, with various interest groups, working together and building an alliance against corruption so that the problem can be approached and resolved from multiple angles.

The advantages of Collective Action:

- Collective Action describes various methods of combating corruption. It is a matter of acting collectively and forming alliances against corruption. Collective Action calls for cooperation on the part of participants from the worlds of politics, business and society at large.
- The ultimate goal is thereby to create fair and equitable market conditions, that is a 'Level Playing Field', for all marketplace participants and to eliminate the temptation of corruption for all those concerned.
- Collective Action helps to set up the conditions for fair competition within a corrupt environment.
- Collective Action promotes innovation, as the bidder is selected solely on the basis of price, quality and capacity to innovate.
- Observance of anti-trust law when collaborating with other companies must be ensured by a neutral monitor (e.g., in the form of a non-governmental organisation).
- Collective Action can, if necessary, cover gaps in legislation or replace or augment inadequate local law.

14.2 Alstom[6]

14.2.1 Text from the US Department of Justice (DoJ) Website[7]

Alstom S.A. (Alstom), a French power and transportation company, pleaded guilty today and agreed to pay a $772,290,000 fine to resolve charges related to a widespread scheme involving tens of millions of dollars in bribes in countries around the world, including Indonesia, Saudi Arabia, Egypt and the Bahamas.

Deputy Attorney General James M. Cole, Assistant Attorney General Leslie R. Caldwell of the Justice Department's Criminal Division, First Assistant US Attorney Michael J. Gustafson of the District of Connecticut and FBI Executive Assistant Director Robert Anderson, Jr. made the announcement.

---

[6]In addition to other proceedings, in November 2019, a jury in US, found Lawrence Hoskins, a former senior vice president of France-based Alstom SA guilty of helping orchestrate a bribery scheme in Indonesia, a verdict that reinforces the reach of the US law prohibiting bribes to foreign government officials. See also FCPA Blog article: 'Jury convicts Hoskins of multiple FCPA and money laundering offenses' by Richard L. Cassin dated November 8, 2019 in which he noted: 'Alstom SA pleaded guilty in December 2014 to violating the Foreign Corrupt Practices Act by bribing officials in Indonesia, Saudi Arabia, Egypt, and the Bahamas.Three other Alstom executives pleaded guilty in the United States to bribing officials in Indonesia'. After the company's FCPA resolution, General Electric bought Alstom's power business in 2015 . . . The DOJ indicted Hoskins in 2013. His trial was delayed while he challenged the reach of the FCPA through motions to the trial court and during government appeals . . . Prosecutors were able to convince the jury that Hoskins, who worked for the Alstom parent company in France, violated the FCPA by acting as an agent for the Connecticut subsidiary when he helped arrange the Indonesia bribes . . . Prosecutors said Hoskins helped hire two 'consultants' who were supposed to bribe Indonesian officials, including a member of parliament. Alstom's Connecticut unit eventually won a $118 million contract from Indonesia's state-owned electricity company . . . After the verdict... the DOJ said it appreciated 'significant cooperation' from 'law enforcement colleagues in Indonesia, Switzerland's Office of the Attorney General and the United Kingdom, as well as authorities in France, Germany, Italy, Singapore, and Taiwan'. See also reports at www.wsj.com. See also FCPA Blog article: "Here's the 'agent' instruction from US v. Hoskins" by Richard L. Cassin, December 20, 2019 about Hoskins' (who worked for Alstom SA, a French company, in Paris, he was a British national and said he never set foot in the United States) challenged whether the U. S.'s Foreign Corrupt Practices Act could apply to him.

Also in November 2019, a UK Judge imposed a fine for bribery in respect of a contract on the Tunis metro—the British division of Alstom was ordered to pay £16.4 m after being convicted of paying bribes to win a contract to supply trams to the metro system in Tunis. The Judge at Southwark crown court in London fined the French multinational's British subsidiary £15 m plus £1.4 m in costs. The company was convicted in April 2018 of conspiracy to corrupt after paying Construction et Gestion Nevco, an intermediary, €2.4 m to secure a contract (worth nearly €80 m with Transtu, the company that runs the metro system in the Tunisian capital). More info on this at www.thetimes.co.uk.

[7]www.justice.gov/opa/pr/alstom-pleads-guilty-and-agrees-pay-772-million-criminal-penalty-resolve-foreign-bribery.

'Alstom's corruption scheme was sustained over more than a decade and across several continents', said Deputy Attorney General Cole. 'It was astounding in its breadth, its brazenness and its worldwide consequences. And it is both my expectation – and my intention – that the comprehensive resolution we are announcing today will send an unmistakable message to other companies around the world: that this Department of Justice will be relentless in rooting out and punishing corruption to the fullest extent of the law, no matter how sweeping its scale or how daunting its prosecution'.

'This case is emblematic of how the Department of Justice will investigate and prosecute FCPA cases – and other corporate crimes,' said Assistant Attorney General Caldwell. 'We encourage companies to maintain robust compliance programs, to voluntarily disclose and eradicate misconduct when it is detected, and to cooperate in the government's investigation. But we will not wait for companies to act responsibly. With cooperation or without it, the department will identify criminal activity at corporations and investigate the conduct ourselves, using all of our resources, employing every law enforcement tool, and considering all possible actions, including charges against both corporations and individuals'.

'Today's historic resolution is an important reminder that our moral and legal mandate to stamp out corruption does not stop at any border, whether city, state or national,' said First Assistant US Attorney Gustafson. 'A significant part of this illicit work was unfortunately carried out from Alstom Power's offices in Windsor, Connecticut. I am hopeful that this resolution, and in particular the deferred prosecution agreement with Alstom Power, will provide the company an opportunity to reshape its culture and restore its place as a respected corporate citizen'.

'This investigation spanned years and crossed continents, as agents from the FBI Washington and New Haven field offices conducted interviews and collected evidence in every corner of the globe', said FBI Executive Assistant Director Anderson. 'The record dollar amount of the fine is a clear deterrent to companies who would engage in foreign bribery, but an even better deterrent is that we are sending executives who commit these crimes to prison'.

Alstom pleaded guilty to a two-count criminal information filed today in the US District Court for the District of Connecticut, charging the company with violating the Foreign Corrupt Practices Act (FCPA) by falsifying its books and records and failing to implement adequate internal controls. Alstom admitted its criminal conduct and agreed to pay a criminal penalty of $772,290,000. US District Judge Janet B. Arterton of the District of Connecticut scheduled a sentencing hearing for June 23 2015, at 3 pm.

In addition, Alstom Network Schweiz AG, formerly Alstom Prom (Alstom Prom), Alstom's Swiss subsidiary, pleaded guilty to a criminal information charging the company with conspiracy to violate the anti-bribery provisions of the FCPA. Alstom Power Inc. (Alstom Power) and Alstom Grid Inc. (Alstom Grid), two US subsidiaries, both entered into deferred prosecution agreements, admitting that they conspired to violate the anti-bribery provisions of the FCPA. Alstom Power is headquartered in Windsor, Connecticut, and Alstom Grid, formerly Alstom T&D, was headquartered in New Jersey.

According to the companies' admissions, Alstom, Alstom Prom, Alstom Power and Alstom Grid, through various executives and employees, paid bribes to government officials and falsified books and records in connection with power, grid and transportation projects for state-owned entities around the world, including in

Indonesia, Egypt, Saudi Arabia, the Bahamas and Taiwan. In Indonesia, for example, Alstom, Alstom Prom, and Alstom Power paid bribes to government officials—including a high-ranking member of the Indonesian Parliament and high-ranking members of Perusahaan Listrik Negara, the state-owned electricity company in Indonesia—in exchange for assistance in securing several contracts to provide power-related services valued at approximately $375 million. In total, Alstom paid more than $75 million to secure $4 billion in projects around the world, with a profit to the company of approximately $300 million.

Alstom and its subsidiaries also attempted to conceal the bribery scheme by retaining consultants purportedly to provide consulting services on behalf of the companies, but who actually served as conduits for corrupt payments to the government officials. Internal Alstom documents refer to some of the consultants in code, including 'Mr. Geneva', 'Mr. Paris', 'London', 'Quiet Man' and 'Old Friend'.

The plea agreement cites many factors considered by the department in reaching the appropriate resolution, including: Alstom's failure to voluntarily disclose the misconduct even though it was aware of related misconduct at a US subsidiary that previously resolved corruption charges with the department in connection with a power project in Italy; Alstom's refusal to fully cooperate with the department's investigation for several years; the breadth of the companies' misconduct, which spanned many years, occurred in countries around the globe and in several business lines, and involved sophisticated schemes to bribe high-level government officials; Alstom's lack of an effective compliance and ethics programme at the time of the conduct; and Alstom's prior criminal misconduct, including conduct that led to resolutions with various other governments and the World Bank.

14.2.2 *Text from the Website of the UK SFO*[8]

Former Alstom Power Global Sales Director sentenced to 4.5 years for corruption, 21 December 2018.[9]

Today, Nicholas Reynolds received 4 years and 6 months imprisonment for his part in a conspiracy to bribe officials in Lithuania's Elektrenai power station and senior Lithuanian politicians in order to win two contracts worth €240 million.

He was also ordered to pay costs of £50,000.

In sentencing the former Global Sales Director for Alstom Power Ltd's Boiler Retrofits unit, HHJ Beddoe said:

> This was sophisticated corruption, planned and executed under your direction over many years. This was a very serious example of the bribery and corruption that beleaguers the

---

[8]www.sfo.gov.uk/2018/12/21/former-alstom-power-global-sales-director-sentenced-to-4-5-years-for-corruption/.

[9]See also other media reports including the FCPA Blog article on March 29, 2016 by Richard Cassin entitled: 'SFO Charges another individual in Alstom corruption case'.

civilised commercial world and is a cancer upon it. Even if you do not create the disease but help it spread, you bear a very heavy responsibility, and the more senior your position, the more serious it obviously is.

Lisa Osofsky, Director of the Serious Fraud Office said:

'The substantial prison sentences imposed in this case reflect the seriousness of the bribery and corruption. We can only hope that this may deter others tempted to resort to illicit means to win contracts'.

'We are grateful for the assistance provided by our international partners across more than 30 countries for helping us deliver these results'.

Reynolds' sentencing follows the conviction and sentencing of Alstom Power Ltd, its former Business Development Manager John Venskus and former Regional Sales Director at Alstom Power Sweden AB Göran Wikström for their part in the conspiracy.

John Venskus was sentenced to 3 years and 6 months imprisonment on 4 May 2018. Göran Wikström was sentenced to 2 years and 7 months imprisonment on 9 July 2018, and was also ordered to pay £40,000 in costs.

Alstom Power Ltd was ordered to pay a total of £18,038,000 which included:

A fine of £6,375,000.

Compensation to the Lithuanian government of £10,963,000.

Prosecution costs of £700,000.

14.2.3 Text Also from the Website of the UK SFO[10]

Five convictions in SFO's Alstom investigation into bribery & corruption to secure €325 million of contracts, 19 December, 2018.

Nicholas Reynolds was found guilty of conspiracy to corrupt today at Blackfriars Crown Court following an extensive investigation and prosecution brought by the Serious Fraud Office.

The conviction brings to four the number of total convictions in relation to this conspiracy to bribe officials in a Lithuanian power station and senior Lithuanian politicians in order to win two contracts worth €240 million. These individuals falsified records to avoid checks in place to prevent bribery and between them, the Alstom companies paid more than €5 million in bribes to secure the contracts.

The conviction of Nicholas Reynolds who is a UK national and former Global Sales Director for Alstom Power Ltd's Boiler Retrofits unit followed a guilty plea from former Business Development Manager at Alstom Power Ltd John Venskus on 2 October 2017 and former Regional Sales Director at Alstom Power Sweden AB

[10] www.sfo.gov.uk/2018/12/19/five-convictions-in-sfos-alstom-investigation-into-bribery-and-corruption-to-secure-e325-million-of-contracts/.

Göran Wikström on 22 June 2018 on the same charge. Alstom Power Ltd entered a guilty plea to conspiracy to corrupt on 10 May 2016.

In sentencing Göran Wikström HHJ Martin Beddoe said:

> This was a very serious example of bribery and corruption that beleaguers the civilised, commercial world and is a cancer upon it

Venskus was sentenced to 3 years and 6 months imprisonment on 4 May 2018. Wikström was sentenced to 2 years and 7 months imprisonment on 9 July 2018. He was also ordered to pay £40,000 in costs.

Alstom Power Ltd was ordered to pay a total of £18,038,000 which included:

A fine of £6,375,000.

Compensation to the Lithuanian government of £10,963,000.

Prosecution costs of £700,000.

Nicholas Reynolds is due to be sentenced at Blackfriars Crown Court on 21 December 2018.

Lisa Osofsky, Director of the Serious Fraud Office said:

> The culture of corruption evident within the Alstom Group was widespread. Their illicit activities to win lucrative contracts were calculated and sustained, undermining legitimate business and public trust.
>
> 'These convictions were a result of a truly global investigation and I thank our case team for their effort and persistence in bringing the individuals and companies involved to justice'.

The SFO's investigation involved cooperation with more than 30 countries including France, Canada, Hungary, Denmark, Austria, Slovakia, Czech Republic, Lichtenstein, Cyprus, Singapore, the Seychelles, India, Sweden, Lithuania, Switzerland and Tunisia.

Due to the lifting of reporting restrictions, the conviction of Alstom Network UK Ltd in a linked case can also now be reported.

Alstom Network UK Ltd were found guilty of one count of conspiracy to corrupt on 10 April 2018 for making corrupt payments to win a tram and infrastructure contract in Tunisia.

In return for its work in securing the €85 million contract, Alstom Network UK Ltd paid €2.4 million to a company called Construction et Gestion Nevco Inc, which Alstom Network UK Ltd itself acknowledged was a front for corruption when it decided not to make a final payment of €240,000 in its contract.

Staff within the Alstom Group helped the consultants produce paperwork to satisfy internal compliance checks, cobbling together 'evidence' of the services provided, which at best were of a nominal nature because the company was, in reality, just a conduit for bribes.

Graham Hill, Robert Hallett and Alstom Network UK Ltd were acquitted of other charges in this case, relating to alleged corruption to win transport contracts in India and Poland, on 10 April 2018.

Alstom Network UK Ltd will be sentenced at Southwark Crown Court on a date to be determined.

Alstom Network UK Ltd along with Michael Anderson, Terence Watson and Jean-Daniel Lainé were acquitted of a charge in a linked investigation into alleged corruption relating to a Budapest Metro rolling stock contract.

14.2.4 Text from the EBRD's Website[11]

EBRD debars GE Power of Sweden for six years By Anthony Williams@ebrdtony, 27 November 2019.

The European Bank for Reconstruction and Development (EBRD) has imposed a 6-year term of debarment on GE Power Sweden AB following an investigation in cooperation with the Serious Fraud Office of the UK.

The 6-year debarment means that GE Power Sweden will not be eligible to be a Bank Counterparty from 27 November 2019 until 26 November 2025.

The EBRD's Office of the Chief Compliance Officer (OCCO) will also submit debarment of GE Power Sweden to the World Bank, the African Development Bank, the Asian Development Bank, and the Inter-American Development Bank, so that this entity is also debarred by these multilateral development banks.

The investigation relates to a project to instal flue gas desulphurisation (FGD) units at the Lithuanian Power Plant, a project financed by donor funds administered by the EBRD.

The investigation found that, from as early as 2002, representatives of Alstom Power Sweden AB, a predecessor company to GE Power Sweden, had conspired with another Alstom entity to manipulate the technical specifications for the FGD contract in their favour by making payments to Lithuanian government officials.

The 6-year debarment is the longest to have been imposed in the history of the Bank, and reflects the egregious nature of the misconduct involved. The action also reflects close collaboration with the European Commission and the International Ignalina Decommissioning Support Fund, the donor fund that provided financing for the project.

The EBRD's Chief Compliance Officer Lisa Rosen said:

> The EBRD's decisive response in this case underscores how seriously the EBRD takes corruption, especially when it involves donor funds.

The Bank's cooperation with UK's Serious Fraud Office also led to the successful prosecution in the UK of three individuals and one entity in relation to the misconduct.

[11] www.ebrd.com/news/2019/ebrd-debars-ge-power-of-sweden-for-six-years.html.

14.2.5 *Text from the AfDB's Website*[12]

Integrity in Development Projects: The African Development Bank and GE Power Reach Settlement on Legacy Alstom Misconduct.

The African Development Bank imposes debarments of 76 months and 12 months on former Alstom companies found to have engaged in bribery and fraud in 2006 and 2011 in relation to two Bank-financed Egyptian power generation projects. GE Power acquired the companies in 2015.

22-Mar-2019.

The African Development Bank Group today announced the conclusion of a settlement agreement with GE Power, thus resolving sanctionable practices committed by former Alstom companies.

An investigation conducted by the Bank's Office of Integrity and Anti-Corruption established that in 2006 and 2011 the companies, then named Alstom Power Generation AG, Alstom Power GmbH and Alstom Egypt for Power and Transport Projects S.A.E., engaged in two instances of corrupt practices and in one instance of a fraudulent practice in the context of the Bank-financed Suez Thermal Power Plant Project and the El Kureimat III Power Project, both in Egypt.

GE Power assumed control over these three companies in 2015, after the misconduct had occurred, when it acquired Alstom's thermal power generation business. As part of the settlement, the Bank imposes on former Alstom Egypt for Power & Transport Projects S.A.E. (now known as Alstom Egypt for Power Projects S.A. E.), based in Cairo, Egypt, and on former Alstom Power Generation AG (now known as GE Power Systems GmbH), headquartered in Mannheim, Germany, a debarment of 76 months.

The debarment period may be reduced to 48 months if the companies comply with all conditions of the agreement early. This debarment may be enforced by other multilateral development banks under the Agreement for Mutual Enforcement of Debarment Decisions, including the Asian Development Bank, the European Bank for Reconstruction and Development, the Inter-American Development Bank and the World Bank Group. Further, pursuant to the settlement, former Alstom Power GmbH (now known as GE Power GmbH), equally based in Mannheim, Germany, is debarred for a period of 12 months.

Among other conditions for release from debarment, GE Power commits to collaborate with the Office of Integrity and Anti-Corruption in the fight against corruption in the power generation and transmission sector.

> Corrupt practices in the power generation sector directly undermine the African Development Bank's operational priority to light up and power Africa. This can never be accepted by the Bank,

[12] www.afdb.org/en/news-and-events/integrity-in-development-projects-the-african-development-bank-and-ge-power-reach-settlement-on-legacy-alstom-misconduct-19116.

says Bubacarr Sankareh, Manager of the Investigations Division within the Office of Integrity and Anti-Corruption.

> We are very pleased that GE Power is joining us today in our efforts to fight corruption and to ensure the delivery of value for money to the Bank's regional member countries.

In 2006, Alstom Egypt for Power & Transport Projects S.A.E. and Alstom Power Generation AG participated in a tender for steam turbine generators in the context of the Bank-financed El Kureimat III Power Project. The companies indirectly paid an amount of 963,477 EURO to their local agent.

The Office of Integrity and Anti-Corruption has concluded that one purpose of the payment was to ensure the support of public officials involved in the procurement process in order to gain an unfair competitive advantage in the tender. Further, the Office of Integrity and Anti-Corruption established that the companies had erroneously only declared 50,000 EURO in fees paid to its local agent.

In 2011, Alstom Egypt for Power & Transport Projects S.A.E., Alstom Power GmbH and Alstom Power Generation AG, by then renamed Alstom Power Systems GmbH, participated in a tender for a steam turbine generator and condensers for the Bank-financed Suez Thermal Power Plant. In the context of this tender, the companies indirectly offered 1.7 million EURO to their local agent. The Office of Integrity and Anti-Corruption has concluded that one objective of the offer was to ensure that public officials would assert undue influence on the procurement process in favour of the companies' bid.

In reaching this settlement, the African Development Bank took into account General Electric's substantial cooperation with the investigation of the legacy cases as well as the high quality of the company's comprehensive compliance programme, which now applies to the Alstom entities acquired by GE Power.

Also, text from an FCPA Blog (www.fcpablog.com) article entitled:

ADB debars GE Power units tied to Alstom offenses, by Harry Cassin, March 25, 2019.

The African Development Bank said Thursday it debarred several former Alstom companies now owned by GE Power for up to 76 months because of fraud and bribery committed on two bank-financed projects in Egypt.

The bank said the offences occurred in 2006 and 2011.

GE Power acquired the former Alstom companies in 2015.

The bank said three former Alstom companies 'engaged in two instances of corrupt practices and in one instance of a fraudulent practice' in connection with two bank-financed power projects in Egypt.

The bank imposed a 76-month debarment on two of the former Alstom units. Those units are now known as Alstom Egypt for Power Projects S.A.E. based in Cairo and GE Power Systems GmbH headquartered in Mannheim, Germany.

And it debarred GE Power GmbH (formerly Alstom Power GmbH), also based in Mannheim, for 12 months.

The bank said GE Power entered into a voluntary settlement of the legacy offences.

The 76-month debarment can be reduced to 48 months based on the companies' compliance with the settlement terms, the bank said.

Among other things, GE Power promised to collaborate with the African Development Bank's Office of Integrity and Anti-Corruption 'in the fight against corruption in the power generation and transmission sector'.

In 2015, an ex-Bechtel Corporation vice president was sentenced to 42 months in prison in the United States for taking $5.2 million in kickbacks to rig bids for state-run power contracts in Egypt.

Asem Elgawhary, 73, of Potomac, Maryland pleaded guilty to mail fraud, conspiracy to commit money laundering, obstruction, and interference with the administration of the tax laws.

The judge also ordered Elgawhary—a dual US and Egyptian citizen—to forfeit $5.2 million.

From 1996 to 2011, Bechtel assigned Elgawhary to be the general manager at a joint venture between Bechtel and Egypt's state-owned and state-controlled electricity company. Elgawhary took a total of $5.2 million from three power companies to rig bids for the project contracts.

One of the power companies that bribed Elgawhary was Paris-based Alstom S.A.

Bechtel wasn't charged in the case.

In December 2014, Alstom paid $772 million in criminal penalties to resolve FCPA offences, including bribing Elgawhary.

The African Development Bank's statement Thursday said in 2006 Alstom companies tendering for a bank-financed project paid their agent in Egypt about $1.1 million.

The African Development Bank said it took into account 'General Electric's substantial cooperation with the investigation of the legacy cases as well as the high quality of the company's comprehensive compliance programme, which now applies to the Alstom entities acquired by GE Power'.

Thursday's 76-month debarment qualifies for cross debarment by other multilateral development banks under their mutual enforcement agreements. The other multilateral development banks include the Asian Development Bank, the European Bank for Reconstruction and Development, the Inter-American Development Bank, and the World Bank Group.

14.3 Oxford University Press

14.3.1 Text from the Website of the UK SFO[13]

14.3.1.1 Oxford Publishing Ltd to Pay Almost £1.9 Million As Settlement After Admitting Unlawful Conduct in Its East African Operations: 3 July 2012

The Director of the Serious Fraud Office (SFO) has taken action in the High Court, which has resulted in an Order that Oxford Publishing Limited (OPL) pay £1,895,435 in

[13] www.sfo.gov.uk/2012/07/03/oxford-publishing-ltd-pay-almost-1-9-million-settlement-admitting-unlawful-conduct-east-african-operations/.

recognition of sums it received which were generated through unlawful conduct related to subsidiaries incorporated in Tanzania and Kenya.

14.3.1.2 Background

OPL is a wholly owned subsidiary of Oxford University Press (OUP), which pursues its mission through five publishing divisions, including the International Division. (See note 1 for editors.) The International Division has ten overseas publishing entities with a head office in Oxford. Oxford University Press East Africa (OUPEA) is based in Kenya but covers a geographical region which includes Kenya, Burundi, Malawi, Rwanda, Sudan and Uganda. Oxford University Press Tanzania (OUPT) is based in mainland Tanzania but also has responsibility for the semi-autonomous Zanzibar archipelago. Both OUPT and OUPEA are wholly owned subsidiaries of OPL and part of the International Division of OUP.

The business of all the International Division entities is focused on the school text book market but most entities also have well established local dictionary programmes and growing higher education lists. The business activities include participating in public tenders for contracts to supply governments with text books and other educational materials for the school curricula. These tenders may lead to contracts which are supported or funded by the World Bank Group which is the collective title for the International Bank for Reconstruction and Development and the International Development Association.

14.3.1.3 Self Referral

In 2011, OUP became aware of the possibility of irregular tendering practices involving its education business in East Africa. OUP acted immediately to investigate the matter, instructing independent lawyers and forensic accountants to undertake a detailed investigation.

As a result of the investigation, in November 2011 OUP voluntarily reported certain concerns in relation to contracts arising from a number of tenders which its Kenyan and Tanzanian subsidiaries, OUPEA and OUPT, entered into between the years 2007 and 2010. The SFO required OUP to follow a procedure based on the guidance contained within its published protocol document—'The Serious Fraud Office's Approach to Dealing with Overseas Corruption'.

Because two of the tenders were funded by the World Bank, OUP also voluntarily reported on a potential breach of the World Bank's Procurement Guidelines to the World Bank.

The SFO remit was broader in its scope than the World Bank investigation in that it required investigation of all public tender contracts whether or not funded by the World Bank.

The costs of the investigation were met by OUP.

The investigation was thorough—involving numerous interviews and an extensive review of documents and electronic data—and completed to the satisfaction of the SFO. The substantial product of those investigations was presented to the SFO and, in a separate presentation, to the World Bank. The product of that work led the SFO and the World Bank to believe that OUPEA and OUPT had offered and made payments, directly and through agents, intended to induce the recipients to award competitive tenders and/or publishing contracts for schoolbooks to OUPEA and OUPT.

14.4 SNC Lavalin[14]

14.4.1 Text Is an Excerpt from Wikipedia (on 30/11/19)[15]

14.4.1.1 Legal Issues

SNC-Lavalin's management team have been investigated in a number of allegations under the Corruption of Foreign Public Officials Act regarding contracts beginning with SNC-Lavalin Kerala hydroelectric dam scandal (1995–2008) [49] through to the allegations involving the bribing of Libyan officials between 2001 and 2011... [50].

14.4.1.2 Libya (2011)

A 2012 CBC News report, said that the first reports of murky affairs surfaced against the company in 2010 in relation to contracts in Libya [6]. According to a CBC News article, a Libyan bribery and fraud scandal involving crimes that took place from 2001 to 2011 led to charges in 'connection with payments of nearly $48 million' to Libyan public officials [58]. In the same article, it was reported that the company was also accused of 'defrauding Libyan organisations of an estimated $130 million' [58, 50].

In 2015, SNC-Lavalin was charged with bribing Libyan officials in exchange for construction contracts between 2001 and 2011 [50]. In 2011, the RCMP began their investigation called Project Assistance which was triggered by a tip from Swiss authorities [59]. According to an August 8, 2013 Financial Post article, Michael Novak who, had been the head of SNC International, had signed 'several of the contracts between SNC and 'unknown commercial consultants to help win contracts' for 'work in Africa' [60, 61]. This included a contract with former Libyan dictator Muammar Gaddafi's controversial government [62]. By the summer of 2013, police alleged that the 'unknown commercial consultants' had never existed and that Ben Aissa had 'set up shell companies so he could pocket the [$56 million] himself' [61, 63]. By July 2014, Aissa was jailed in Switzerland for 'suspicion of corruption, fraud and money-laundering in North Africa' [64, 65][Notes 4].

---

[14]See also FCPA Blog article: Former SNC-Lavalin Chief Pleads Guilty in Bribery Case by Richard Cassin, dated February 4 2019 noting 'In 2012, the Royal Canadian Mounted Police filed an affidavit that tied former SNC-Lavalin executive Riadh Ben Aissa to more than $160 million in alleged bribes paid to Libyan officials in exchange for contracts'. and 'In 2013, the World Bank barred SNC-Lavalin from bank-funded projects for ten years because of alleged corruption in Bangladesh and Cambodia' and the FCPA Blog article: SNC-Lavalin Blowback: Reconsidering corporate criminal liability by Lincoln Caylor and Nathan Shaheen, May 8, 2019. In addition to other proceedings, in December 2019, a division of SNC-Lavalin Group Inc. pleaded guilty to fraud in relation to the company's activities in Libya. SNC-Lavalin Construction paid $127 million to two shell companies between 2001 and 2011, according to an agreed statement of facts presented in a Montreal court. Duvel Securities Inc. and Dinova International Inc. both listed as the sole beneficial owner Riadh Ben Aissa. He was a former top executive of the company who pleaded guilty in Switzerland to bribery and laundering funds to win SNC-Lavalin contracts in Libya. About $47 million of the money was then used to reward Saadi Gadhafi, son of the late dictator Moammar Gadhafi, for helping SNC-Lavalin secure lucrative construction projects. More info is also at www.cbc.ca.

[15]www.en.wikipedia.org/wiki/SNC-Lavalin.

When SNC-Lavalin pulled out of Libya in 2011, it left behind $22.9 million in Libyan banks [66]. In 2013, Roy filed a countersuit for wrongful dismissal, claiming lost wages and damages to his reputation, alleging that he had been framed and scapegoated by higher-level executives whose directives he was obliged to follow [67–70][Notes 5].

By February 2012, SNC investors had found out that audited financial statements had been delayed to accommodate an internal review relating to SNC's operations. The internal review probed $35 million of unexplained payments in Libya. Prior to the launch of the investigation, there had been months-long media speculation about the company's work in Libya and its ties to the Muammar Gaddafi family [71–73]. In 2012, the Royal Canadian Mounted Police investigated the company on these charges in the Project Assistance investigation and [74], in 2015, they charged SNC-Lavalin with 'fraud and corruption', which the company indicated they would contest in court [75].

14.4.1.3 McGill University; The Arthur Porter Kick-Back Scandal (2011–2014)

Charges were laid against senior executives from 2014 through 2019 in the bribery cases involving Arthur Porter at the McGill University Health Centre. According to a 2012 article in The Globe and Mail, these reports prompted calls for Canada to tighten bribery laws [76].

According to the National Post, SNC-Lavalin employees allegedly were involved in fraud and forgery in relation to a $22.5 million kick-back described as 'consulting fees' to Arthur Porter [77][Notes 6] on the contract to build the new $1.3 billion hospital at the McGill University Health Centre's CEO in violation of the Quebec Health Act. SNC-Lavalin were awarded the contract even though they were outbid by $60 million [36]. The case led to an investigation by the Charbonneau Commission. Porter resigned from the post on December 5, 2011 in light of substantial public pressure [78–80]. Porter was arrested in Panama on fraud charges on May 27, 2013, which alleged that he took part in the kick-back scheme [81]. The Canadian Broadcasting Corporation called it the biggest fraud investigation in Canadian history [82, 83]. SNC CEO, Pierre Duhaime in March 2012 [84, 6, 85] Duhaime was arrested on fraud charges by Quebec authorities on November 28, 2012 [86, 87][Notes 7][Notes 8][88].

SNC-Lavalin sued Duhaime for millions of dollars in damages, claiming that he stained its goodwill by means of the McGill University Health Centre super hospital scandal. The company claims that Duhaime 'facilitated the execution of the embezzlement' of $22.5 million of company funds. Duhaime was charged with several counts related to the bribe. In February 2019 he pleaded guilty to one count of breach of trust. The prosecution vacated some 15 further charges [89].

14.4.1.4 Padma Bridge (Since 2011)

An investigation into an alleged graft related to 2011 bids for the construction of the 6.51 km (four-mile) US$3 billion road—rail bridge crossing the Padma River in Bangladesh [90], resulted in the former SNC-Lavalin employees being cleared of all charges by a Canadian court. In May 2011, two former SNC-Lavalin International Inc. (SLII) employees Ramesh Shah and Mohammad Ismail met government officials in Bangladesh to discuss a bid for the $50-million supervision contract to build the Padma Bridge, a project estimated to be worth US$3 billion [49]. Part of the allegations were related to SLII common practice of list project consultancy costs (PCC), also known as project commercial cost, as a line item in internal budgets documents related to the bidding process [49][Notes 9][49]. As a result of the original investigation by World Bank investigators who worked with RCMP officers, in September 2013, the World Bank blacklisted SNC-Lavalin and its affiliates from bidding on the World Bank's global projects.[91] The World Bank had originally offered to fund $1.5 billion of the $3 billion but pulled back following the allegations. However, on February 11, 2017, the Ontario Superior Court found no proof of the Padma bridge bribery conspiracy, dismissed the case, and acquitted the ex-SNC-Lavalin executives [92]. According to the Dhaka Tribune, Justice Ian Nordheimer rebuked the Canadian police, saying: ‘Reduced to its essentials, the information provided in the [wiretap applications] was nothing more than speculation, gossip, and rumor [92]’.

Text from the World Bank website (January 2020)

World Bank Debars SNC-Lavalin Inc. and its Affiliates for 10 years

This represents the longest debarment period that has ever been agreed to in a World Bank settlement.

WASHINGTON, April 17, 2013—The World Bank Group today announced the debarment of SNC-Lavalin Inc.—in addition to over 100 affiliates—for a period of 10 years following the company’s misconduct in relation to the Padma Multipurpose Bridge Project in Bangladesh, as well as misconduct under another Bank-financed project. SNC-Lavalin Inc. is a subsidiary of SNC-Lavalin Group, a Canadian company, and represents more than 60% of its business.

The debarment is part of a Negotiated Resolution Agreement between the World Bank and SNC-Lavalin Group following a World Bank investigation into allegations of bribery schemes involving SNC-Lavalin Inc. and officials in Bangladesh.

Whilst the investigation was ongoing, the World Bank’s Integrity Vice Presidency also learned of misconduct by SNC-Lavalin Inc. in relation to the World Bank-financed Rural Electrification and Transmission project in Cambodia.

The debarment can be reduced to eight years if the companies comply with all conditions of the agreement. The remainder of the SNC-Lavalin Group has been conditionally non-debarred for the same period of time. Under this sanction, the remainder of SNC-Lavalin Group faces debarment if they fail to comply with the terms and conditions of the Agreement.

‘This case is testimony to collective action against global corruption’, **said Leonard McCarthy, World Bank Integrity Vice President.** ‘Once we had evidence of the company’s misconduct, we referred the matter to the Royal Canadian Mounted Police whilst the World Bank finalized its investigation. Going forward, I hope that SNC-Lavalin’s commitment under this agreement represents meaningful action in deterring the risks of fraud and corruption to development projects’.

SNC-Lavalin’s misconduct involved a conspiracy to pay bribes and misrepresentations when bidding for Bank-financed contracts in violation of the World Bank’s procurement guidelines. Under the Agreement, the SNC-Lavalin Group and its affiliates commit to cooperating with the World Bank’s Integrity Vice Presidency and continuing to improve their internal compliance programme. The debarment of SNC-Lavalin Inc. qualifies for cross-debarment by other MDBs under the Agreement of Mutual Recognition of Debarments that was signed on April 9, 2010.[16]

[16]www.worldbank.org/en/news/press-release/2013/04/17/world-bank-debars-snc-lavalin-inc-and-its-affiliates-for-ten-years.

14.5 Wasim Tappuni

14.5.1 Text from the UK's City of London Police Website[17]

22 September 2017—Man sentenced for £1.7 million corruption involving the World Bank.

Today (22 September 2017) a man has been sentenced to 6 years imprisonment at Southwark Crown Court after an investigation led by the City of London Police's Overseas Anti Corruption Unit (OACU) found that he had entered into corrupt agreements with 12 medical supply companies that had submitted tenders for projects mostly financed by the World Bank.

Wasim Tappuni, 64, of Coombe Neville in Kingston upon Thames, was sentenced to 6 years imprisonment following a 6 week trial. A 74 year old man who also stood trial was found not guilty of money laundering and false accounting.

Tappuni, who was an independent medical procurement consultant, was employed by the World Bank between August 2007 and October 2011. He acted as an independent advisor on their medical procurement projects. Over the course of 4 years, Tappuni received payments from companies based in the Netherlands, Germany, France, Austria, and Kazakhstan, of approximately £1.7 million.

Following an anonymous tip in 2011, the World Bank began an internal investigation into a Dutch medical supply company and made a referral to the Dutch authorities. The Dutch investigation identified Tappuni as the 'insider' at the World Bank and led to a criminal investigation being carried out on the company in the Netherlands.

It was suspected that Tappuni provided these companies with confidential information held by the World Bank which was not in the public domain, including tender documents and competitors' bids, prior to the information becoming public. This information allowed these companies an unfair advantage in the tendering process. He also offered to amend the criteria to suit particular suppliers and unfairly reject competitors, allowing them to unfairly win the contract.

Tappuni would then benefit from the corrupt arrangement and receive a pre-arranged percentage of the contract value, should the company, with whom he had the corrupt arrangement, be successful.

In September 2011 the Dutch authorities made OACU aware of their investigation which resulted in a joint operation team being set up by Eurojust on 21 October 2011 to further investigate Tappuni and the Dutch medical supply company.

On 25 October 2011 coordinated searches took place in the Netherlands and at Tappuni's home address in Kingston where a large amount of documentation and material from his computer were recovered. Tappuni was arrested and interviewed on the same day.

As a result of this search and extensive international enquiries, it was discovered that Tappuni had received approximately £1.7 million in corrupt payments from

[17]http://news.cityoflondon.police.uk/r/914/man_sentenced_for__1_7_million_corruption_involvi.

12 medical companies relating to 44 corrupted contracts totalling £42 million in value. For all but two of these contracts Tappuni was engaged by the World Bank as an independent advisor. For the remaining two, he was similarly engaged by the United Nations Development Programme (UNDP). Most of these corrupt monies had been paid into accounts, held in Switzerland that he controlled.

Acting Detective Superintendent Peter Ratcliffe, Head of the City of London Police's Overseas Anti Corruption Unit (OACU), said:

> This corrupt manipulation of the tendering process meant that the reputation of the World Bank would be tarnished and taxpayers money wasted, as the medical supply companies that won the contracts did so having been unfairly assisted in the process. This case and subsequent sentencing highlights the severity of this crime and demonstrates that such acts will not go unpunished.
>
> The Overseas Anti Corruption Unit and the World Bank have worked together on this case and by sharing information, we have been able to successfully uncover Tappuni's crimes and expose the sheer extent of his corruption. The investigation led to not only the identification of a large number of corrupt relationships, but also the 12 medical suppliers being investigated by and in most cases barred from bidding on World Bank contracts.
>
> This case should serve as a warning to those who engage in such crimes that justice will be served.

14.6 VW

14.6.1 Text from EIB's Website[18]

The European Investment Bank has today published a detailed summary of the investigation report by the European Anti-Fraud Office (OLAF) into alleged misuse of EIB loan by Volkswagen AG. This was done in accordance with the EIB Group Transparency Policy and considering the strong public interest in this highly exceptional case.

The summary includes all information relevant to the public interest and also includes extracts of the report, providing the public with an informative and meaningful account of the OLAF investigation. The investigation concerns practices which have been the centre of controversy and legal action ever since 2015, when environmental authorities in the US issued a notice of violation against Volkswagen AG for producing and selling diesel cars that featured sophisticated software to circumvent emissions standards for air pollutants. Notably, the report states: "The investigation established that VW never informed the EIB throughout the duration of the loan from 24 February 2009 to 24 February 2014 about the continuous use and implementation of this 'defeat device' on the EA 189 engine in the context of the Research and Development activities financed by the EIB loan." OLAF's report further indicates that this information should have been communicated to the EIB

[18] www.eib.org/en/press/all/2019-049-eib-publishes-a-summary-of-the-european-anti-fraud-office-report-into-alleged-misuse-of-eib-loan-by-volkswagen-ag.

and, had the EIB been informed of this relevant information, the EIB would not have granted the loan or would have requested full repayment.

OLAF opened its investigation in November 2015. The OLAF investigation focused on one sub-project under the loan 'VW Antrieb RDI', which was granted to Volkswagen AG by the EIB in February 2009. The aim of EIB loan 'Antrieb RDI' was to provide financing for the development of power engines and power train components for passenger cars and commercial vehicles. The notion of 'defeat device' was used in the OLAF report to refer to VW's sophisticated "software which aimed at circumventing emissions standards for air pollutants, in particular nitrogen oxides (NOx) [...] The 'defeat device' deployed on the EA 189 engine detected if the car was operated under testing conditions and accordingly activated and deactivated certain functionalities in order to meet emission standards during tests while offering full performance of the vehicle under normal driving conditions."

The end of legal proceedings arising from the OLAF investigation and the implementation by the Bank of OLAF's recommendation gives the possibility to the Bank to publish the summary of the OLAF report.

EIB and Volkswagen AG finalised an agreement in December 2018, following the OLAF investigation. As part of the agreement Volkswagen AG voluntarily committed to contribute EUR 10 million to environmental and/or sustainability projects in Europe. In addition, according to this agreement, the European Investment Bank concluded its investigation and Volkswagen AG in turn agreed voluntarily not to participate in any European Investment Bank project for an exclusion period of 18 months. Since October 2015, the consideration of loans by the European Investment Bank to Volkswagen AG had been under suspension.

Summary of the European Anti-Fraud Office (OLAF) report on the European Investment Bank (EIB) loan 'Antrieb RDI' to Volkswagen AG.

Agreement reached between the European Investment Bank and Volkswagen AG in relation to EIB loan 'Antrieb RDI'.[19]

14.7 Odebrecht

14.7.1 Text from BBC News Website[20]

17 April 2019.

For years, Latin America's construction giant, Odebrecht, built some of the region's most crucial infrastructure projects.

---

[19]See also FCPA Blog article: Compliance dialogue: What happens when an 'air of innocence' fills the halls? by Richard Bistrong, dated June 27, 2019.

[20]www.bbc.com/news/amp/business-39194395.

But then it became well-known for another superlative: its involvement in one of the biggest corruption cases in history.

In 2016, the Brazilian-based group signed what has been described as the world's largest leniency deal with US and Swiss authorities, in which it confessed to corruption and paid $2.6bn (£2.1bn) in fines.

Seventy-seven company executives agreed to plea bargains with Brazilian authorities, and their statements to investigators were made public.

Their revelations had strong political and economic repercussions throughout Latin America...

14.7.2 Text from the US DoJ Website[21]

Wednesday, December 21, 2016.

Odebrecht and Braskem Plead Guilty and Agree to Pay at Least $3.5 Billion in Global Penalties to Resolve Largest Foreign Bribery Case in History.

Odebrecht S.A. (Odebrecht), a global construction conglomerate based in Brazil, and Braskem S.A. (Braskem), a Brazilian petrochemical company, pleaded guilty today and agreed to pay a combined total penalty of at least $3.5 billion to resolve charges with authorities in the United States, Brazil and Switzerland arising out of their schemes to pay hundreds of millions of dollars in bribes to government officials around the world.

Deputy Assistant Attorney General Sung-Hee Suh of the Justice Department's Criminal Division, U.S. Attorney Robert L. Capers of the Eastern District of New York, Assistant Director Stephen Richardson of the FBI's Criminal Investigative Division and Assistant Director in Charge William F. Sweeney of the FBI's New York Field Office made the announcement.

"Odebrecht and Braskem used a hidden but fully functioning Odebrecht business unit—a 'Department of Bribery,' so to speak—that systematically paid hundreds of millions of dollars to corrupt government officials in countries on three continents," said Deputy Assistant Attorney General Suh. 'Such brazen wrongdoing calls for a strong response from law enforcement, and through a strong effort with our colleagues in Brazil and Switzerland, we have seen just that. I hope that today's action will serve as a model for future efforts'.

'These resolutions are the result of an extraordinary multinational effort to identify, investigate and prosecute a highly complex and long-lasting corruption scheme that resulted in the payment by the defendant companies of close to a billion dollars in bribes to officials at all levels of government in many countries', said U.S. Attorney Capers. 'In an attempt to conceal their crimes, the defendants used the global financial system – including the banking system in the United States – to

[21] www.justice.gov/opa/pr/odebrecht-and-braskem-plead-guilty-and-agree-pay-least-35-billion-global-penalties-resolve.

disguise the source and disbursement of the bribe payments by passing funds through a series of shell companies. The message sent by this prosecution is that the United States, working with its law enforcement partners abroad, will not hesitate to hold responsible those corporations and individuals who seek to enrich themselves through the corruption of the legitimate functions of government, no matter how sophisticated the scheme'.

'This case illustrates the importance of our partnerships and the dedicated personnel who work to bring to justice those who are motivated by greed and act in their own best interest', said Assistant Director Richardson. 'The FBI will not stand by idly while corrupt individuals threaten a fair and competitive economic system or fuel criminal enterprises. Our commitment to work alongside our foreign partners to root out corruption across the globe is unwavering and we thank our Brazilian and Swiss partners for their tireless work in this effort'.

'No matter what the reason, when foreign officials receive bribes, they threaten our national security and the international free market system in which we trade', said Assistant Director in Charge Sweeney. 'Just because they're out of our sight, doesn't mean they're beyond our reach. The FBI will use all available resources to put an end to this type of corrupt behavior'.

Odebrecht pleaded guilty to a one-count criminal information filed today by the Criminal Division's Fraud Section and the U.S. Attorney's Office in the U.S. District Court for the Eastern District of New York, charging the company with conspiracy to violate the anti-bribery provisions of the Foreign Corrupt Practices Act (FCPA). Odebrecht agreed that the appropriate criminal fine is $4.5 billion, subject to further analysis of the company's ability to pay the total global penalties. In related proceedings, Odebrecht also settled with the Ministerio Publico Federal in Brazil and the Office of the Attorney General in Switzerland.

Under the plea agreement, the United States will credit the amount that Odebrecht pays to Brazil and Switzerland over the full term of their respective agreements, with the United States and Switzerland receiving 10% each of the principal of the total criminal fine and Brazil receiving the remaining 80%. The fine is subject to an inability to pay analysis to be completed by the Department of Justice and Brazilian authorities on or before March 31, 2017, because Odebrecht has represented it is only able to pay approximately $2.6 billion over the course of the respective agreements. Sentencing has been scheduled for April 17, 2017.

Braskem, whose American Depositary Receipts (ADRs) are publicly traded on the New York Stock Exchange, separately pleaded guilty to a one-count criminal information filed in the Eastern District of New York charging it with conspiracy to violate the anti-bribery provisions of the FCPA. Braskem agreed to pay a total criminal penalty of $632 million. Sentencing has not yet been scheduled. In related proceedings, Braskem also settled with the U.S. Securities and Exchange Commission (SEC), the Ministerio Publico Federal in Brazil and the Office of the Attorney General in Switzerland. Under the terms of its resolution with the SEC, Braskem agreed to a total of $325 million in disgorgement of profits. Braskem agreed to pay Brazilian authorities 70% of the total criminal penalty and agreed to pay the Swiss authorities 15%. The department has agreed to credit the criminal penalties paid to

Brazilian and Swiss authorities as part of its agreement with the company. The United States will receive $94.8 million, an amount equal to 15% of the total criminal fines paid by Braskem.

Under their respective plea agreements, Odebrecht and Braskem are required to continue their cooperation with law enforcement, including in connection with the investigations and prosecutions of individuals responsible for the criminal conduct. Odebrecht and Braskem also agreed to adopt enhanced compliance procedures and to retain independent compliance monitors for 3 years. The cases are assigned to U.S. District Judge Raymond J. Dearie of the Eastern District of New York.

The combined total amount of United States, Brazilian and Swiss criminal and regulatory penalties paid by Braskem will be approximately $957 million. The combined total amount of penalties imposed against Odebrecht will be at least $2.6 billion and up to $4.5 billion. With a combined total of at least $3.5 billion, today's resolutions with Odebrecht and Braskem are the largest-ever global foreign bribery resolution.

The Bribery Schemes.

According to its admissions, Odebrecht engaged in a massive and unparalleled bribery and bid-rigging scheme for more than a decade, beginning as early as 2001. During that time, Odebrecht paid approximately $788 million in bribes to government officials, their representatives and political parties in a number of countries in order to win business in those countries. The criminal conduct was directed by the highest levels of the company, with the bribes paid through a complex network of shell companies, off-book transactions and off-shore bank accounts.

As part of the scheme, Odebrecht and its co-conspirators created and funded an elaborate, secret financial structure within the company that operated to account for and disburse bribe payments to foreign government officials and political parties. By 2006, the development and operation of this secret financial structure had evolved such that Odebrecht established the 'Division of Structured Operations', which effectively functioned as a stand-alone bribe department within Odebrecht and its related entities. Until approximately 2009, the head of the Division of Structured Operations reported to the highest levels within Odebrecht, including to obtain authorisation to approve bribe payments. After 2009, this responsibility was delegated to certain company business leaders in Brazil and the other jurisdictions. To conceal its activities, the Division of Structured Operations utilised an entirely separate and off-book communications system, which allowed members of the Division of Structured Operations to communicate with one another and with outside financial operators and other co-conspirators about the bribes via secure emails and instant messages, using codenames and passwords.

The Division of Structured Operations managed the 'shadow' budget for the Odebrecht bribery operation via a separate computer system that was used to request and process bribe payments as well as to generate and populate spreadsheets that tracked and internally accounted for the shadow budget. These funds for the company's sophisticated bribery operation were generated by the Odebrecht Finance Department through a variety of methods, as well as by certain Odebrecht subsidiaries, including Braskem. The funds were then funnelled by the Division of

Structured Operations to a series of off-shore entities that were not included on Odebrecht's balance sheet as related entities. The Division of Structured Operations then directed the disbursement of the funds from the off-shore entities to the bribe recipient, through the use of wire transfers through one or more of the off-shore entities, as well as through cash payments both inside and outside Brazil, which were sometimes delivered using packages or suitcases left at predetermined locations.

Odebrecht, its employees and agents took a number of steps whilst in the United States to further the scheme. For instance, in 2014 and 2015, whilst located in Miami, two Odebrecht employees engaged in conduct related to certain projects in furtherance of the scheme, including meetings with other co-conspirators to plan actions to be taken in connection with the Division of Structured Operations, the movement of criminal proceeds and other criminal conduct. In addition, some of the off-shore entities used by the Division of Structured Operations to hold and disburse unrecorded funds were established, owned and/or operated by individuals located in the United States. In all, this conduct resulted in corrupt payments and/or profits totaling approximately $3.336 billion.

Braskem also admitted to engaging in a wide-ranging bribery scheme and acknowledged the pervasiveness of its conduct. Between 2006 and 2014, Braskem paid approximately $250 million into Odebrecht's secret, off-book bribe payment system. Using the Odebrecht system, Braskem authorised the payment of bribes to politicians and political parties in Brazil, as well as to an official at Petróleo Brasileiro S.A.—Petrobras (Petrobras), the state-controlled oil company of Brazil. In exchange, Braskem received various benefits, including: preferential rates from Petrobras for the purchase of raw materials used by the company; contracts with Petrobras; and favourable legislation and government programmes that reduced the company's tax liabilities in Brazil. This conduct resulted in corrupt payments and/or profits totaling approximately $465 million.

The Corporate Resolutions.

The department reached these resolutions with Odebrecht and Braskem based on a number of factors, including: the failure to voluntarily disclose the conduct that triggered the investigation; the nature and seriousness of the offence, which spanned many years, involved the highest levels of the companies, occurred in multiple countries and involved sophisticated schemes to bribe high-level government officials; the lack of an effective compliance and ethics programme at the time of the conduct; and credit for each company's respective cooperation. The companies also engaged in remedial measures, including terminating and disciplining individuals who participated in the misconduct, adopting heightened controls and anti-corruption compliance protocols and significantly increasing the resources devoted to compliance.

The criminal penalty for Odebrecht reflects a 25% reduction off the bottom of the U.S. Sentencing Guidelines fine range because of Odebrecht's full cooperation with the government's investigation, whilst the criminal penalty for Braskem reflects a 15% reduction off the bottom of the U.S. Sentencing Guidelines as a result of its partial cooperation.

Odebrecht has represented its ability to pay a maximum of $2.6 billion of the total fine amount. The department and Brazilian authorities are engaged in further analysis regarding the company's claimed inability to pay, which will be completed on or before March 31, 2017.

* * *

The FBI's New York Field Office is investigating the case. Chief Dan Kahn and Trial Attorneys Christopher Cestaro, Sarah Edwards, David Fuhr, Kevin R. Gingras, Lorinda Laryea and David Last of the Criminal Division's Fraud Section and Assistant U.S. Attorneys Julia Nestor and Alixandra Smith of the Eastern District of New York are prosecuting the case.

The Criminal Division's Office of International Affairs also provided substantial assistance. The SEC and the Ministerio Publico Federal in Brazil the Departamento de Polícia Federal and the Office of the Attorney General in Switzerland provided significant cooperation.[22]

The Criminal Division's Fraud Section is responsible for investigating and prosecuting all FCPA matters.[23]

14.7.3 From IDB's Website[24]

September 4, 2019.

Odebrecht Reaches Settlement Agreement with IDB Group Resulting in Sanctions.

Sanctions include debarment and contributions of US$50 million to go to NGOs and charities serving vulnerable communities in IDB member countries.

---

[22]See also FCPA Blog article 'Former Braskem CEO charged with FCPA and money laundering conspiracies' by Richard L. Cassin dated November 21, 2019 in which notes that the US DoJ charged: '... the former chief executive officer of Braskem S.A. with helping his company and Odebrecht S.A. amass a giant slush fund and use it to bribe officials and political parties in Brazil. Jose Carlos Grubisich, 62, a Brazil citizen, was charged in federal court in Brooklyn, New York. He faces one count of conspiracy to violate the anti-bribery provisions of the Foreign Corrupt Practices Act, one count of conspiracy to violate the FCPA's books and records provisions and falsely certifying financial reports, and one count of conspiracy to commit international money laundering ... Braskem's controlling shareholder is Odebrecht, a Brazilian construction firm, with nearly 40 percent ownership and just over 50 percent of the voting shares. Brazil's state energy company, Petroleo Brasileiro S.A. (Petrobras), owns about a third of Braskem ... In December 2016, Odebrecht and Braskem pleaded guilty to bribing officials around the world. The companies agreed to pay $3.5 billion for a global settlement with authorities in the United States, Brazil, and Switzerland...'

[23]Additional information about the Justice Department's Fraud Section FCPA enforcement efforts can be found at www.justice.gov/criminal/fraud/fcpa.

[24]www.iadb.org/en/news/odebrecht-reaches-settlement-agreement-idb-group-resulting-sanctions-0.

Following an extensive investigation by the Office of Institutional Integrity (OII, an independent office of the Inter-American Development Bank), with the cooperation of the Brazilian company Odebrecht S.A. (Odebrecht), OII announced today the debarment of CNO S.A. (CNO), a subsidiary of Odebrecht, for 6 years in connection with prohibited practices in two IDB-financed projects. The debarment makes CNO ineligible to participate in IDB Group-financed projects.

The OII investigation uncovered bribes paid in two IDB-financed projects: the Tocoma Hydroelectric Power Plant Program in Venezuela and the Highway Rehabilitation Program in the State of São Paulo in Brazil.

As part of the Settlement, Odebrecht does not contest the evidence obtained by OII demonstrating that in both projects CNO committed corrupt practices when it made payments to public officials in order to facilitate either the award, contract execution payments and/or contract amendments.

According to OII's evidence, the illicit payments amounted to upward of 5–6% of each contract amount, including amendments. Specific to the Highway Rehabilitation Program, between 2006 and 2008, CNO paid government officials a total amount equivalent to approximately US$380,000. In the case of the Tocoma Hydroelectric Power Plant Program, evidence obtained by OII indicates that between 2007 and 2015, illicit payments and transactions of up to US$118 million were made utilising a complex network of agents and offshore financial payment schemes.

The sanctions are the result of a Negotiated Resolution Agreement (the Settlement) between the IDB, the Inter-American Investment Corporation (IDB Invest) and Odebrecht on behalf of its subsidiaries, CNO and Odebrecht Engenharia e Construção S.A. (OEC). The Settlement also includes a conditional non-debarment applied to OEC for 10 years and CNO for 4 years directly following CNO's 6-year period of debarment. When conditionally non-debarred, a company remains eligible to participate in IDB Group-financed projects but only if it fully meets the conditions of the Settlement. If any of the conditions are not met, the company will be debarred.

As part of the sanctions, Odebrecht commits to make a total contribution of US$50 million, starting in 2024, directly to NGOs and charities managing social projects with the purpose of improving the quality of life of vulnerable communities in the IDB's developing member countries.

In addition to the sanctions against CNO and OEC, 19 CNO subsidiaries will be subject to debarment and a further 41 OEC subsidiaries will be subject to conditional non-debarment. CNO branches in Africa are excluded from the sanction. Separately, the Odebrecht group commits to comply with certain conditions necessary to demonstrate its reforms.

The Settlement allows for a reduced period of debarment in light of Odebrecht's continued cooperation, including internal investigations that are intended to uncover systemic integrity risks to IDB Group-financed activities. Under the terms of the Settlement, Odebrecht commits to report on its compliance programme through an independent monitor.

The Settlement was negotiated by OII in accordance with the IDB Group's Sanctions Procedures. Settlements of this nature are used by the IDB Group and other multilateral development banks as an effective means to resolve investigations related to prohibited practices in exchange for cooperation and disclosures of systemic integrity risks.

The debarment of CNO and listed subsidiaries qualifies for cross-debarment by other multilateral development banks (MDBs) under the Agreement for Mutual Enforcement of Debarment Decisions that was signed on April 9, 2010.

For additional information on the IDB's Office of Institutional Integrity and its sanctions system, please click here.

Chapter 15
Sources of Further Information

There are a number of organisations, foundations and public sector entities that provide guidance, advice and assistance on governance and integrity issues. Some of these are longer-term (and may require academic study); others are accessible from the office desktop. There are others that make useful/relevant documents available to interested parties.

These are in addition to those organisations mentioned already, who may also be able to provide guidance, suggestions and other assistance. The list is, of course, not intended to be a complete list on how to prevent and to deter or (if it does occur) to deal with fraud, corruption and broader integrity and misconduct issues. There are many other sources of similar information[1] that can be found but it is a list of the sites that I have found useful.

The following list is in no particular order:

15.1 Open Contracting Partnership

As referred to in Chap. 9, the website of Open Contracting contains articles on various transparency initiatives, blogs and news.[2] In particular, open contracting is trying to raise accountability, as follows:

> **Open Contracting for Infrastructure Data Standards Toolkit**
>
> The Open Contracting Data Standard (OCDS) is already used to describe millions of procurement processes around the world relating to goods, services and public works. The CoST Infrastructure Data Standard (CoST IDS) has been used to guide what data and

[1] Such as the UNDP's report (a downloadable document) on 'Tackling Integrity Risks in Government Contracts' dated December 28, 2017: www.asia-pacific.undp.org/content/rbap/en/home/library/democratic_governance/tackling-integrity-risks-in-government-contracts.html.

[2] www.open-contracting.org.

D. Smith, *Promoting Integrity in the Work of International Organisations*,
Contributions to Finance and Accounting,
https://doi.org/10.1007/978-3-030-73916-4_15

information should be disclosed at each stage of the project cycle on over 25,000 infrastructure projects.[3]

This site describes how to combine **contract level disclosures using OCDS** with **project-level disclosure based on the CoST IDS**, in order to support scalable disclosure and monitoring of infrastructure project identification, preparation, implementation and delivery.

Trillions of dollars are spent every year on infrastructure and estimates suggest between 10 and 30% of infrastructure investment is lost through inefficiency, mismanagement and corruption. Access to better and more joined up data is essential to drive better quality, more affordable and more accessible infrastructure for government, citizens and business.[4]

15.2 OECD

The OECD is an inter-governmental organisation that brings together 36 countries to promote economic growth, prosperity and employment through cooperation and policy dialogue. It was founded in 1961 to stimulate economic progress and world trade; most of its members are high-income countries. It is based in Paris (in the Château de la Muette, near Bois de Boulogne).

The OECD has developed Principles of Corporate Governance, Guidelines for Multilateral Enterprises and a Convention on Combating Bribery of Foreign Public Officials in International Business Transactions.

Its website[5] notes:

> Although no bribery can take place without two parties participating in the corrupt transaction, the payers and receivers, there is generally less focus on the corrupt recipients. International conventions such as the OECD Anti-Bribery Convention and the UN Convention Against Corruption encourage state parties to address both sides of bribery in their national legislation but this does not occur in, for example, the USA's Foreign Corrupt Practices Act (FCPA). Of course many of the corrupt relationships are international and many of the corrupt recipients are therefore unlikely to be the subject of a US federal court jurisdiction; if they were, there are other possibilities to charge both participating sides (such as mail fraud or money laundering).
>
> Unfortunately, the OECD's study of prosecutions of foreign bribe takers, Foreign Bribery Enforcement: What Happens to the Public Officials on the Receiving End?, said that public officials were sanctioned in only one in five cases of the corrupt schemes covered by the survey.
>
> Prosecuting foreign bribe receivers could also not be possible on the grounds that it could subject U.S. industry and possibly the government as well to political fallout and maybe even retaliation from foreign governments. The US's Trump Administration recently reaffirmed this policy in its National Security Strategy, which states 'the United States will continue to target corrupt foreign officials'.

[3] www.standard.open-contracting.org/infrastructure/latest/en/.

[4] https://standard.open-contracting.org/infrastructure/latest/en/.

[5] www.oecd.org/.

15.3 B20 Collective Action Hub

The B20 is a forum and dialogue platform of business representatives, policymakers and civil society and has direct communications with the G20 world leaders from 20 major economies. (19 member states and the EU). In 2020, Saudi Arabia holds the G20 presidency and the B20 has created task-forces to address six priorities: integrity and compliance; digitalisation; energy, sustainability and climate change; finance and infrastructure; future of work and education; and trade and investment.[6] The B20 task-forces would normally prepare policy papers with recommendations for G20 leaders.

The Collective Action website[7] refers to the various initiatives undertaken and includes a link to 'Collective Action guidance for SMEs' and notes as follows:

> The International Centre for Collective Action
>
> Building on the Basel Institute on Governance's decade long track record of support to and research into Collective Action initiatives against corruption, and to formalise and further strengthen the impact of this engagement, the Basel Institute in 2012 launched the International Centre for Collective Action (ICCA). The purpose of the ICCA is to assist companies and other concerned stakeholders in enhancing their ability to reduce the risk of corruption through Collective Action.
>
> The promotion of Collective Action against corruption was one of the key objectives of the Basel Institute when it was founded in 2003, formalising an engagement of the Institute's President Professor Mark Pieth and other leading Institute members in this area that dates back to the early 1990s.
>
> Our track record
>
> Highlights of the Basel Institute's track record include:
>
> - Global cross-sectoral initiatives:
>
>   Founding (and current) Member of the Board of the World Economic Forum Partnering Against Corruption Initiative (PACI)
> - Global sector/specific initiatives:
>
>   Founding (and current) member of the Wolfsberg Group on Money Laundering
>
>   Founder and facilitator of several sectoral Collective Action initiatives, including in the defence, logistics and transport, art trade, finance, and transport & energy sectors
> - National/local cross-sectoral initiatives:
>
>   High Level Reporting Mechanism (with OECD)
>
>   Facilitation of a high-level Collective Action anti-corruption initiative in Ukraine
>
> Institutional partners
>
> - Institutional partners of the ICCA, which jointly form the ICCA's Steering Committees include
> - International Anti-Corruption Academy (IACA);
> - Organisation for Economic Cooperation and Development (OECD);
> - TRACE;
> - Transparency International (TI);
> - World Economic Forum (WEF);
> - Universidad de San Andrés Argentina.

[6]See FCPA Blog article: 'Integrity & compliance continues as a B20 priority' by Mirna Adjami November 7, 2019.

[7]www.collective-action.com; see also www.baselgovernance.org/collective-action.

Funding

The ICCA is partially funded through a grant by the Siemens Integrity Initiative (SII) and through Basel Institute core funding. In addition, members of sectoral Collective Action initiatives moderated by the ICCA will be required to contribute to the funding of these efforts over time. Finally, additional corporate sponsoring is sought from global companies actively engaged in Anti-Corruption Collective Action.

15.4 Basel Institute on Governance (Based in Basel, Switzerland)

The Basel Institute on Governance is an independent, not-for-profit organisation based in Basel, Switzerland. It works worldwide with the public and private sector to improve the quality of governance and to counter corruption and other financial crimes.

A number of relevant aspects are addressed on their website[8] including:

> The International Centre for Asset Recovery (ICAR) is dedicated to strengthening and supporting the capacities of developing and transition countries to recover stolen public assets.
>
> Our global network and team of asset recovery specialists is made up of former prosecutors, lawyers and financial investigators.
>
> Flexible and fast-moving, we are uniquely placed to provide hands-on support to partner agencies across the world in tackling complex financial crime schemes.
>
> (B) The International Centre for Collective Action (ICCA) is an independent centre of excellence specialising in anti-corruption Collective Action initiatives in a variety of industries and, with the UN Global Compact, is home to the B20 Collective Action Hub.
>
> We help to develop and facilitate Collective Action initiatives that bring together businesses and other stakeholders in a variety of industries worldwide.
>
> Collective Action is an innovative approach to tackle corruption, raise standards of business integrity and level the playing field between competitors. It involves collaboration and sustained cooperation between stakeholders in the private and public sectors, civil society and international organisations. Because working together, we can overcome corruption challenges more effectively than working alone.
>
> … Our B20 Collective Action Hub offers a range of anti-corruption publications and tools, plus a database of over 100 anti-corruption Collective Action initiatives around the world.

15.5 Transparency International (TI)

TI is a significant player in the global anti-corruption fight by undertaking research, adopting policies, undertaking international initiatives and offering advice to counteract new forms of corruption as well as conducting their well-known yearly

[8] http://www.baselgovernance.org/asset-recovery.

ranking of countries based on the risk of corruption. They stated as follows on their website[9] (October 2019):

> 'Transparency International e.V. (TI) is an international non-governmental organization which is based in Berlin, Germany, and was founded in 1993'. Its nonprofit purpose is to take action to combat global[1] corruption with civil societal anti-corruption measures and to prevent criminal activities arising from corruption. It publishes for example the Global Corruption Barometer and the Corruption Perceptions Index. Transparency International has the legal status of a German registered voluntary association (Eingetragener Verein) and serves as an umbrella organization. Its members have grown from a few individuals to more than 100 national chapters which engage in fighting corruption in their home countries.[2] TI is a member of UNESCO Consultative Status[3], United Nations Global Compact[4] and United Nations Sustainable Development Goals for Peace, Justice and Strong Institutions and Partnerships For the Goals.[5] TI confirmed the dis-accreditation of the national chapter of United States of America in 2017.[6]

It has an International Secretariat based in Berlin and national chapters in many countries. The International Secretariat also acts as a knowledge centre.

They have produced in July 2019 their assessment of the '25 Corruption Scandals That Shook The World' which they claim are the following:

1. Siemens: corruption made in Germany
2. Draining Nigeria of its assets
3. Fujimori's Peru: death squads, embezzlement and good public relations
4. Kadyrov's Chechnya: bikers, boxers, bribes
5. Shutting down competition in Tunisia
6. Ukraine's missing millions
7. Ricardo Martinelli's spy-game in Panama
8. The 1MDB fund: from Malaysia to Hollywood
9. The Russian Laundromat (with a little help from Moldova)
10. Spain's largest corruption scandal: Gürtel
11. Venezuela's currencies of corruption
12. The Panama Papers
13. Maldives: a paradise lost
14. Teodorín Obiang's #LuxuryLiving in Equatorial Guinea
15. How the Gupta family captured South Africa through bribery
16. Lebanon's garbage: the stench of corruption
17. FIFA's football parallel universe
18. Myanmar's dirty jade business
19. Fighting impunity in Guatemala
20. Turkey's 'gas for gold' scheme
21. The Azerbaijani Laundromat
22. Paradise Papers: where the rich and powerful hide their money
23. Operation Lava Jato: clean cars, dirty money
24. The Troika Laundromat

---

[9] www.transparency.org.

25. Andrej Babiš's conflict of interest in Czechia
*Listed in no particular order.

15.6 Integrity Action

This is an international development NGO based in London, UK Their website[10] states (in October 2019) that:

> Integrity Action is an organisation and an active network of committed NGOs, universities and policy makers, working closely with governments, media organisations, businesses and our peers to identify ways of making integrity work in some of the world's challenging settings.
>
> We help citizens to monitor and improve the delivery of vital projects and services, like education or infrastructure. Working with partners, we do this in places where securing improvements to services like these is tough. And yet these citizens get results.

15.7 US FBI

This US investigation organisation gives details of Common Fraud Schemes: Scams and Safety. Their website also has a section dedicated to corruption, part of which is replicated here:[11]

> Public corruption, the FBI's top criminal investigative priority, poses a fundamental threat to our national security and way of life. It can affect everything from how well our borders are secured and our neighbourhoods protected to how verdicts are handed down in courts to how public infrastructure such as roads and schools are built. It also takes a significant toll on the public's pocketbooks by siphoning off tax dollars—it is estimated that public corruption costs the US government and the public billions of dollars each year. The FBI is uniquely situated to combat corruption, with the skills and capabilities to run complex undercover operations and surveillance.
>
> **Overview**
>
> The Bureau's Public Corruption programme focuses on:
>
> - Investigating violations of federal law by public officials at the federal, state, and local levels of government;
> - Overseeing the nationwide investigation of allegations of fraud related to federal government procurement, contracts, and federally funded programmes;
> - Combating the threat of public corruption along the nation's borders and points of entry in order to decrease the country's vulnerability to drug and weapons trafficking, alien smuggling, espionage, and terrorism.
> - Addressing environmental crime, election fraud, and matters concerning the federal government procurement, contracts, and federally funded programmes.
>
> In 2008, the FBI created the International Corruption Unit (ICU) to oversee the increasing number of investigations involving global fraud against the US government and the

[10]www.integrityaction.org.

[11]www.fbi.gov.

corruption of federal public officials outside of the continental US involving US funds, persons, businesses, etc. The ICU's tasks include:

- Overseeing the Bureau's Foreign Corrupt Practices Act (FCPA) and antitrust cases;
- Maintaining operational oversight of several International Contract Corruption Task Forces, which investigate and prosecute individuals and firms engaged in bribery, illegal gratuities, contract extortion, bid rigging, collusion, conflicts of interest, product substitution, items and/or services invoiced without delivery, theft, diversion of goods, and individual and corporate conspiracies on every level of US government operations.

No other law enforcement agency has attained the kind of success the FBI has achieved in combating corruption. This success is due largely to the cooperation and coordination from a number of federal, state, local, and tribal law enforcement agencies to combat public corruption. These partnerships include, but are not limited to the Department of Justice, Agency Offices of Inspector General; law enforcement agencies' internal affairs divisions; federal, state and local law enforcement and regulatory investigative agencies; and state and county prosecutor's offices.

There is also a specific section on International Corruption, as follows:

The FBI's International Corruption Unit (ICU) is the leading investigative entity in combating foreign corruption. ICU manages five programmes:

- Foreign Bribery/Foreign Corrupt Practices Act (FCPA)
- Foreign Corruption/Kleptocracy Program
- Antitrust
- International Fraud Against the Government
- International Corruption of Federal Public Officials

Foreign Corrupt Practices Act

ICU has management responsibility and programme oversight for FBI investigations under the FCPA. The 1977 legislation has two main provisions. The first deals with bribery of foreign officials, and the second deals with accounting transparency requirements under the Securities Exchange Act. The dual elements were designed to facilitate parallel criminal and civil enforcement to stem corruption and promote fair business practices worldwide. The anti-bribery provision makes it illegal for US companies and certain foreign companies to bribe foreign officials to obtain or retain business. The bribes can be in the form of money or any other items of value. The accounting provision of the FCPA focuses on the Securities Exchange Act requirements applying to all foreign companies whose securities are listed on the US stock exchanges and US companies.

The United States cannot charge the foreign official under the FCPA; rather, the United States works together with international law enforcement partners to investigate US subjects who are complicit in paying bribes to foreign officials. The supply and demand equation of bribe paying and receiving illustrates the FCPA and kleptocracy violations as two sides of the same coin. For more information, see this detailed FCPA Resource Guide.

Kleptocracy

Kleptocracy, literally meaning 'the rule by thieves', is a form of political corruption in which the ruling government seeks personal gain and status at the expense of the governed. Through graft and embezzlement of state funds, corrupt leaders amass tremendous wealth at the expense of the broader populace. Some of the most egregious examples have occurred in countries with very high rates of poverty...

Antitrust

ICU has programme management responsibility for the FBI's antitrust investigations, both domestic and international, which target conspiracies among competitors to fix prices, rig bids, or allocate markets or customers. These conspiracies deprive US consumers of true competition, an economic bedrock of our free and democratic society. Perpetrators often operate in multinational companies that bask in illegal profits at the expense of US consumers. Stolen by cartels, the ill-gotten gains and competitive advantages reduce supply, eliminate incentives to compete by offering better and more innovative products and services, and destabilise economic markets.

International Contract Corruption

ICU has programme management responsibility over cases involving international fraud against the government and international corruption of federal public officials. The FBI was a co-founder of the International Contract Corruption Task Force, which was created in 2006 with the goal of addressing contract fraud concerns. These concerns stemmed from overseas US government spending during the wars in Afghanistan and Iraq. These cases typically involve bribery, gratuities, contract extortion, bid rigging, collusion, conflicts of interest, product substitution, items/services invoiced without delivery, diversion of goods, and corporate and individual conspiracies at various levels of US government operations.

ICU's programme extends beyond the war effort to include worldwide contingency operations involving US military actions, foreign aid and development, and humanitarian aid in any international region. Spending on these programmes is highly susceptible to corruption and fraud by those wishing to take advantage of the chaotic circumstances surrounding these benevolent endeavours. Misuse of US funds overseas poses a threat to the United States and other countries by promoting corruption within the host nation, damaging diplomatic relations, inadvertently supporting insurgent activity, and potentially strengthening criminal and terrorist organisations.

15.8 UK Action Fraud: National Fraud and Cyber Crime Reporting Centre

The website[12] describes Action Fraud as follows:

> Action Fraud is the UK's national reporting centre for fraud and cybercrime where you should report fraud if you have been scammed, defrauded or experienced cyber crime in England, Wales and Northern Ireland.
>
> We provide a central point of contact for information about fraud and financially motivated internet crime. People are scammed, ripped off or conned everyday and we want this to stop.
>
> The service is run by the City of London Police working alongside the National Fraud Intelligence Bureau (NFIB) who are responsible for assessment of the reports and to ensure that your fraud reports reach the right place. The City of London Police is the national policing lead for economic crime.
>
> Fraud is when trickery is used to gain a dishonest advantage, which is often financial, over another person. Cyber crime is any criminal act dealing with computers and networks.
>
> **Online hacking**
>
> There are many words used to describe fraud: Scam, con, swindle, extortion, sham, double-cross, hoax, cheat, ploy, ruse, hoodwink, confidence trick.
>
> These are just a few words you might hear in relation to fraud. Fraud can be committed against individuals or businesses. Have a look in our A-Z of fraud for information about different types of fraud.
>
> Cyber crime is any criminal act dealing with computers and networks (called hacking). Additionally, cyber crime also includes traditional crimes conducted through the Internet.
>
> Facts about fraud and cyber crime

[12] www.actionfraud.police.uk/.

The Annual Fraud Indicator 2017 estimates the cost of fraud to the UK is £190bn a year. The Office for National Statistics (ONS) says that people are more likely to fall victim to fraud or cyber offences above any other crime.

Between October 2017 and March 2018 there were:

- 332,570 crimes were reported to Action Fraud.
- £706 million lost by victims.
- 62% of reports were from businesses and 39% from individuals.

Action Fraud is the UK's national reporting centre for fraud and cyber crime where you should report fraud if you have been scammed, defrauded or experienced cyber crime.

Reporting a live cyber attack 24/7

If you are a business, charity or other organisation which is currently suffering a live cyber attack (in progress), please call 0300 123 2040 immediately. This service is available 24 hours a day, 7 days a week. Please note, if you are a member of the public you must call to report through our core opening hours below....

Reporting fraud and cyber crime

You can report fraud or cyber crime to Action Fraud any time of the day or night using our online fraud reporting tool. You can also report and get advice about fraud or cyber crime by calling 0300 123 2040.

The times above represent our core contact centre opening hours, although from time to time we do extend the service we provide to you...

15.9 Financial Fraud Action, UK

Financial Fraud Explained has a website[13] which notes:

Financial Fraud Action UK is now integrated into UK Finance.

From 1 July 2017, the finance and banking industry operating in the UK is represented by a new trade association, UK Finance. It represents around 300 firms in the UK providing credit, banking, markets and payment-related services. The new organisation takes on most of the activities previously carried out by the Asset Based Finance Association, the British Bankers' Association, the Council of Mortgage Lenders, Financial Fraud Action UK, Payments UK and the UK Cards Association.

Please go to www.ukfinance.org.uk for new content and updates from UK Finance.

The website also provides access to an article entitled:

A Dance of Deceit - A Report on Techniques Used by Vishing Fraudsters To Establish Patterns of Trust, a report by Dr Paul Breen, The University of Westminster

This article states as follows:

As a constituent part of UK Finance, Financial Fraud Action UK is responsible for leading the collective fight against financial fraud on behalf of the UK payments industry. Our membership includes banks, credit, debit and charge card issuers, and card payment acquirers in the UK.

Human beings have evolved with the instinctive 'willingness to accept someone at his or her word' and this 'leaves many of us vulnerable to attack' (Granger, 2001). That is particularly true in the online context, where the cost of fraud committed in the UK in 2016 'topped £1bn for the first time since 2011' (Treanor, 2017). Today's fraudsters are

[13]www.equifax.co.uk.

operating with increasing sophistication at the intersection of our physical and online lives, taking advantage of trust and data readily accessible in the public domain. They ensnare their victims by engaging in a carefully plotted masquerade in which they engineer a suspension of belief on the part of victims akin to the way we suppress our sense of reality when watching actors play the part of characters in a TV show.

Such 'clever manipulation of the natural human tendency to trust' (Granger, 2001) is referred to as social engineering; 'a euphemism for non-technical or low-technology means – such as lies, impersonation, tricks, bribes, blackmail, and threat – used to attack information systems' (McDowell, 2007). Increasingly, bank customers have been a favoured target of fraudsters and human beings represent 'the weak spot' in the security of our financial institutions (Keyworth, 2016). This is because our innate tendency is to trust others, especially those in authority, and to view ourselves as being 'too clever to be caught out' (ibid). After all, if human beings did not evolve with a natural disposition to trust, then everyday relationships, such as those in the workplace or the selection of a marriage partner would prove difficult.

The meaning of trust

Though the meaning of trust is a 'complex multidimensional construct' (Jones & George, 1998) encompassing 'moral, cognitive, and emotional elements' (Barber, 1983), the basic signification remains entrenched in the origins of the word. Coming from the Old Norse word treysta, the core definition is one of 'confident expectation' and 'fidelity' in the course of interaction with others. By the late 15th century, 'trust' had found its way into legal parlance, meaning 'confidence placed in one who holds or enjoys the use of property entrusted to him by its legal owner' (Etymology Online). Such a definition is particularly apt for the banking context, where institutions are expected and legally obliged to safeguard their customers' financial interests.

However, there is also a responsibility on the part of customers and this has become an Achilles Heel through which fraudsters can attack customers' security, using the affordances of the digital age. Today's digital technologies are characterised by their 'protean', 'unstable' and 'opaque' nature (Koehler & Mishra, 2009, p. 61); making them hard to trace, and capable of constant adaptation. This leaves the authorities engaged in a constant battle to guard their customers from compromising situations, and has stimulated debate about the best ways to address this growing challenge. Several theorists including Song, Kim & Gkelias argue that 'for the time being, the best option is to try to educate users about these attacks and the associated risks' (2014, p. 865), even though 'many security researchers' have also 'warned that the effectiveness of such education is inherently limited' (ibid).

Other theorists such as Hasan et al acknowledge that even though technology serves as the vehicle for fraud, 'user education is the first and most powerful defence against social engineering' (2010, p. 21). This is because technological resources alone cannot facilitate a fraud, any more than fishing rods and reels guarantee a catch, on their own. The human element is essential, and it all boils down to the basic human predisposition towards trust. Hasan et al (ibid, p. 18) suggest that such a basic manipulation of trust has been going on since ancient times, charting the example of the Trojan horse which was 'one of the most ingenious social engineering tricks in the history of humankind'.

In that story, it was not just the design of an unsuspected weapon that gave the enemy entrance to the gates of Troy, but also the fact that the Trojans failed to heed warnings about Greeks bearing gifts (ibid). If the Trojans had heeded the signs, the horse outside the city walls would have proven useless, just as malware is useless without the human curiosity of being seduced by clickbait. Had they been fully aware of the dangers, the Trojans would have fortified their city, rather than making guests of their enemies. It is such awareness that is crucial to people's self-protection.

15.10 FCPA Blog

Articles can be submitted to the Editor, Harry Cassin, which (once reviewed and approved) are then sent by email to the many thousands of subscribers and stored for searching on the website. It provides 'News and commentary from a range of contributors about white-collar crime, enforcement, and compliance', extremely useful for compliance and investigations purposes, as can be seen for the number of articles referred to in the footnotes above.

In addition, there is a section entitled **Job Board** which lists a number of compliance jobs and positions that are being recruited and another section entitled **FCPA Tracker**, as follows:

> **Searchable real-time disclosures of FCPA-related investigations**
>
> FCPA Tracker scans for and analyses public disclosures by companies and agencies about FCPA-related investigations. Analysts sort over 20 unique fields for each investigation.
>
> Public disclosures are complex and vary from company to company. That's why FCPA Tracker's expertise is essential.
>
> FCPA Tracker '<update@fcpatracker.com>'

15.11 Fraud.org: A Project of the UK's National Consumer League

This is a fraud awareness website[14] which includes the following report:

> **Top ten scams of 2018**
>
> Imposter scams, romance frauds, and bogus loans showed big gains in 2018

Overall Top Ten Scams

Rank	Scam type	% of total
1	Internet: General Merchandise	31.25%
2	Prizes/Sweepstakes/Free Gifts	16.97%
3	Fake Check Scams	13.09%
4	Recovery/Refund Companies	7.63%
5	Advance Fee Loans, Credit Arrangers	7.37%
6	Phishing/Spoofing	4.84%
7	Friendship & Sweetheart Swindles	2.81%
8	Computers: Equipment/Software	2.23%
9	Scholarships/Grants	1.63%
10	Family/ Friend Imposter	1.41%

[14]www.fraud.org.

Internet merchandise scams continued to be the top category of complaint to Fraud.org in 2018. However, scams like the advance fee loans (where swindlers offer you a loan in exchange for a large up-front fee) saw a 29.1 percent year-over-year gain. Friendship scams (also known as 'sweetheart swindles') showed the biggest gain of any of our top 10 fraud categories in 2018, increasing by more than 45 percent. Imposter scams like the infamous 'grandparent scam' grew rapidly in 2018, with a 30.61 percent increase.

Phishing/spoofing scams continue to rise

When we analysed our data last year, we spotted a worrying sign: an increase in complaints about phishing/spoofing. In 2018, the trend accelerated. This year's report shows a 10.49 percent increase in year-over-year phishing/spoofing-related complaints. This marks the third consecutive year we've seen such an increase in complaints about these scams. With fraudsters having access to more information about potential targets thanks to data breaches, we anticipate that this trend will continue in 2019 and beyond.

The Web is now the most likely place to be contacted by scammers

In 2017, we noticed that scammers seemed to be turning away from the phone as their preferred method of reaching their victims. That trend continued in 2018, and the Web is now the most likely place for scammers to find victims. Complaints where victims indicated they'd first been approached on the Web increased by 8.85 percent in 2018; the Web as a source for victims is followed by the phone, email, and in person.

Gift cards are becoming a bigger target

It should come as no surprise that wire transfer and credit cards continue to be the most popular ways for scammers to get paid by their victims. However, 2018 saw a rise in the use of gift cards as a payment method. In 2018, we detected a 25.25 percent year-over year increase in scams where alternate payment methods, particularly gift cards, were demanded by the fraudsters.

Seniors continue to be at risk

More than one in every five complaints received at Fraud.org in 2018 came from someone over the age of 65. Whilst seniors have historically been popular targets for scam artists, the 19.6 percent year-over-year increase in complaints from seniors suggests that the scammers may be becoming more aggressive in their pitches to older adults.

Meet the scams: The worst of 2018

Internet: General Merchandise Sales (not auctions)

Goods purchased are either never delivered or misrepresented

Prizes/Sweepstakes/Free Gifts

Requests for payment to claim fictitious prizes, lottery winnings, or gifts

Fake Check Scams

Consumers paid with phony checks for work or for items they're trying to sell, instructed to wire money back to buyer

Recovery/Refund Companies

Scammers contact victims and claim they owe money on a fictitious debt or offers to recover money lost in a previous scam

Advance Fee Loans, Credit Arrangers

False promises of business or personal loans, even if credit is bad, for a fee upfront

Phishing/Spoofing

Emails pretending to be from a well-known source ask consumers to enter or confirm personal information

Friendship & Sweetheart Swindles

Con artist nurtures an online relationship, builds trust, and convinces the victim to send money

Computers: Equipment and Software

Scammers claim to offer 'technical support' for computer problems and charge a fee to fix a nonexistent problem

Scholarships/Grants

For a fee, a 'search company' offers to conduct customised search for scholarships or grants for students. Scammers take money and run or provide a worthless list

Family and Friend Imposters

A scammer calls or emails, claiming that a friend or family member is in distress (in jail, in the hospital, etc.) and urgently needs funds to help.

The bottom line

Regardless of the type of scam, many instances of fraud can be avoided by remembering the old rule of thumb: If something seems too good to be true—it probably is.

If you ever do have questions about a potential fraud or think you might be a victim of a scam, report it immediately via Fraud.org's secure online complaint form. Embarrassment or fear of friends and relatives finding out about the crime causes many victims of fraud to remain silent. Only by speaking out can we give law enforcement the tools they need to bring these criminals to justice.

About this report

Fraud.org's Top Ten Scams report is compiled annually from complaints received directly from consumers. We do not attempt to verify the authenticity of these complaints, nor do they represent a scientific sample. To get more information on these scams or report suspected fraud, please visit Fraud.org.

15.12 Ethical Alliance

Ethical Alliance provides email updates on top criminal cases of white collar fraud and compliance.[15] The website states the following:

Global Anti-Corruption Compliance News

ethiXbase is committed to stamping out corruption and increasing transparency across the globe and for this reason created the Ethical Alliance, a global community of companies and individuals dedicated to anti-corruption compliance, corporate transparency and ethical business dealings. The Ethical Alliance Daily News and free Associate membership stands testament to this and delivers our members a daily digest of the latest news and alerts related to bribery and corruption from around the world. When it comes to fighting corruption, knowledge is power and we are dedicated to providing the business community with up to date information about initiatives and investigations to combat bribery and corruption globally. Our news feed irrefutably proves two things about the corporate world; that there is no country, industry or echelon of business that is immune to corruption, and that organisations over the world are becoming more astute at uncovering and stamping out unsavoury practices in the corporate world.

We believe that our corporate compliance news database performs an important function in that it promotes awareness of current trends in corporate crimes and prompts businesses to look more closely at their own supply chains and practices. The ultimate goal of the Ethical Alliance is to rescue corruption by achieving greater transparency and awareness.

[15]https://ethixbase.com/ethical-alliance-daily-news/.

15.13 Ethikos Weekly

This website[16] provides the Ethikos Weekly Newsletter sent to recipients by email - interesting articles about corporate ethics, business governance, accountability and compliance. Their website says 'Subscribe to ethikos weekly and stay up-to-date of (sic) the latest ethics. Each week we scour the major news sources and summarise the top ethics-related stories for you'.

15.14 The Ethics Institute

This is a not-for-profit organisation that, according to their website,[17] tries to 'build an ethically responsible society' in Southern Africa by forming partnerships with the public and private sectors by undertaking research, assessment of various approaches, offering a range of services and products related to organisational ethics and training.

15.15 The International Anti-corruption Conference

The IACC website[18] states the following:

> The International Anti-Corruption Conference (IACC) is (a) . . . forum for bringing together heads of state, civil society, the private sector and more to tackle the increasingly sophisticated challenges posed by corruption.
>
> Established in 1983, the IACC takes place usually every two years in a different region of the world, and hosts from 800 to 2000 participants from over 135 countries worldwide

An IACC conference is scheduled to take place in Seoul, South Korea in June 2020.

There are links between the IACC and Transparency International. Huguette Labelle (the former head of TI) is Chair of the IACC Council and the IACC website says the following in relation to TI:[19]

> Transparency International (TI) is the Secretariat to the IACC Council and has a dedicated IACC team in its Berlin offices. On behalf of the IACC Council, the IACC team designs the conference agenda and provides advice and assistance to the host of each conference. Other responsibilities include advising the host country on logistics and raising funds for the participating delegates.

---

[16] www.corporatecompliance.org/publications/newsletters/ethikos-weekly-newsletter.

[17] www.tei.org.za/index.php/about-us/who-we-are.

[18] https://iaccseries.org/.

[19] https://iaccseries.org/about/governance-accountability/.

TI is also responsible for the engagement of international stakeholders whilst preparing and implementing the conference programme. This includes communicating with organisations and individuals involved at the forefront of anti-corruption work. TI collates programme suggestions, and prepares the conference's plenary sessions and workshops.

15.16 International Anti-corruption Academy (IACA), Laxenberg (Near Vienna), Austria

According to their website:[20]

> The International Anti-Corruption Academy (IACA) is an international organisation based in Laxenburg, Austria. It is the first global institution of its kind, dedicated to overcoming current shortcomings in knowledge and practice in the field of anti-corruption and seeking to empower professionals for the challenges of tomorrow.
>
> The Academy offers standardised and tailor-made trainings, academic degree programmes, opportunities for dialogue and networking, and anti-corruption think-tank and benchmarking activities. It provides a new, holistic approach to anti-corruption education and research, delivers and facilitates anti-corruption training for practitioners from all sectors of society, and provides technical support and assistance to a wide variety of stakeholders. International cooperation, the sharing of knowledge and experiences, and mutual support are fundamental aspects of IACA's mandate.
>
> The organisation was initiated by the United Nations Office on Drugs and Crime, INTERPOL, the European Anti-Fraud Office (OLAF), the Republic of Austria, and other stakeholders. It became an international organisation on 8 March 2011 and currently has a constituency of 77 Parties, including three international organisations. IACA is an observer to the UN General Assembly, the Council of Europe's Group of States against Corruption, the United Nations Economic and Social Council, and the International Organization for Migration, and has explicitly been welcomed by an array of international resolutions.
>
> IACA is a signatory to the UN-backed Principles for Responsible Management Education (PRME) initiative, which aims to realise the UN Sustainable Development Goals (SDGs) through responsible management education and to raise the profile of sustainability in schools around the world.
>
> IACA observes geographical and cultural diversity and seeks broad partnerships with public and private sector institutions, international and non-governmental organisations, and civil society. It works together with these partners to co-organise anti-corruption trainings, and participates in other international events as a co-sponsor or expertise provider. In addition, IACA's Dean, faculty members, and senior representatives regularly (guest) lecture and contribute to international anti-corruption consultations and working groups, advisory boards, conferences, and meetings.
>
> In providing anti-corruption education and research, IACA draws on an unwavering drive towards excellence, a spirit of innovation, and a commitment to rendering itself accessible to individuals from all over the globe.

The IACA runs a number of specialised anti-corruption courses such as regional summer schools in Asia and Latin America, as well as postgraduate (master's) degrees such as the Master in Anti-Corruption Studies (MACS) and the International Masters in Anti-Corruption Compliance and Collective Action (IMACC). Students

[20] www.iaca.int/.

can join coming from the private sector, public sector or civil society and can apply to join from anywhere in the world.

> Since its inception, IACA has been recognised by numerous international bodies and other fora for its work in the area of anti-corruption and compliance education and capacity-building.
>
> Most recently, IACA's anti-corruption capacity-building activities and specialised curricula are, along with those of the United Nations Office on Drugs and Crime (UNODC), explicitly noted with appreciation in Resolution 35/25 of the Human Rights Council of the UN General Assembly, adopted on 23 June 2017, in recognising that the negative impact of corruption on human rights and sustainable development can be addressed and prevented through anti-corruption education.

15.17 Construction Transparency (CoST)

The CoST website[21] states:

> We work globally, disclosing, validating and interpreting data on infrastructure projects so that decision makers are held to account.
>
> Since 2015 our achievements include
>
> - 24,830 projects disclosed in line with the CoST Infrastructure Data Standard
> - 370 projects reviewed by CoST members
> - 3880 government representatives trained

The CoST website has links to a number of resources including a

> Powerpoint on the CoST approach and how we use our core features of disclosure, assurance, multi-stakeholder working and social accountability to promote infrastructure transparency globally. The powerpoint outlines concrete successes from our work in Afghanistan, Malawi and other countries.

The contact details for CoST and their Infrastructure Transparency Initiative are:

- Address: 5th Floor, Woolgate Exchange, 25 Basinghall Street, London, EC2V 5HA, UK.
- Phone: +44 (0)20 3206 0488
- Email: CoST@infrastructuretransparency.org

15.18 The Stolen Asset Recovery Initiative (StAR)

According to their website,[22] the Stolen Asset Recovery Initiative is a partnership between the World Bank Group and the United Nations Office on Drugs and Crime (UNODC) that:

---

[21] www.constructiontransparency.org.

[22] www.star.worldbank.org.

supports international efforts to end safe havens for corrupt funds. StAR works with developing countries and financial centres to prevent the laundering of the proceeds of corruption and to facilitate more systematic and timely return of stolen assets.

StAR provides platforms for dialogue and collaboration and also facilitates contact among different jurisdictions involved in asset recovery. Since its establishment ten years ago, StAR has assisted many countries in developing legal frameworks, institutional expertise, and the skills necessary to trace and return stolen assets.

StAR works with partners around the world to develop the most effective tools to tackle and prevent the theft of assets critical to development. StAR works with global organisations, including the Conference of States parties to UNCAC, the G8, the G20, and the Financial Action Task Force to influence and liaise with policymakers.

15.19 Government Transparency Institute (GTI)

Government Transparency Institute (GTI) website[23] states that:

> It is a non-partisan think tank researching and advocating good governance. Born from the research and civil society activism of its founder Mihály Fazekas,[24] the Institute was founded in 2015 to provide an independent, research-driven voice to the causes of transparency, anti-corruption, and good-governance in Europe and beyond. It is financed by private donations, European research funds, and government contract work, and works independently of political parties or special interest groups. The aim of the Institute is to better understand the causes, characteristics, and consequences of low-quality governance with interdisciplinary analysis, drawing on political science, economics, law, and data science.
>
> We help citizens hold their governments accountable through the publication of novel datasets and robust analyses. Our unique research approach uses Big Data, statistical analysis, and qualitative methods to understand the paths from micro-behaviour to macro-outcomes. Our research topics include anti-corruption, public procurement, legislative processes, and competition. We believe that the combination of qualitative understanding and quantitative measurement of the state is the foundation of good governance.
>
> Contact:
> info@govtransparency.eu
> https://twitter.com/GovTranspInst
> https://www.linkedin.com/company/government-transparency-institute

15.20 The Pearl Initiative

Founded in 2010, this is a not-for-profit, independent organisation bringing business, government and civil society together to share best practice, maximise economic opportunities and is working in the Gulf Region of the Middle East to improve corporate accountability, governance and transparency. Their website[25] notes:

---

[23] www.govtransparency.eu/.

[24] See earlier, page 14 and footnote 27 in the Introduction.

[25] www.pearlinitiative.org.

The Pearl Initiative believes that proactively raising standards in these areas enhances business innovation, opportunity and value creation. In other words, at the company level, it simply makes good business sense. At the sector and regional level, high standards of corporate governance and integrity are key drivers of competitiveness, investment, job creation and sustainable economic growth.

15.21 Corporate Data Quality

CDQ's website[26] states that:

> We enable global organisations throughout Europe to achieve their business goals with the help of professional data management and data quality management. In addition, we help our customer to adequately address current and future trends and challenges (as e.g. IoT, AI, Big Data, ontologies/semantics and Industry 4.0) with excellent corporate data quality. For us, data is more than an enabler of operational excellence – it is essential for designing and offering new, data-driven products and services. Consequently, data is a value driver and needs to be managed as any other corporate asset. Well-managed data is also the starting point for innovative digital business models.
>
> We believe that all data management activities should be aligned with the requirements of business. Data management should act as a service provider for (internal) data customers. Therefore, we support our customers with a comprehensive range of data management services such as data management consulting, training or data quality as a service (DQaaS) solutions including data cleansing and data enrichment. We also offer access to a well-established co-innovation & research data quality management community (CC CDQ). Our solutions are scientifically substantiated, practice-proven and sustainably effective

15.22 INTERPOL's Integrity in Sport

It is very sad to say that fraud and corruption have extended even into international sport. Perhaps it is no surprise given sizeable reputations are in potential jeopardy and large sums of money for winning (as well as for the gamblers) can be obtained.

National and international sporting organisations have teams to try to regulate the behaviour of sportsmen and women, so that the 'best person wins'. They seek to prevent and deter fraud and corruption from taking a meaningful hold and punish those who are found to have engaged in misconduct.

If Integrity in Sport is of particular interest, it is possible to subscribe and receive regular updates from INTERPOL.[27]

---

[26]www.cdq.ch.

[27]the Integrity in Sport Bi-Weekly Bulletin comes from integrityinsports@interpol.int.

15.23 US Department of Justice (DoJ) Website

Apart from detailed summaries of completed cases (like those cited above in Chap. 14), there are many other interesting issues addressed on the US DoJ website. For example, when the Department of Justice published the 'Evaluation of Corporate Compliance Programs', it provided compliance officers with considerable guidance on how companies can define and evaluate the effectiveness of various parts of their compliance programme.

The Evaluation Guidance addresses third-party oversight in one dedicated section, that explores four main topics:

- Risk-based and integrated processes
- Appropriate controls
- Management of relationships
- Real actions and consequences

How are compliance officers considering this guidance, to reverse engineer third-party compliance programmes that regulators would deem effective?

Dated Tuesday 30 April 2019, the website[28] has the following announcement:

> Criminal Division Announces Publication of Guidance on Evaluating Corporate Compliance Programs
>
> The Criminal Division announced today the release of a guidance document for white-collar prosecutors on the evaluation of corporate compliance programmes. The document, entitled 'The Evaluation of Corporate Compliance Programs', updates a prior version issued by the Division's Fraud Section in February 2017. It seeks to better harmonise the guidance with other Department guidance and standards whilst providing additional context to the multifactor analysis of a company's compliance programme.
>
> 'Effective compliance programs play a critical role in preventing misconduct, facilitating investigations, and informing fair resolutions', Assistant Attorney General Brian A. Benczkowski said. 'Today's guidance document is part of our broader efforts in training, hiring, and enforcement to help promote corporate behaviors that benefit the American public and ensure that prosecutors evaluate the effectiveness of compliance in a rigorous and transparent manner'.
>
> The guidance document sets forth topics that the Criminal Division has frequently found relevant in evaluating a corporate compliance programme, organising them around three overarching questions that prosecutors ask in evaluating compliance programmes: First, is the programme well-designed? Second, is the programme effectively implemented? And, third, does the compliance programme actually work in practice?
>
> To that end, Part I of the document discusses various hallmarks of a well-designed compliance programme relating to risk assessment, company policies and procedures, training and communications, confidential reporting structure and investigation process, third-party management, and mergers and acquisitions. Part II details features of effective implementation of a compliance programme, including commitment by senior and middle management, autonomy and resources, and incentives and disciplinary measures. Finally, Part III discusses metrics of whether a compliance programme is in fact operating effectively, exploring a programme's capacity for continuous improvement, periodic testing, and review, investigation of misconduct, and analysis and remediation of underlying misconduct.

---

[28] www.justice.gov.

The document was compiled with the input of components across the Division, including attorneys from the Office of the Assistant Attorney General, Fraud Section, and the Money Laundering and Asset Recovery Section. For the full guidance document, click here.

15.24 Foundation for the Global Compact

According to their website, this foundation undertakes fundraising, outreach and engagement with business stakeholders in support of the UN Global Compact to try to find lasting solutions to pressing global problems.[29] Further:

> Its relationship with the United Nations is set out in a Memorandum of Understanding (MOU). A summary of the main provisions of the MOU follows:
>
> The Foundation's main functions are:
>
> - Fundraising to support the Global Compact initiative
> - Providing financial and programme support for the Global Compact initiative and its activities
> - Promotion and advocacy of the Global Compact initiative and its principles.
>
> The MOU provides that the Global Compact and the Foundation work together in the following ways:
>
> - They collaborate in the planning and implementation of fundraising activities for the Global Compact initiative
> - The Global Compact Office keeps the Foundation informed of its ongoing and planned activities
> - The Global Compact Office invites representatives of the Foundation to relevant Global Compact meetings
> - The Global Compact Office provides appropriate recognition and acknowledgement to the Foundation...

15.25 Partnership for Transparency

Their website[30] states that their aim is to 'advance innovative citizen-led approaches to improve governance, increase transparency, promote the rule of law and reduce corruption in developing and emerging countries'.

Moreover, they state that:

> Governance will only improve if citizens organise themselves to demand reform. Governments respond to internal, not external pressures. We aim to help local civil society organisations (CSOs) to acquire the knowledge, skills, abilities and tools to campaign effectively for reform, to help development agencies to better assist local CSOs to have voice, and to encourage governments agencies to respond constructively to the demands of citizens as a way to strengthen their legitimacy.

---

[29] www.unglobalcompact.org.

[30] www.ptfund.org/about/.

15.26 Coalition for Integrity

Coalition for Integrity (or C4I as it styles itself on its website[31]) is a 'non-profit, non-partisan . . . organisation' based in the US. They work 'in coalition with a wide range of individuals and organisations to combat corruption and promote integrity in the public and private sectors'.

They released a report in 2019 entitled: 'Enforcement of Ethics Rules by State Agencies: Unpacking the S.W.A.M.P. Index' which demonstrates 'tremendous differences in United States' ethics enforcement and a lack of transparency in actions taken by state ethics agencies'. In addition, there is an interactive map on their website.[32]

15.27 Spotlight on Corruption

This is an organisation based in the UK that works 'to end corruption'.[33]

Their website notes that they 'track how the UK enforces its anti-corruption laws, we research ways in which they can be improved, we investigate cases where anti-corruption laws have been broken, we hold the government and enforcement bodies to account for ensuring anti-corruption laws work properly'.

15.28 Corruption Watch UK

This organisation, also based in the UK, states on it's website that it 'details and exposes the impact of bribery and corruption, predominantly but not exclusively in the global arms trade, on democracy governance and development'.[34]

Moreover, it says that:

> By tracking and monitoring major bribery and corruption cases, pushing for effective enforcement of global and national anti-corruption legislation, and building an international network of anti-corruption partners and activists. The organisation also assists prosecutors, law enforcement agencies, NGOs, journalists, activists and legislators in their efforts to fight corruption.

---

[31] www.coalitionforintegrity.org.

[32] See FCPA Blog article: 'Coalition for Integrity releases new report on U.S. states' by Laurie Sherman and Shruti Shah, September 24, 2019.

[33] www.spotlightcorruption.org.

[34] www.cw-uk.org.

15.29 ACFE

The Association of Certified Fraud Examiners (ACFE) has a motto 'Together, Reducing Fraud Worldwide' and notes 'we are the world's largest anti-fraud organisation and premier provider of anti-fraud training and education'.[35]

It has a number of 'Fraud Headlines' and carries links to its Fraud Magazine, as well as a list of upcoming training events, in particular for those who wish to be accredited 'CFE'.

[35] www.acfe.com.

Chapter 16
Conclusion

Fraud is a widespread problem and can occur frequently in all sorts of contexts, the implementation of contracts for development projects are not alone and in some ways, other situations are more vulnerable. Dishonesty can form the basis of such behaviour, and if the person or people concerned can get away with it in the short and long term, it can result in sizeable rewards sometimes instantaneously. If they get away with a clearly fraudulent act but circumstances change, in many cases an investigation and prosecution can result, in part because of the political desire to demonstrate that their predecessors were not as honest and law-abiding as was their image at the time.

Collusion and corruption are more sophisticated issues where multiple parties are required to agree to participate and to act accordingly over a length of time following the agreement, but again the rewards are potentially high and attractive if there is only a low risk of being (1) discovered (2) investigated (3) prosecuted and (4) convicted and sentenced.

To the extent that fraud and corruption can be exposed and brought out into the open, the public (and especially those directly affected) can seek explanations and those responsible can be held accountable, not just criminally (in a court of law) but also politically, socially and economically.

Of course, entities that trade in part on their image, do not wish to have such situations identified and discussed so will try to avoid it; if they play hard ball and don't mind the negative coverage, they might fight the legal proceedings, if successfully they can rely on the acquittal, if not, then seek to minimise the damaging after-effects with low sentence if convicted.

Despite the abundance of potential issues and the possibility that corrupt people will seek extra payment whenever possible, individuals and entities that want to play (and thereby enforce) the rules in order to minimise the occurrence of fraud and corruption in vulnerable projects with appropriate safeguards. For example, bids in a procurement process can be accompanied by positive statements of the entity or individual's previous behaviour and intentions if performing this contract. A stated

D. Smith, *Promoting Integrity in the Work of International Organisations*, Contributions to Finance and Accounting,
https://doi.org/10.1007/978-3-030-73916-4_16

willingness to make all of their books and records available for inspection by third parties (enforcement agencies or the international organisation funding the project) can reduce suspicion—the only concern for a clean company is that to allow their books to be reviewed directly or indirectly gives away information about their profit margins. This is confidential information and not normally of concern in the least to investigators who are looking for records of fraud or corruption and who accept that firms in the commercial world are entitled to earn a profit from the work they have done, the exception would be investigators seeking evidence of excessive profits based on a breach of competition law.

For those who have paid bribes to secure the award of a contract they would not have otherwise won, they need to assess the cost-benefit ratio: does the cost of the payment and the risk of getting caught, investigated and prosecuted (together with some, potentially extensive, negative publicity that can be generated as a result) outweigh or exceed the benefits of winning the contract (and the feedback and reports that follow as a result)?

Depending on the sector, the country in which the entity is based and is trading and what other work it does (and media coverage it gets), the implications may become very negative and serious. Such reports can also provide details of who has been paid and what for (commissions, etc.) and can be found not just at the time but for years to come as background information identified during due diligence by others and maybe a useful starting point if there is an allegation that the contract was awarded corruptly.

The Future In future years, it would be fantastic if there was no fraud or corruption subversively committed, leaving people's lives, professionally and personally, unaffected. Unfortunately, this is highly unlikely to be the case—more likely, there will be threats in the future similar to those that have occurred in the past. To predict ahead of time the nature and details of the frauds or corrupt agreements that will become a major threat is extremely difficult.

Of course, there are likely to be the same types (and new, different variations of earlier versions) of the frauds that have been successful in recent years, as well as new types of frauds in new sectors, with much human inventiveness and based on new technologies/products. As the list above (in Chap. 12) demonstrates, there is no limit to the ingenuity of the human race in fraud terms. Consequently, there are likely to be many major risks of fraud and corruption in the future.

In addition to existing risks, new areas may include:

- Food fraud (in particular, various/different types of food being misdescribed) for purchase in a shop or consumption in a restaurant or fast food provider;
- Cosmetics fraud (cosmetics and drugs available on the internet claiming falsely to achieve certain results);
- Identity theft (affecting people with ownership/use of a range of high-tech products);
- Sport, athletic behaviour and associated gambling;

- Environmental fraud (especially construction projects and the supply of false or distorted data); and
- Climate change prevention/mitigation fraud (misleading or false data used to seek finance and/or the funding being misused or misapplied).

Also, there may be new ways (through the use or application of new technologies) that older types of fraud such as pyramid schemes and 'phishing' emails/phone calls are made to people. Indeed, there are likely to be people who have not previously been exposed and therefore are somewhat less cautious.

Prevention Prevention[1] would be a big step forward: not having fraud or corruption infect the development work that the MDBs and other organisations are doing could allow significant improvements in a much shorter time; to spend a lot of time and resources to detect or uncover, investigate, sanction and/or resolve fraud and corruption would be a much better way but, of course, prevention is not so easy. Human nature, being what it is especially with criminals, always develops to try to make a 'quick buck'. So deterrence then starts to play a role: acknowledging that they might

[1]AfDB has an Integrity and Prevention Division that: '...leads the Department's proactive role in deterring and preventing corruption and other harmful practices in operations financed by the Bank. (They) develop and implement proactive measures, including campaigns and outreach programs to train and assist operational staff and other partners of the Bank Group'. The Division also develops due diligence tools and risk assessment programs to reduce vulnerability of Bank's projects as well as mainstream integrity concerns into project implementation processes... https://www.afdb.org/en/about-us/organisational-structure/integrity-and-anti-corruption/divisions.

World Bank INT has a Prevention Unit that has publications on their website: https://www.worldbank.org/en/about/unit/integrity-vice-presidency#41

- Warning Signs of Fraud and Corruption in Procurement (Formerly known as Common Red Flags of Fraud and Corruption in Procurement)—There are multiple warning signs that can help identify the risk of fraud, corruption, collusion or coercion in procurement. This brochure, Warning Signs of Fraud and Corruption in Procurement, elaborates on these warning signs, which, if spotted, might be cause for concern in a World Bank Group-funded project.
- Preventing Fraud and Corruption for Greater Development Impact—Taking a more comprehensive approach to targeting fraud and corruption, INT provides World Bank Group staff and clients with guidance on how to build preventive measures into projects. The Preventive Services Unit (PSU), working in partnership with operational teams, turns the unique knowledge gained from INT investigations into practical measures that can deter or stop corruption in World Bank Group-financed projects.
- Fraud and Corruption in Engineering Consultancy Contracts—This is a study by investigators, for investigators. It focuses not on the big picture but on the small details. It follows a typical procurement process and details the corrupt negotiations and transactions that take place and that have been discovered during investigations. It reports on indicators at all stages that investigators should look for and act on.
- Curbing Fraud, Corruption and Collusion in the Roads Sector—This report covers global corruption trends in the roads sector and includes recommendations based on the experience of developed and developing countries. It draws from what INT has learned from its investigations of World Bank Group-financed roads projects; borrowing country governments' investigations and reports; and the experience of developed countries.

be those who try to manipulate the processes for their own benefit but dissuaded from doing so because of the possible costs/punishment if caught.

After what has been a significant stream of consciousness, perhaps I should end on an optimistic note? I can do so by relying on a single sentence (a quote from the UK's SFO) to stress the fundamental importance of the need to deter and prevent corruption (as well as fraud, collusion and other types of misconduct affecting the MDBs and international organisations more broadly) and for such issues to be investigated and prosecuted as fully as possible (and therefore punished) under the law of the jurisdiction affected by the courts if and when it occurs:

> Tackling bribery and corruption creates more prosperous and healthy communities and a better business environment.

Cases/Issues Involving

D. Smith, *Promoting Integrity in the Work of International Organisations*,
Contributions to Finance and Accounting,
https://doi.org/10.1007/978-3-030-73916-4

Appendix: A List of Films About or Involving Fraud and Corruption

There are a number of films that have been produced over the last few years with a high degree of interest and relevance to the battle against fraud and corruption. No doubt you will have your own favourites from the following list (the details are reproduced from the IMDB film website) and maybe there are others that I have failed to mention:

1. **Rogue Trader** (1999)—The story of Nick Leeson, an ambitious investment broker who single-handedly bankrupted one of the oldest and most important banks (Barings Bank) in Britain. Director: James Dearden; Starring: Ewan McGregor, Anna Friel, Yves Beneyton, Betsy Brantley
2. **The Wolf of Wall Street** (2013)—Based on the true story of Jordan Belfort, from his rise to a wealthy stockbroker living the high life to his fall involving crime, corruption and the federal government. Director: Martin Scorsese; Starring: Leonardo DiCaprio, Jonah Hill, Margot Robbie, Matthew McConaughey
3. **The Wizard of Lies** (2017)—The fall of Bernie Madoff, whose Ponzi scheme robbed $65 billion from unsuspecting victims; the largest fraud in US history. Director: Barry Levinson; Starring: Robert De Niro, Michelle Pfeiffer, Alessandro Nivola
4. **The Big Short** (2015) In 2006-7 a group of investors bet against the US mortgage market. In their research they discover how flawed and corrupt the market is. Director: Adam McKay; Starring: Christian Bale, Steve Carell, Ryan Gosling, Brad Pitt
5. **Catch Me If You Can** (2002)—A seasoned FBI agent pursues Frank Abagnale Jr. who, before his 19th birthday, successfully forged millions of dollars' worth of checks whilst posing as a Pan Am pilot, a doctor, and a legal prosecutor. Director: Steven Spielberg; Starring: Leonardo DiCaprio, Tom Hanks, Christopher Walken, Martin Sheen
6. **Margin Call** (2011)—Follows the key people at an investment bank, over a 24-hour period, during the early stages of the 2008 financial crisis. Director:

D. Smith, *Promoting Integrity in the Work of International Organisations*, Contributions to Finance and Accounting,
https://doi.org/10.1007/978-3-030-73916-4

J.C. Chandor; Starring: Zachary Quinto, Stanley Tucci, Kevin Spacey, Paul Bettany

7. **Enron: The Smartest Guys in the Room** (2005)—Corporate audio and videotapes tell the inside story of the scandal involving one company's manipulation of California's energy supply and its, and how its executives wrung a billion dollars out of the resulting crisis. Director: Alex Gibney; Starring: Kenneth Lay, Peter Coyote, John Beard
8. **Matchstick Men** (2003) A phobic con artist and his protégé are on the verge of pulling off a lucrative swindle when the former's teenage daughter arrives unexpectedly
9. **Wall Street** (1987)—A young and impatient stockbroker is willing to do anything to get to the top, including trading on illegal inside information taken through a ruthless and greedy corporate raider who takes the youth under his wing. Director: Oliver Stone; Starring: Charlie Sheen, Michael Douglas, Tamara Tunie, Franklin Cover
10. **Wall Street 2: Money Never Sleeps** (2010)—Now out of prison but still disgraced by his peers, Gordon Gekko works his future son-in-law, an idealistic stock broker, when he sees an opportunity to take down a Wall Street enemy and rebuild his empire. Director: Oliver Stone; Starring: Shia LaBeouf, Michael Douglas, Carey Mulligan, Josh Brolin
11. **Too Big To Fail** (2011)—Chronicles the financial meltdown of 2008 and centres on Treasury Secretary Henry Paulson. Director: Curtis Hanson; Starring: James Woods, John Heard, William Hurt, Erin Dilly
12. **Working Girl** (1988)—When a secretary's idea is stolen by her boss, she seizes an opportunity to steal it back by pretending she has her boss' job. Director: Mike Nichols; Starring: Melanie Griffith, Harrison Ford, Sigourney Weaver, Alec Baldwin
13. **The Bank** (2001)—The Bank is a thriller about banking, corruption and alchemy. Director: Robert Connolly; Starring: David Wenham, Anthony LaPaglia, Sibylla Budd, Steve Rodgers
14. **Boiler Room** (2000)—A college dropout, attempting to win back his father's high standards he gets a job as a broker for a suburban investment firm, which puts him on the fast track to success, but the job might not be as legitimate as it once appeared to be. Director: Ben Younger; Starring: Giovanni Ribisi, Vin Diesel, Nia Long, Nicky Katt
15. **The Laundromat** (2019)—A widow investigates an insurance fraud chases leads to a pair of Panama City law partners exploiting the world's financial system. Director: Steven Soderbergh; Starring: Meryl Streep, Gary Oldman, Antonio Banderas
16. **Betting on Zero** (2016, Documentary) Writer-Director: Ted Braun—about hedge fund titan Bill Ackman and Herbalife
17. **Dirty Money** (2018 documentary series, Netflix)
18. **L'Argent** (1983)—A forged 500-franc note is passed from person to person until carelessness leads to tragedy. Director: Robert Bresson, Writer: Leo

Tolstoy (inspired by "Faux billet"), Stars: Christian Patey, Sylvie Van den Elsen, Michel Briguet

19. **Inside Job** (2010)—Takes a closer look at what brought about the 2008 financial meltdown. Stars: Matt Damon, Gylfi Zoega, Andri Snær Magnason. Director: Charles Ferguson
20. **To Live and Die in LA** (1985)—A fearless Secret Service agent will stop at nothing to bring down the counterfeiter who killed his partner. Director: William Friedkin, Stars: William Petersen, Willem Dafoe, John Pankow
21. **Floored** (2009)—For some people, risking everything is nothing. Director: James Allen Smith, Stars: Bobby Ansani, Jeff Ansani, Ron Beebe
22. **The Inventor: Out for Blood in Silicon Valley** (2019)—The story of Theranos, a multi-billion dollar tech company, its founder Elizabeth Holmes, the youngest self-made female billionaire and the massive fraud that collapsed the company. Director: Alex Gibney, Stars: Alex Gibney, Elizabeth Holmes, Dan Ariely
23. **Panic: The Untold Story of the 2008 Financial Crisis** (2018)—This documentary looks at the factors that led to the 2008 financial crisis and the efforts made by then Treasury Secretary Henry Paulson, Federal Reserve Bank of New York President Timothy Geithner, and Federal Reserve Chair Ben Bernanke to save the United States from an economic collapse. Director: John Maggio, Stars: Gary Ackerman, Ben Bernanke, Jill Biden
24. **Michael Clayton** (2007)—A law firm brings in its "fixer" to remedy the situation after a lawyer has a breakdown while representing a chemical company that he knows is guilty in a multibillion-dollar class action suit. Director: Tony Gilroy, Stars: George Clooney, Tilda Swinton, Tom Wilkinson
25. **American Hustle** (2013)—A con man, Irving Rosenfeld, along with his seductive partner Sydney Prosser, is forced to work for a wild F.B.I. Agent, Richie DiMaso, who pushes them into a world of Jersey powerbrokers and the Mafia. Director: David O. Russell, Stars: Christian Bale, Amy Adams, Bradley Cooper
26. **Can You Ever Forgive Me?** (2018)—When Lee Israel falls out of step with current tastes, she turns her art form to deception. Director: Marielle Heller, Stars: Melissa McCarthy, Richard E. Grant, Dolly Wells
27. **Chasing Madoff** (2010)—A look at how one investigator spent 10 years trying to expose Bernie Madoff's massive Ponzi scheme that scammed an estimated $18 billion from investors. Director: Jeff Prosserman, Stars: Bernie Madoff, Frank Casey, Gaytri Kachroo
28. **The Insider** (1999)—A research chemist comes under personal and professional attack when he decides to appear in a 60 Minutes exposé on Big Tobacco. Director: Michael Mann, Stars: Russell Crowe, Al Pacino, Christopher Plummer
29. **Money Monster** (2016)—Financial TV host Lee Gates and his producer Patty are put in an extreme situation when an irate investor takes them and their crew as hostage. Director: Jodie Foster, Stars: George Clooney, Julia Roberts, Jack O'Connell
30. **Bad Banks** (2018)—TV mini-series (12 episodes). Ambitious Jana is confronted with the unscrupulous machinations of the world of finance. Her

working life is determined by egotism, the pressure to succeed and machismo. She soon has to decide how far she is prepared to go for her career. Creator: Oliver Kienle, Stars: Paula Beer, Barry Atsma, Désirée Nosbusch

31. **Madoff** (2016)—TV mini-series. The rise and fall of Bernie Madoff, whose Ponzi scheme bilked $65 billion from unsuspecting victims; the largest fraud in US history. Stars: Drew Gregory, Bruce Altman, Anthony Arkin

1: **Hard Nox**—VW's corporate deceit. VW's 'clean diesel' cars seemed like a dream come true for carbon conscious drivers—until a fraud of staggering proportions came to light.

2: **Payday**—Targeting unsuspecting Americans, a group of payday lenders made millions off small loans with undisclosed charges, inflated interest rates and incomprehensible rules. But the way the laws are written, is that a crime or just business? Targeting unsuspecting Americans, a group of payday lenders made millions off small loans with undisclosed charges, inflated interest rates and incomprehensible rules. But the way the laws are written, is that a crime or just business?

3: **Drug Short**—Wall Street short-sellers expose a scam that regulators overlook: how Big Pharma gouges patients in need of life-saving drugs.

4: **Cartel Bank**—For decades, HSBC, one of the world's largest banks, laundered hundreds of millions of dollars for Mexican drug cartels. Senator Elizabeth Warren, dogged journalists and prosecutors try to hold the bankers to account.

5: **The Maple Syrup Heist**—In Canada, maple syrup is worth more than oil. When $20 million of syrup goes missing, the trail leads back to an epic battle between cartels and the little guy.

6: **The Confidence Man—**Weaving together a tapestry of tales in real estate booms and busts, Stevens lays out how Donald Trump's business career transformed from epic failures into a consummate branding machine that propelled him into office.

The manufacturer's authorised representative in the EU is Springer Nature Customer Service Centre GmbH, Europaplatz 3, 69115 Heidelberg, Germany. If you have any concerns regarding our products, please contact ProductSafety@springernature.com

Printed and bound by CPI Group (UK) Ltd, Croydon, CR0 4YY
30/09/2026
02225497-0005